Group work applications
across the social work curriculum
Selected and updated papers
from the IASWG Proceedings archive

Group work applications across the social work curriculum

Selected and updated papers from the IASWG Proceedings archives

Edited by
Carol S. Cohen and Mark J. Macgowan

w&b
MMXXI

About the Editors

Carol S. Cohen and Mark J. Macgowan are the Co-Chairs of the Commission on Group Work in Social Work Education of the International Association for Social Work with Groups.

Dr. Carol S. Cohen is Professor, Adelphi University School of Social Work in New York. In addition to social work with groups, her interests include international social work, professional education, supervision and community development. She is past chair of the US Council on Social Work Education's Commission on Global Social Work Education, co-chair of the CSWE Group Work Track, IASWG board member, and a Fulbright Scholar. Among her numerous publications is *Practicing as a Social Work Educator in International Collaboration* with Alice Butterfield, and she is co-editing the Routledge *International Handbook on Social Work with Groups* with Mark J. Macgowan, Ronald Toseland and an esteemed International Advisory Team.

Dr. Mark J. Macgowan is Professor of Social Work and Associate Dean, Robert Stempel College of Public Health and Social Work at Florida International University, Miami. He serves on the Executive Committee of the International Association for Social Work with Groups. He has numerous awards for excellence in teaching and research and was Fulbright-Scotland Visiting Professor, University of Edinburgh. Among other books, he is author of *Guide to Evidence-Based Group Work* and co-author with Charles Garvin and Rich Tolman of Group Work Research, both with Oxford Press, and currently co-editor with Carol Cohen and Ron Toseland of the *Routledge International Handbook on Social Work with Groups*.

© The Contributors and Whiting & Birch Ltd 2021
Published by Whiting & Birch Ltd,
Forest Hill, London SE23 3HZ
ISBN 9781861771476

Contents

Incorporating groupwork as co-curricular activity or as part of implicit curriculum

Introduction

Carol S. Cohen and Mark J. Macgowan

Overview

The International Association for Social Work with Groups (IASWG) and its Commission on Group Work in Social Work Education is continually attempting to expand group work education. As many have noted, focused education in group work has been on the decline in parts of the world (e.g., Birnbaum & Auerbach, 1994; Simon & Kilbane, 2014). As Co-Chairs of the IASWG Commission, we have joined with colleagues in seeking ways to ensure that social group work as a unique and complex method of practice gets its time and place in the social work curricula and in social work institutions.

When the idea of this book was raised, we thought about how many presentations there have been through the years at the IASWG annual symposia related to group work education. We knew that not every presenter chose to submit their paper for the proceedings, and that the content of many presentations may appear in other publications. However, as we searched the contents of the volumes of selected proceedings, we were excited to find numerous presentations about teaching group work in traditional and non-traditional ways across the curriculum. Indeed, we were delighted to find a veritable gold mine of presentations offering practices that keep group work alive and evolving in their institutions, across nations!

Serving as editors of this book has been a significant and humbling honor, affording the opportunity to bring renewed attention to the sixteen chapters in this volume. Coupled with contemporary prefaces to each chapter, each paper provides important insights, inspiration and evidence of the essential nature of group work in social work education. These peer reviewed papers originally appeared in selected proceedings of annual symposia from 2003 to 2013 of the International Association for Social Work with Groups (IASWG). In our selection, we sought to identify exemplary papers with enduring themes, which, collectively, provide a broad picture of the role, diversity, effectiveness and potential for group work investment at multiple levels of social work education.

When contacted, the authors were enthusiastic about this re-publication, and avidly contributed new prefaces to their work which include updates on their evolving programs and ideas. Sadly, given the passage of time since the original publication, we found that four of the authors had died, Anna Fritz, Annette Gerten, John Mansfield, and Stephen J. Yanca. In two chapters, the remaining co-authors wrote a new preface. In two chapters where this was not possible due to the passing of the authors, we authored the prefaces. Along with their colleagues, we and the group work community honor their enduring contributions.

This is the first formal compilation of previously published IASWG Symposium papers, an auspicious event in the long history of the IASWG and its Proceedings. The genesis of this volume was over 40 years ago, in 1979 when the first symposium of what is now called IASWG was held in Cleveland, Ohio, in the United States (Abels & Abels, 1981). The inaugural symposium organizers Paul and Sonia Abels committed themselves to the publication of a volume of selected papers and commentary from the conference, which they believed would convey the "contributions and differences that shaped group work's major themes" (Abels, 2013, p. 262).

Nearly all volumes remain available, including some early proceedings and a small number of later collections that were self-published by the main organization or by a local IASWG Chapter. The IASWG Collection at the Social Welfare History Archive in Minnesota (https://www.lib.umn.edu/swha) is an excellent source of unpublished and informally published materials and related materials. Formal publication appears to have begun in 1983 through arrangements with the Haworth Press. With Haworth, the proceedings were first published as supplements to the journal Social Work with Groups, and then as both stand-alone books and as special issues of the journal. From 1990 through 2010, Haworth Press and Routledge/Taylor and Francis (after their merger), published only stand-alone volumes of the proceedings. Whiting and Birch Ltd, assumed the role of proceedings publishers in 2010, and has published all proceedings since then.

Year by year, volume by volume, IASWG has continued the tradition of publishing annual selected proceedings, amassing an extraordinary archive over forty years. The proceedings provide an irreplaceable guide to how group work in social work education, practice and research has evolved dramatically over time. The proceedings illuminate periods of challenge, decline, re-emergence and change. This long track record is itself a remarkable achievement in organizational longevity and commitment. However, beyond being admirable for sheer endurance, the collection provides a unique window to the historical development through which readers can indeed immerse themselves in the "contributions and differences" to "group work's major themes" as the Abels (Abels, 2013) first intended.

Organization

To encompass the multiple dimensions of group work in social work education, we divided the papers into four sections. We thought the papers would fit well into an arrangement based on four contexts of delivery; namely, a traditional group work focused class, generalist practice class, across the curriculum, and as part of co-curricular or implicit curriculum.

Teaching social work practice with groups in a group work practice focused class
The papers in this first section are innovative examples of teaching in classes dedicated to social work with groups. Casstevens and Cohen describe an empirical study of teaching using reflecting teams as a small group exercise, valuable for group work and other courses. Mansfield and Hull explore the use of video recordings to learn group work skills, through a critical process of examining the recordings. Clements and Benbow describe a manual they developed that included activities for learning group work, helping to fill the gap between the classroom and the field.

Teaching social work practice with groups in a generalist social work practice or foundation practice class
This second section includes readings about educational initiatives that take place in social work practice classes that are not limited to group work, with a common theme of teaching about diversity through group work. Yanka's chapter offers a group work approach to increase diversity competence using research/focus groups with undergraduate

social work students. Prinsloo describes the use of group work to help teach first year undergraduate students in a social work practice course about diversity in South Africa. Graham's chapter presents literature groups to teach about diversity in early foundation practice courses.

Teaching classes using groups and groupwork across the curriculum
The chapter authors in this third section describe using groups outside of dedicated group work courses and social work practice classes. Exum and Yanisko articulate the model they developed to teach about task groups across multiple courses and in community settings. Frank describes using community social service projects to help students learn to work in task groups in the community. Gerten's chapter provides an exciting vision of cooperative group learning to help students learn and appreciate the connection between research and practice. Canning uses the classroom as a case study about group work, through the lens of British school of object relations. The final chapter in this section's collection is Mesbur's, which describes using group work in delivering a field education training program in Russia.

Incorporating groupwork as a co-curricular activity
The chapters in this final section describe ways group work is taught in classes that are part of the implicit curriculum of social work curricula, and not in a specific course. Wilson presents how group work is used for gatekeeping with non-traditional students in social work education in Ireland, in maintaining professional standards, collaborative relationships, and inclusive structures. Atchinson and colleagues in a qualitative study present how group work is used to mentor social work faculty, using a feminist perspective. Using the stages of group development, Silver and Fritz describe the formation and work of an ad-hoc task group linked to IASWG, to expand group work education at a local university in the Midwest, U.S.A. Lee and Montiel show how extra-curricular group work clubs located in a social work program, can help students gain not only skills related to group work but also a commitment to the modality and to the international organization (IASWG). The final paper in this section is Berteau and Warin's paper about developing a culture of group work among students, even in environments where there is a paucity of opportunities.

Conclusion

This volume's wide array of group work approaches and applications in social work education will be useful to faculty members, scholars and trainers. The 16 chapters, clustered by the role that group work plays in four key arenas can be studied individually, by section, or in total. We believe this book provides a strong justification and foundation for the essential role of social group work within and throughout the social work curriculum. We chose to focus on papers published from 2003-2012, since it represents the first ten years of Whiting and Birch's publication of the Proceedings. This volume sets the stage of additional volumes, both in time period and in focus. At present, a compilation volume focusing on social work practice is being developed, and it is our hope that follow up volumes will be published on a periodic basis.

In 2016, the IASWG Board of Directors published a call to action, *The Time for Group Work*, which declared in part:

> There has never been a more urgent time to bring communities together towards a mutual understanding and a respect, not just for humanity, but for the planet as a whole .... As social groupworkers, we stand for and advocate for creating spaces for respectful dialogue to expand our worldviews and perspectives in community with each other. (IASWG, 2016)

This book is evidence of IASWG's commitment to the importance of ethical and rigorous group-focused practice in all settings, especially in professional social work education. We must consider the academic world a critical environment for mobilizing the power of groups for promoting justice and building community well-being. Unless we apply and expand group work knowledge and practice in the classroom and broader academy, we diminish the competencies and commitment of all its constituents, and those they will serve.

Note

The International Association of Social Work with Groups has been known by two previous names. First, as the Committee for the Advancement of Social Work with Groups in 1978 and, second, a few years later as the Association for the Advancement of Social Work with Groups. The current name, the International Association for Social Work with Groups was approved in 2012 to more clearly indicate the organization's international identity.

References

Abels, P. (2013). History of the Standards for Social Work Practice with Groups: A partial view. *Social Work With Groups, 36*, 259-269. doi: 10.1080/01609513.2012.763009

Abels, S.L. and Abels, P., Editors. (1981). *Social Work with Groups: Proceedings of the 1979 Symposium, Cleveland Ohio.* Louisville, KY: Committee for the Advancement of Social Work with Groups.

Birnbaum, M. L., & Auerbach, C. (1994). Group work in graduate social work education: The price of neglect. *Journal of Social Work Education, 30,* 325-335.

IASWG (2016) *A Time for Group Work.* Retrieved May 11, 2019 at www. iaswg.org.

Simon, S. R., & Kilbane, T. (2014). The current state of group work education in U.S. graduate schools of social work. *Social Work with Groups, 37,* 243.

Using a reflecting team as a small group exercise in the social work classroom

Preface to the 2021 reprint

The authors' original study surveyed social work students to evaluate the use of reflecting teams in social work with groups and human behavior courses (n = 52; 86.5% response rate). Reflecting teams (Andersen, 1987) were an innovative clinical strategy for counselors and family therapists in the late twentieth century. Since that time, they have moved into widespread use among practitioners using collaborative narrative and/or social constructionist approaches (e.g., Chang, 2010; Cole, Demeritt, Shatz, & Sapoznik, 2001; Fine, 2003; Haley, 2002). The strategy is also used in clinical training and supervision, as well as classroom settings (e.g., Shurts, Cashwell, Spurgeon, Degges-White, Barrio, & Kardatzke, 2006).

A good deal of additional research has been identified since the authors completed their original study, including material focusing on counselor education at the graduate level. Shurts et al. (2006) observed that "reflecting teams allowed students to practice offering tentative impressions, hypotheses, and suggestions in a nonthreatening manner" (p. 154). They also addressed the group aspect of the approach, noting that in some instances "the power of the group nature of the reflecting teams and class processing sessions led to a powerful learning experience. In other cases, the group nature of the experience led to difficulties" (Shurts et al., p. 155). Any difficulties were addressed through instructor follow-up after a reflecting team exercise. Thus reflecting teams, while a valuable educational strategy, are best used with an instructor present in the event follow-up debriefing is needed.

The authors' ongoing examination of the literature indicates that social work has been aware of the use of reflecting teams in both clinical work (e.g., Smith, Sells, & Clevenger, 1994) and educational settings for decades. Carrillo, Gallant, and Thyer (1993) explored reflecting team role-play techniques when teaching social work students interviewing skills, and Woit and Brownlee (1995) explored reflecting team use in teaching social work students clinical skills. More recently, Sloan-Power (2013) reported on the strategy's usefulness in teaching spiritual diversity to social work graduate students. All these studies, while exploratory, reported positive outcomes.

Additionally, Fine (2003) has identified the reflecting team's use of a *power with* (as opposed to *power over*) perspective and observed that this is at odds with the competitive (as opposed to collaborative) use of power that predominates in traditional academic settings. Academe notwithstanding, the use of a *power with* approach resonates both for social workers and social work educators, due to the profession's emphasis on social justice. The concept of social justice involves equity and fairness for those who do not share equal power in society (Lee, Smith, & Henry, 2013; NASW, 2017), and reflecting teams can be used to explore power, dominance and intersectionality in social work classrooms at both graduate and undergraduate levels of education. This implies that reflecting teams can be constructively used as a teaching tool in courses across the social work curriculum, not merely in the group work classroom, and supports conclusions drawn in the authors' original study.

Willa J. Casstevens and M. B. Cohen

Willa J. Casstevens is now Program Director and Associate Professor of Social Work, Buena Vista University, Storm Lake, Iowa

M. B. Cohen is now Professor Emerita, University of New England

References

Andersen, T. (1987). The reflecting team: Dialogue and meta-dialogue in clinical work. *Family Process, 26,* 415-428.
Carrillo, D. F., Gallant, J. P., & Thyer, B. A. (1993). Training MSW students in interviewing skills: An empirical assessment. *Arete, 18*(1), 12-19.

Chang, J. (2010). The reflecting team: A training method for family counselors. *The Family Journal: Counseling and Therapy for Couples and Families, 18*(1), 36-44.

Cole, P. M., Demeritt, L. A., Shatz, K., Sapoznik, M. (2001). Getting personal on reflecting teams. *Journal of Systemic Therapies, 20*(2), 74-87. doi. org/10.1521/jsyt.20.2.74.23038

Fine, M. (2003). Reflections on the intersection of power and competition in reflecting teams as applied to academic settings. *Journal of Marital and Family Therapy, 29*(3), 339-351.

Haley, T. (2002). The fit between reflecting teams and a social constructionist approach. *Journal of Systemic Therapies, 21*(1), 20-40. doi.org/10.1521/ jsyt.21.1.20.23095

Lee, M. A., Smith, T. J., & Henry, R. G. (2013). Power politics: Advocacy to activism in social justice counseling. *Journal for Social Action in Counseling and Psychology, 5*(3), 70-94.

NASW (1996, revised 2017). *NASW Code of Ethics.* Retrieved November 24, 2017 from: www.socialworkers.org/About/Ethics/Code-of-Ethics/ Code-of-Ethics-English

Shurts, W. M., Cashwell, C. S., Spurgeon, S. L., Degges-White, S., Barrio, C. A., & Kardatzke, K. N. (2006). Preparing counselors-in-training to work with couples: Using role-plays and reflecting teams. *The Family Journal: Counseling and Therapy for Couples and Families, 14*(2), 151-157.

Sloan-Power, E. (2013). Diversity education and spirituality: An empirical reflecting approach for MSW students. *Journal of Religion & Spirituality in Social Work, 32*(4), 330-348.

Smith, T. E., Sells, S. P., & Clevenger, T. (1994). Ethnographic content analysis of couple and therapist perceptions in a reflecting team setting. *Journal of Marital and Family Therapy, 20*(3), 267-286.

Woit, J., & Brownlee, K. (1995). Reflecting teams in the classroom: An effective educational tool? *Journal of Teaching in Social Work, 11*(1/2), 67-84.

Using a reflecting team as a small group exercise in the social work classroom

W. J. Casstevens and Marcia Cohen

Introduction

Reflecting teams developed in the postmodern, constructionist environment of narrative therapy, embedded in systems theory and family therapy. Andersen developed the reflecting team approach in family therapy (Brownlee, Vis, & McKenna, 2009) and it has since been used as both a clinical and a teaching tool (Griffith, 1999; Kleist, 1999; Wahlstroem, 2006). Cox, Bañez, Hawley, and Mostade (2003) recommended using reflecting teams for training group workers in classroom settings. They suggested two formats for classroom exercises noting "that there could be many variations of this process and that it could be used in a variety of situations (Anderson, 1991, 1995)" (Cox, et al., p. 104). This is perhaps not surprising, since reflecting teams are themselves small groups.

The authors applied this small group approach to developing critical thinking and collaboration in the social work classroom, and evaluated these reflecting team exercises through anonymous student questionnaires. This chapter presents reflecting teams, reflective learning, and an approach to formatting reflecting team exercises in human behavior and group work classrooms. It also reports results from student feedback questionnaires that were used to evaluate these classroom exercises.

The reflecting team in therapy

As used in therapy, the reflecting team model consists of a three-step sequence: (a) Client – Therapist interaction, (b) Listening/Reflecting Consultants interaction, and (c) Client – Therapist interaction resumes, and Client reacts to the Consultants' interaction (Griffith, 1999). In this model, the Listening/Reflecting Consultants comprise the reflecting team. In narrative therapy, if either therapeutic discourse reaches an impasse, or widening their audience would benefit clients, a reflecting team may be invited into a therapy session (Monk, 1997). Team members are generally selected through therapist-client consultation: "A reflecting team/audience may consist of individuals who are family/friends to the client or strangers to the client, e.g., colleagues or interns of the client's therapist and/or relevant other specialists such as a priest or minister; or members of the community who have been through similar experiences (White, 2007)" (Taliaferro, Casstevens, & Decuir-Gunby, 2013).

The carefully selected reflecting team members observe session dialog, then the therapist and client remove themselves to observe the team as it reflects on the observed interaction. After this occurs, the team departs and client and therapist resume their session. It is hoped that reflecting team input will result in a shift in the client system, that is, in change (O'Connor, Davis, Meakes, Pickering, & Schuman, 2004; Wahlstroem, 2006).

Brownlee, Vis, and McKenna (2009) challenged researchers to further examine the effectiveness of this model, as it involves extensive use of time and resources on behalf of clients. Both Kleist (1999) and Brownlee et al., (2009) while recommending further research, agreed that the evidence on the use of reflecting teams in family and couple counseling by and large supports the model's continued use. Griffith (1999) expanded the model's application, and used reflecting teams in the classroom as "an alternative case teaching model" (p. 343) in graduate level business education.

Reflective learning in professional education

Reflective learning plays an important part in professional education in a variety of disciplines, including social work. Platzer, Blake, and Ashford (2000), for example, evaluated reflective learning in nursing education, using reflective practice groups that "enabled some of the students to develop their critical thinking and professionalism" (p. 694). Platzer et al. (2000) suggested that group work "could further enhance a learner's opportunities to consider different viewpoints and reflect on their own experiences" (p. 691). Charalambous (2003) agreed that reflection can facilitate teaching, pointing out that it "has increasingly become a cornerstone of nursing professionalism" (p. 1 of 8), and connecting it to "helping students learn about and from clinical experience" (p. 3 of 8). Although Charalambous discussed counseling in the context of reflection, narrative therapy and reflecting teams were not mentioned. In social work education, Noble (2001) and Rai (2006) explored reflective writing and student narratives. Rai noted that: "Reflection remains at the core of social work education, although its face may have evolved" (p. 795). Holland and Kilpatrick's (1993) work with using narrative analysis and reflective questions to teach a multicultural approach to practice is yet another example of how narrative and reflection have been used in social work education. Incorporating reflecting team activities within the social work classroom could be viewed as one more step in this evolution.

Classroom implementation

The first author of this article introduced the reflecting team into an undergraduate classroom in an experiential exercise on group work: The instructor took the role of group leader or facilitator, student volunteers participated as members in the group process, and a panel of observers (the remainder of the class) watched the group, then discussed their observations among themselves while the group members and leader observed. This exercise was enthusiastically received. The first author then used a reflecting team activity in a small graduate level class, again as an experiential exercise on group work. In this situation, however, student volunteers requested a follow-up dialog to process the observers' reflection, and class ran overtime attending to this request. Anecdotally, both BSW and MSW students found these reflecting teams to be engaging and constructive aids to experiencing and reflecting on the use of groups in social work practice. This informal feedback led the authors to more systematically evaluate the usefulness of reflecting team activities in social work classrooms. Griffith (1999) explicitly adapted the reflecting team model for use in the classroom, and summarized six major rules for reflection as guidelines for student use (a slightly modified version of these is provided in Figure 1). The authors used the modified guidelines to help standardize the process for reflecting team activities in this study.

Figure 1. Reflecting Team Activity Handout Paraphrased from Griffith (1999).

Guidelines for consultations (based on Griffith, 1999):

1. Restrict speculations to conversations that take place during the activity in this room today
2. Present ideas tentatively, e.g., starting with "I was wondering..." or "perhaps..."
3. Comments are to be positive or logical, rather than negative or blaming
4. Share perceptions without evaluation, judgment, or explanation/ justification of team member perceptions
5. Attempt to present both sides of any dilemma, moving from "either-or" to a "both-and" position
6. Maintain eye contact with fellow team members during the team consultation

---

Method

The authors used Griffith's (1999; see Figure 1) reflecting team approach in two social work courses (a total of three course sections) at two universities, as part of a broader study that had Institutional Review Board approval at the first author's university. The courses were graduate level, semester-long courses; one of the courses was group work specific. The group work specific course was an advanced level practice course with two sections (*Social Work Practice with Groups*; n = 14 and n = 17, respectively). Each section of *Social Work Practice with Groups* incorporated two reflecting team activities during the semester. The other course was a foundation level human behavior course with one section (*Human Behavior & the Social Environment: Individuals, Families, & Groups*; n = 21). The human behavior course incorporated three reflecting team activities during the semester. Because of the larger class size (n = 21), two process group/reflecting team dyads convened concurrently to allow all students to participate in each of the three activities.

Figure 2. Anonymous End-of-Semester Questionnaires.

Human Behavior	Practice with Groups
Recall the 3 Reflecting Team exercises, focusing on what defines social class, teen suicide and sexual orientation, and aging and care-giving. Did the Reflecting Team format contribute to the enhancement or development of your: ___ Yes ___ No Critical thinking skills	Recall the 2 Reflecting Team exercises, focusing on the role plays. Did the Reflecting Team format contribute to the enhancement or development of your: ___ Yes ___ No Critical thinking skills
___ Yes ___ No Small group collaboration	___ Yes ___ No Small group collaboration
___ Yes ___ No Ability to see issues from the perspective of others	___ Yes ___ No Awareness of group process and group facilitation
___ Yes ___ No Ability to critically reflect upon your own process	___ Yes ___ No Ability to critically reflect upon your own process
	___ Yes ___ No Do you think this was a useful format?
	Please explain below:
Please explain below: Thank you for your feedback on this type of group exercise!!	Thank you for your feedback on this type of group exercise!!

Anonymous in-class questionnaires administered at the end-of-semester were used to evaluate the impact of reflecting team activities (see Figure 2). The questionnaires offered three identical questions; the *Practice with Groups* questionnaire added two questions, and the *Human Behavior* questionnaire added one question. For the *Practice with Groups* course the added questions (1) related to group process and facilitation, and (2) asked whether this was a useful format. For the *Human Behavior* course the added question related to students' abilities to see things from the perspective of others.

The instructor provided students with a handout of Griffith's (1999) slightly modified guidelines (Figure 1) for reference during each reflecting team activity. In order to address any sensitive feelings that might surface, the instructors also added a fourth step to the reflecting team classroom activity. This led to the following small group format: (1) Small Group – Facilitator interaction; (2) Reflecting Team interaction; (3) Small Group – Facilitator interaction resumes and reacts to the Reflecting Team interaction; (4) Reflecting Team interaction resumes and reacts to the second Small Group – Facilitator interaction.

In the classroom, instructors had students divide into small groups of 5 – 8 students each, which became (1) a process group, and (2) a reflecting team. The process group facilitator was either selected by group members or assigned by the instructor. The process group was provided either with a role-play scenario (in the group work course), or with structured questions on current course material for discussion (in the human behavior course). During the ensuing small group activity, the reflecting team observed and took notes. The groups then switched places, and the reflecting team discussed what it observed, with appropriate related commentary that followed the handout guidelines "major rules for reflection" (Griffith, 1999, p. 354-355; refer to Table 1). Finally, the original process group reconvened and concluded the exercise, discussing group members' thoughts and/or feelings on the reflecting team's discussion and commentary.

Each group segment took between 10 and 20 minutes (segment lengths were determined in advance, so students knew what to expect). The entire exercise initially took about one hour and 15 minutes, including the initial explanation, coaching, and group formation. Once students were familiar with the guidelines for the activity, a reflecting team exercise could be completed in approximately one hour.

The way a reflecting team handles its comments is central to the success of any reflecting team exercise. In the classroom, for example, while demonstrating critical thinking in role plays and/or discussion amongst team members, reflecting teams also need to avoid negativity. This has an added benefit of making reflecting teams excellent experiential exercises in strengths-based discourse.

Table 1.1 Social Work Practice with Groups – Section 1.

Question n = 12	Yes	No
Critical thinking skills	12 (100%)	0
Small group collaboration	9 (75%)	3 (25%)
Awareness of group process and facilitation	10 (83%) 1(8%) "somewhat"	1 (8%)
Ability to critically reflect on own process	11 (92%) 1(8%) "somewhat"	0
Useful format?	11 (92%) 1(8%) "somewhat"	0

Table 1.2 Social Work Practice with Groups – Section 2.

Question n = 14	Yes	No
Critical thinking skills	12 (86%)	2 (14%)
Small group collaboration	8 (57%) 1 (7%) "maybe"	5 (36%)
Awareness of group process and facilitation	14 (100%)	0
Ability to critically reflect on own process	11 (79%) 1(7%) "maybe"	2 (14%)
Useful format?	13 (93%)	1 (7%)

Table 2. Human Behavior and the Social Environment: Individuals, Families, and Groups.

Question n = 19	Yes	No
Critical thinking skills	10 (53%)	9 (47%)
Small group collaboration	17 (89%)	2 (11%)
Ability to see issues from perspective of others	15 (79%)	4 (21%)
Ability to critically reflect on own process	14 (74%)	5 (26%)

Results

Responses from the anonymous questionnaires for each class are tabulated for reference (Table 1.1, Table 1.2 and Table 2). The group work students were second year MSW students at a medium-sized private university in the American northeast. In Section 1 of the *Practice with Groups* course, 12 of the 14 students responded for a response rate of 85.7% (see Table 1.1). All respondents reported that the reflecting team exercises contributed to the enhancement or development of their critical thinking skills. Ninety-two percent reported that this was a useful format, and the exercises contributed to the enhancement or development of their ability to critically reflect upon their own process. Eighty-three percent reported that the exercises enhanced their awareness of group process and facilitation. Finally, 75% reported that the reflecting team exercises contributed to the enhancement or development of group collaboration.

In Section 2 of the *Practice with Groups* course, 14 of 17 students responded for a response rate of 82.4% (see Table 1.2). All respondents reported that the reflecting team exercises contributed to the enhancement or development of their awareness of group process and facilitation, though only 57% reported the exercises contributed to the enhancement or development of group collaboration. Ninety-three percent reported that this was a useful format; 86% reported the exercises contributed to the enhancement or development of their critical thinking skills; and 79% reported it contributed to their ability to critically reflect upon their own process.

Students in both course sections provided comments. In Section 1 of *Practice with Groups*, three students (25%) commented on the "lack of authenticity" involved with role-play scenarios. Two students (17%) requested more structure while one student (8%) suggested less (this student also commented on the format's helpfulness). In total, 10 of the 12 students (83.3%) commented on the helpfulness of the reflecting team exercises. In Section 2 of *Practice with Groups*, six students (43%) commented that doing this exercise when classmates were more comfortable with one another and/or with role-playing would have been less intimidating. In addition, seven of the 14 students (50%) commented on the helpfulness of the exercises. Two students (14%) commented that the reflecting team exercises were difficult to remember at the end of semester. (While it is possible these two students were absent during relevant class sessions, obtaining feedback immediately following class exercises – rather than at the end of the course – is suggested for future studies.) It may be mentioned that students in both sections of the group work course added notes to the yes/no options provided in the first five questions, writing in "somewhat" or "maybe" in response to some questions; these are noted on Tables 1.1 and 1.2. Overall, students in Section 1 of the group work course appeared to respond more favorably to the reflecting team activities than did students in Section 2.

In the human behavior class, 19 of 21 students responded to the questionnaire, for a response rate of 90.5% (see Table 2). These were first-year MSW students at a large southern state university. Eighty-nine percent of respondents reported that the reflecting team exercises contributed to the enhancement or development of group collaboration. Seventy-nine percent of respondents reported that the exercises contributed to the enhancement or development of their ability to see issues from the perspective of others, and 74% reported the exercises contributed to the enhancement or development of their ability to critically reflect upon their own process. However, only 53% of respondents reported the exercises contributed to the enhancement or development of critical thinking skills (discussed further below).

Students provided comments on the questionnaires. In the foundation level human behavior class, three of the 19 students (16%) commented that the reflecting team portion of the activity was not helpful, while seven students (37%) commented on its helpfulness. Four students (21%) commented that the second reflecting team process (Step 4) was unnecessary.

Discussion

Study limitations include the addition of course specific questions to the questionnaire that was used to obtain student feedback, and it is recommended that questionnaires used across courses be identical in future research. In addition, the questionnaires would optimally have been administered immediately following each reflecting team exercise. Although the intention was to reduce social desirability bias, waiting until the end of the course to administer the instrument may have led to diminished recollection of reflecting team exercises and their impact.

Some interesting differences in between-course responses were noted. An overall 65% of respondents in the two sections of the group work course (n = 26) reported that reflecting team exercises enhanced or developed small group collaboration, contrasting with the 89% of respondents in the human behavior course (n =21) who reported this. This marked difference may be due in part to the strong emphasis on small group collaboration that was present from day one in *Practice with Groups*. Since students were already accustomed to having this content emphasized, their perception of the proportionate contribution that reflecting team exercises made may have been less than it otherwise could have been. The human behavior course did not emphasize group collaboration as heavily, and these students may have perceived reflecting team experiences as contributing proportionately more to enhancing or developing group collaboration.

An overall 92% of respondents in the two sections of the group work course (n = 26) reported that reflecting team exercises enhanced or developed their critical thinking skills, which contrasts dramatically with the 53% of respondents in the human behavior course (n =21) who reported this. At the same time, 79% of respondents in the human behavior course reported that these exercises contributed to their ability to see issues from the perspective of others, and 74% reported these exercises contributed to their ability to critically reflect upon their own process. Paul and Elder (2010) defined critical thinking as "the art of analyzing and evaluating thinking with a view to improving it" (p. 2), a definition that would appear to include both seeing issues from multiple perspectives and critical self-reflection. While the concept "critical thinking" was explicitly discussed and defined during the group work course, this did not occur during the human behavior course. It is possible that the human behavior students did not interpret the term as was intended – to remedy this in subsequent human behavior classes the instructor has added a presentation on critical thinking that is followed by class discussion.

Although this was a relatively small study with accompanying limitations, the authors find it had distinct implications for teaching. Almost all of the students viewed the reflecting team exercises as beneficial to their learning. In terms of lessons for the future, results suggest that this activity should not be undertaken without a prior discussion of critical thinking and self-reflection, to familiarize students with these concepts before engaging them in reflecting team exercises. The feeling of intimidation expressed by some of the *Practice with Groups* Section 2 students suggests a need for instructors to be sensitive to the level of class cohesion, co-creating with students a sense of safety and mutuality in the classroom before introducing reflecting team exercises. Comments from human behavior students that the reflecting team's second round of reflection (i.e., Step 4) was unnecessary would appear to support this suggestion, particularly given this human behavior class was a cohesive entity prior to its first reflecting team exercise.

Implications for group work education

The social group work education literature has consistently emphasized the importance of experiential teaching and learning (Berger, 1996; Birnbaum, 1984; Cohen, 1996; Dennison, 2005). Cohen (2011) found that a variety of experiential teaching methods have been used successfully to teach group work assessment and practice skills. Reflecting team exercises are a versatile teaching tool likely to benefit most social work students. Possible applications of this teaching tool in group work education include its use in: (a) role-playing, (b) addressing sensitive topics using open-ended questions as a focus for small group discussions, (c) enhancing critical thinking skills, and (d) providing experiential practice in strengths-based dialog. With any of these applications, the way the reflecting team handles its comments is central to the success of the exercise – the team needs to demonstrate critical thinking in discussion amongst team members, yet at the same time needs to remain strengths based. As discussed previously, student participants in two social work courses (two sections of *Practice with Groups* and one of *Human Behavior*) reported an increased ability to critically reflect upon their own process after participating in reflecting team activities.

References

Andersen, T. (Ed.) (1991). *The reflecting team: Dialogues and dialogues about the dialogues.* New York: Norton.

Anderson, T. (1995). Reflecting processes; acts of informing and forming: You can borrow my eyes, but you must not take them away from me! In S. Friedman (Ed.), *The reflecting team in action: Collaborative practice in family therapy* (pp. 11- 37). New York: Guilford.

Berger, R. (1996). A comparative analysis of different teaching methods of teaching group work. *Social Work with Groups, 19*(1), 79–89.

Birnbaum, M. L. (1984). The integration of didactic and experiential learning in the teaching of group work. *Journal of Education for Social Work, 20,* 50–58.

Brownlee, K., Vis, J., & McKenna, A. (2009). Review of the reflecting team process: Strengths, challenges, and clinical implications. *The Family Journal, 17*(2), 139-145.

Charalambous, A. (January – March, 2003). Reflective practice as a facilitator for learning. *ICUS NURS WEB J,* Issue 13, 1-8.

Cohen, M. B. (1996). Bringing the mountain to Mohammed: An experiential approach to teaching group dynamics in the classroom. In B. Stempler, M. Glass, & C. M Savinelli (Eds.), *Social group work today and tomorrow* (pp. 71–85). Binghamton, New York: Haworth Press.

Cohen, M. B. (2011). Using student task groups to teach group process and development. *Social Work with Groups,* 34(1), 51-60.

Cox, J. A., Bañez, L., Hawley, L. D., & Mostade, J. (2003). Use of the reflecting team process in the training of group workers, *Journal for Specialists in Group Work,* 28(2), 89-105.

Dennison, S. (2005). Enhancing the integration of group theory with practice: A five-part teaching strategy. *Journal of Baccalaureate Social Work, 10*(2), 53–68.

Griffith, W. (1999). The reflecting team model as an alternative case teaching model: A narrative conversational approach. *Management Learning, 30*(3), 343-362.

Holland, T. P., & Kilpatrick, A. C. (1993). Using Narrative Techniques to Enhance Multicultural Practice, *Journal of Social Work Education,* 29(3).

Kleist, D. M. (1999). Reflecting on the reflecting process: A research perspective. *The Family Journal, 7*(3), 270-275.

Monk, G. (1997). How narrative therapy works. In G. Monk, J. Winslade, K. Crocket, & D. Epston (Eds.). *Narrative therapy in practice: The archaeology of hope (pp. 331).* San Francisco: Jossey-Bass.

Noble, C. (2001). Researching field practice in social work education: Integration of theory and practice through the use of narratives. *Journal of Social Work, 1*(3), 347-360.

O'Connor, T. S., Davis, A., Meakes, E., Pickering, R., & Schuman, M. (2004). Narrative therapy using a reflecting team: An ethnographic study of therapists' experiences. *Contemporary Family Therapy,* 26(1), 23-39.

Paul, R., & Elder, L. (2009). *The miniature guide to critical thinking: Concepts and tools*. USA: Foundation for Critical Thinking Press.

Platzer, H., Blake, D., & Ashford, D. (2003). An evaluation of process and outcomes from learning through reflective practice groups on a post-registration nursing course. *Journal of Advanced Nursing, 31*(3), 689-695.

Rai, L. (2006). Owning (up to) reflective writing in social work education. *Social Work Education, 25*(8), 785-797.

Taliaferro, J. D., Casstevens, W. J., & DeCuir-Gunby, J. T. (2013). Working with African American clients using narrative therapy: An operational citizenship and critical race theory framework. *The International Journal of Narrative Therapy and Community Work, 1*, 34-45.

Wahlstroem, J. (2006). Narrative transformations and externalizing talk in a reflecting team consultation. *Qualitative Social Work, 5*(3), 313-332.

White, M. (2007). *Maps of narrative practice*. New York: W. W. Norton.

History

Based on a presentation at the XXXIII AASWG Symposium, Long Beach, CA, 2011. First published in the Proceedings series in: Lee, C.D. (Ed.) (2014) *Social Group Work: We are all in the same boat*. London: Whiting & Birch (pp.63-75)

Notes on authors (at time of first publication)

Willa J. Casstevens, PhD, LCSW is Associate Professor, Department of Social Work, North Carolina State University, Raleigh, North Carolina, USA. She is a licensed clinical social worker. Dr. Casstevens worked in mental health in south Florida for approximately 15 years, and her research focuses on psychosocial and alternative treatment approaches and prevention.

Marcia B. Cohen, PhD, LCSW, is Professor, School of Social Work, University of New England, Portland, Maine, USA. She teaches courses in organizational change, social group work, and multilevel practice. Marcia also provides consultation to and serves on the board of several local agencies, is a member of the International Association for the Advancement of Social Work with Groups (IASWG), and is Co-Editor of the *Journal of Progressive Human Services*.

Exploring group work concepts presented on video in an undergraduate group work course

Preface to the 2021 reprint

The following paper was conceived by my professor Dr. John Mansfield. John was an Associate Professor at Mansfield University of Pennsylvania where I attended as a non-traditional Bachelor of Social Work candidate between 2005-2006. Dr. Mansfield was also my advisor and was among the very first contacts I had with the Department Faculty.

Dr. Mansfield taught several of the practice courses, including Social Work With Groups. His method was to utilize didactic instruction followed up with a role played group-facilitation, which was recorded on video. The purpose of this activity was to play the videos in class and present the facilitation for the scrutiny of fellow students. Each student was to present a video of their respective facilitation experience and then receive feedback.

Dr. Mansfield believed that a student would take their feedback more readily from their peers. He also believed that the exercise taught students the necessary skills to be an effective facilitator when practicing Social Work with Groups. My experience in the post-academic world informed me that the method of teaching group skills was effective. I have utilized the skills taught in this course during several of my career stops, which includes addictions counseling and working with children and adolescents with mental health diagnoses.

I graduated in 2006 and then earned a Masters Degree in Social Work from the State University of New York at Buffalo where Dr. Mansfield served as an Adjunct Professor, teaching a research statistics course, among others. Dr. Mansfield and I enjoyed a close relationship and he indeed not only became my friend, but a mentor. We often met when time permitted, usually over lunch or breakfast and would discuss matters of our profession, especially those concerned with men in the social work field. John was always encouraging, always funny, always sincere. We spoke often on the phone as well.

John told me several years ago that he had a cancer diagnosis and a few years later, after it seemed he was out of the woods, he received an additional, separate cancer diagnosis. John succumbed to the illness in January 2018, immediately prior to his Philadelphia Eagles winning the Super Bowl. He left behind a wonderful spouse, two daughters, two step-daughters, and several hundred, if not a few thousand, grieving students.

John was involved in the faculty union (APSCUF), led his students in various organizations, and was tirelessly preoccupied with providing social work services in the local community. John was instrumental in my growth as a student and as a professional Social Worker, both by the lessons he provided in the classroom and the counsel he so graciously offered in private moments over coffee.

I will miss my friend and mentor and I will certainly miss our conversations.

Patrick Hull

Patrick Hull, LCSW is a Licensed Clinical Social Worker in North Carolina, currently employed by Mecklenburg County Public Health as a Mental Health Licensed Clinician for Child Development-Community Policing program (CDCP).

Exploring group work concepts presented on video in an undergraduate group work course

John Mansfield and Patrick Hull

All accredited schools of social work require courses that teach group work theory and skills. Social work educators have been offering group work courses for over 130 years (Wilson, 1976). The Council on Social Work Education (CSWE) educational policies and standards (EPAS) requires that social work educators incorporate the teaching of theories and skills relevant to group work as part of social work curriculum. According to Kurland and Salmon (1999), group work is a key component of social work practice. Furthermore, the proportion of social workers experienced in facilitation of groups is inadequate and does not seem to be increasing. Berger (1996) posits that many social workers will facilitate a group at some time during their careers; therefore, group work knowledge and skills are essential for all social workers, especially those just entering the profession.

This paper will explore and compare group work concepts presented on videos produced by BSW students enrolled in a Social Work Practice with Small Groups class during the academic year of 2004-2005 at Mansfield University. Mansfield University, a liberal arts institution, is located in North-Central Pennsylvania and is part of the state university system. The Social Work Program is accredited by the CSWE.

Literature review

The Social Work profession has been teaching group work knowledge and skills relevant to working with small groups for quite some time.

Many social work educators have been interested in studying the impact of teaching different theories and methods on the student in the classroom, in field placements, and in employment settings (Berger, 1996; Manor, 1988; Parry, 1988; Wayne & Garland, 1990). Undergraduate social work educators continue to be challenged with preparing students to enter the profession after graduation with the knowledge and skills necessary to function within an agency where, increasingly, group work is a preferred treatment modality.

Manor (1988) suggests that videotape assignments are used extensively for learning skills. According to Toseland & Rivas (2005), videotaping can be an excellent teaching tool. It allows students to use the skills learned in class to actively develop their own personal styles of conducting groups. By viewing the videotaped group sessions, the student is able to critique his or her work and gain insight into the behaviors that require improvement. In cases where there are multiple video sessions, videotapes are an excellent measurement tool for the student in determining the extent to which his or her skills have improved.

The focus of this paper is to determine whether the concepts taught in the aforementioned Social Work Practice with Small Groups class were portrayed in a class video assignment that involved conducting and participating in a small group. There were two questions that guided this analysis: (1) what concepts were apparent in the video assignment?; and (2) were the concepts portrayed in the video assignment consistent with those taught in class throughout the semester?

Method

The intent of this project was to analyze the videotape assignments to discover the concepts portrayed by each group. Once the concepts were identified from each of the eight videotapes individually, they were compared with one another to identify the emergent themes. The sample of videotapes was derived from two sections of a required BSW course entitled, 'Social Work Practice with Small Groups'. Section one had an enrollment of 34 students and section two had 20 students. The students were asked to form groups consisting of four to six members.

Between the two sections, there were nine small groups in total. This paper investigated videos from eight of the nine groups. One group's video was excluded due to an actual therapeutic session that was prompted by inappropriate self-disclosures.

As mentioned, the video assignment was the culminating event in this class; however, there were two assignments which preceded the video assignment. The first assignment was a research paper, the purpose of which was to familiarize the student with a particular theory. Students were instructed to cite the journal *Social Work with Groups* exclusively to emphasize the literature that supported the profession of Social Work with groups. Assignment number one was stated in the syllabus as follows:

Assignment #1

Each student will write a content paper focusing on one group work theory or model. The paper will be 10-12 typewritten pages. A minimum of five references is necessary. The American Psychological Association (APA) format will be adhered to strictly. Check the Mansfield University Library's website for additional information.

The paper will address the following:

1. What is the most appropriate context for the application of the group theory/model?
2. Explain the rationale for choosing this theory/model. Please include any empirical evidence that supports this theory/model and ethical standards and principles that should inform the rationale.
3. Explain the group process. Please include how the process is related to generalist social work practice.
4. How does the theory/model view the members? Please include any forms of oppression and discrimination, if applicable.
5. How does the theory/model treat the individual and the group? Please include any forms of oppression and discrimination, if applicable.
6. What is important in the pre-group phase?
7. Describe and explain the various stages or phases. How is supervision for the social worker addressed?
8. Who would benefit the most from this approach?

9. With what population (if any) should this theory not be used? Please include any forms of oppression and discrimination, if applicable.

Grounding the student in a specific theory or model of the student's choice was intended to familiarize him or her with the literature and increase the student's understanding of social work with groups (Berger, 1996; Gitterman, 1988; Parry, 1988). Furthermore, each student had the option of basing the video assignment on any theory or model as long as it was supported by social work literature. Before the student conducted his or her research, the instructor taught several models and theories (for example, the Remedial Model, Cognitive-Behavioral Theory, and Systems Theory) during the first several weeks of the class. These models or theories taught in class were used in the video assignment, but not always.

The second assignment required the student to discuss the group process of completing the video assignment over the course of the semester. The second assignment was as follows:

Assignment #2

Each student will write a process paper describing the small group process over the course of the semester. The focus will be on the meetings that occurred in order to produce the videotapes (assignment #3). The paper will be 10-12 pages and will include a minimum of five references. The American Psychological Association (APA) format will be adhered to strictly. Check the Mansfield University Library's website for additional information.

The paper will address the following:

1. Describe the rationale for joining this group. Please include any ethical standards and principles that should inform the rationale.
2. Explain the small group process.
    a. Were the group stages clearly identifiable? Explain.
    b. Did the group have a leader? Explain.
    c. How were meetings conducted?
    d. How was conflict handled?
    e. Did each member have the opportunity to participate? Explain.

    f.   When the project was complete how did the group end?

3.   Compare this group experience with other types of groups found in the literature.

The student should have gained a thorough understanding of group content and process as a result of assignments #1 and #2. This understanding was to promote the student's ability to complete assignment #3, which is the video assignment. The third assignment was stated in the syllabus as follows:

Assignment #3

Each group will produce a videotape to be viewed in class. The video will portray a group based on one particular model/theory. The group may role play either a task-focused group or a treatment group. Each member will facilitate the group for approximately 15 minutes. The group will simulate a specific type of group that is indicated by the theory or model chosen. The class will view each of the videotapes. After the tapes have been viewed there will be a discussion based on a critical analysis. A handout will be provided prior to viewing the tapes. The handout or instrument will help organize the discussion and provide key ideas upon which to focus.

The instrument allows the observer to identify the following: group title, group purpose, pre-group, group stages, verbal and non-verbal cues, conflict/resistance, member participation, and termination. The instructor collected and organized data from the videotapes using the instrument in assignment #3. Additionally, one student from each section of the class volunteered to participate with the instructor on this project. The two students viewed the videotapes independently and organized the concepts in the videos using the instrument. Using the data organized on the basis of the instrument, the instructor and two students performed a content analysis to identify any themes that emerged from the videotapes.

Results

The content analysis identified many themes derived from classroom instruction. Although the groups demonstrated different theories, each exhibited some variation of the beginning, middle, and ending stages. The content themes most frequently displayed were introductions, confidentiality, rules, icebreakers, round robin (participation), homework, role-playing, cohesion, and conflict/resistance. The themes will be discussed within the context of stages.

Beginning stage

In the beginning stage, all videos incorporated many important concepts related to group work. These concepts centered around four main themes. The first concept demonstrated in the beginning stage was *introductions*. The students understood the necessity to use a formal introductory procedure to start the group process. The second theme that emerged was *confidentiality*. The instructor expected to see this portrayed in each of the videos. The students often reviewed confidentiality prior to starting each group, demonstrating that each student understood the importance of this critical social work value. The third theme was *rules*. It appeared that the students understood the importance of expressing clear rules at the beginning of each session. This emphasis on rules allowed for smoother group interactions; however, it may have also impacted the ability to portray a variety of conflict scenarios. The fourth theme that emerged was the *'ice-breaker'*. Again, every group had some form of an ice-breaker. By including these activities, the students demonstrated a firm grasp of the importance of using an ice-breaker to aid in putting the members at ease.

Middle stage

Several worthwhile concepts were also demonstrated in the middle stage. The first was *group participation*. Most groups demonstrated the principle of member participation by utilizing round-robin, a concept taught in class. The facilitator called on each member to share in order to assure equal participation. All eight of the groups incorporated a round robin format, regardless of the stage being portrayed. However, as the group progressed, the use of round-robin diminished as free-flowing interactions became the norm, especially during the ending stage.

The second concept demonstrated in the middle stage was *homework*. The importance of homework assignments was emphasized in class and demonstrated by the students. The groups used homework to relate experiences outside of group into the group. The third concept portrayed was *role-playing*. Groups that did emphasize the importance of using role-plays (not all did) encouraged their use outside of group as well. This made the role play similar to a homework assignment.

Ending stage

The ending stage, as presented in the group videos, contained important themes. The first is *cohesion*, which was portrayed by most groups in the ending stage. Cohesion was primarily defined as group members interacting and supporting one another verbally. Although the video assignment was a role play, the group members engaged one another frequently during the ending stage. Their interactions in this stage were clearly distinct from the other stages, especially the beginning stage.

The next common theme was *conflict/resistance*. Again, not every group portrayed conflict and resistance but when demonstrated, it occurred in this stage. The conflict/resistance most often occurred between group members. For example, a group member who was habitually late was reminded by another group member of the group's rule to be on time. Conflict/resistance was often mediated by the facilitators. This particular conflict caused the facilitator to ask the group for feedback. This lead to the group sanctioning the late member by stating the importance of being on time.

Additionally, the groups emphasized *referrals*. Most groups understood the necessity to refer the members for continuing treatment or some other social work resource. This was always performed by the facilitator. The students that facilitated this stage understood the importance of referrals from social workers.

In summary, the skills portrayed were adequate to facilitate a small group. The students presented a clear understanding of necessary skills and the basic knowledge expected from beginning social work practitioners. However, not all concepts discussed in class were witnessed on the videos. There were several concepts which were seldom used or not represented at all in the videos which serve to help inform this analysis and future instruction.

Under-emphasized concepts

The concepts not emphasized included pre-group stage, a strengths perspective, termination, and clear and concise goal formation. The first under-utilized concept was that of a *pre-group interaction*. Although each group began with introductions, only two of the eight group videos decided to demonstrate a formal pre-group phase on camera. The use of a pre-group stage in these videos was done to assure confidentiality and state the reason for the group. The absence of a pre-group stage in the remaining videos left the instructor and the class guessing as to how the members were referred into their respective groups. However, many group videos attempted to incorporate what should have happened in the pre-group stage during the initial session by referencing an implied pre-group interview.

The second theme not portrayed was a focus on a *strengths perspective* by the facilitator. Although the strengths perspective is emphasized across the curriculum, the students did not demonstrate this important concept. There was no attempt to utilize client strengths, which was especially obvious during role-plays. Social work interventions are based on a client's strengths and a role-play provides an excellent opportunity to identify these strengths.

Termination was seldom demonstrated throughout the videos. However, termination was represented in the ending stage, where students would make referrals and affirm the hard work that occurred. The problem existed in the other stages in which the facilitator often ended the group abruptly without, as instructed in class, summarizing the session. Student facilitators often ended group sessions by stating, 'it looks like we are out of time'. Again, the motivated and agreeable members quickly accepted this fact and responded by saying, 'goodbye'.

Finally, several groups struggled with forming *clear and concise goals*. It appears the groups recognized the importance of discussing goal formation but struggled with the ability to set clear, observable, and measurable goals. This is a concept emphasized in all practice courses at Mansfield University.

Overall, many important concepts emerged as themes. There were also some concepts that should have emerged as important themes, but the students did not choose to portray them. The time limit inherent in the assignment could be a reason why more concepts were not demonstrated. The students needed to make decisions based on what they could realistically include within the time allotted. It would have been impossible to portray all concepts in each video.

Implications

In order to become an effective group worker, the emphasis should not be placed solely upon the knowledge base of a particular stage (Berger, 1996). Furthermore, Goldberg and Lamont (1986) posit that, according to students, practice competence is enhanced and more knowledge is gained when various practice methods are taught instead of a generic model. The results of the present project have multiple implications for group work education and practice. In particular, special attention given to those concepts not adequately demonstrated in the group videos will enhance the group work experience for future social work students in this program. These particular concepts were evident in the students' groups and four were inadequately presented.

Concepts clearly addressed

The first concept for discussion is *confidentiality*. Social workers learn the importance of confidentiality early in an undergraduate social work program. The National Association of Social Workers (NASW, 1999) states:

> When social workers provide counseling services to families, couples, or groups, social workers should seek agreement among the parties involved concerning each individual's right to confidentiality and obligation to preserve the confidentiality of information shared by others. (p.11)

Toseland and Rivas (2005) suggest that confidentiality should be addressed either in the pre-group stage or the beginning stage.

Every group addressed confidentiality in at least one of these stages; therefore, the students recognized the importance of establishing and emphasizing this essential ethical principle.

Group cohesion was a content area taught in class and portrayed in each of the videos. However, because prior relationships were already established, some groups appeared to be very cohesive and trusting right from the beginning. In fact, one video was not used in the content analysis due to the nature and frequency of some self-disclosures. In this case, attempts by particular members to derive a therapeutic environment from the educational purpose may be attributed to this prior familiarity with one another. Otherwise, cohesion among members of the remaining groups was demonstrated by both verbal and non-verbal cues. Although the members did not regularly interact verbally, they used non-verbal cues, such as shaking their heads, in an affirming manner. Moreover, members addressed the facilitator rather than speaking directly to other group members, which indicated that members had a desire to help the member currently speaking, but were reluctant to do so directly. For a minority of students, group cohesion was a process demonstrated by increasing trust and self-disclosure, which creates a more accurate simulation of natural group processes. Therefore, cohesion could be considered a latent concept derived from the group process.

Another concept important to understand and routinely demonstrated was that of *conflict/resistance*. Understanding conflict/resistance is often part of the process and will need to be dealt with in a positive, effective manner. Rose (1989) states that it is imperative for a group leader to recognize the normality of conflict in order to allow a group to develop to its full potential. Accordingly, avoiding conflict/resistance hinders the process and leads to a roadblock of self-discovery. Cohen and Garrett (1995) state: 'conflict resolution is the process through which members negotiate disagreements between and among members and workers' (p. 13). For the most part, the conflict that occurred in the videos was among members. The students were not in conflict with the facilitator. Furthermore, Toseland and Rivas (2005) suggest that facilitators should assist the members in viewing conflict as conducive to a proper functioning group and helpful in clarifying group purpose and goals. However, if a social worker has not had much practice in handling conflict/resistance successfully, it poses two problems. First, when a facilitator is unsure how to proceed in the face of conflict, he or she may lose confidence in leading that group. Second, the worker may not acquire the ability to focus and regain control of the group during a conflict. Group workers consider conflict/resistance an important part of the group process because it often facilitates change within the group (Toseland & Rivas, 2005; Garvin, 1997).

Concepts inadequately addressed

There were several concepts that were expected to manifest in the videos but were portrayed minimally or not at all. First, *clear and concise goal formation* was weakly demonstrated. According to Berman-Rossi (1992), it is of primary importance for the group facilitator to state the purpose of the group, learn why each member has chosen to attend, and to what end each client is working. When the facilitator fails to explain the reason for the group, each member is forced to independently discern purpose, and therefore group goals. Consequently, the group may lose its focus and its work may carry no real importance to the members. Although attempts were made to establish clear goals, this was not a theme common to all videos in the sample.

The second concept not demonstrated is the *strengths perspective.* Toseland and Rivas (2005) posit that leaders should explore strengths, especially in culturally diverse groups. However, Toseland and Rivas (2005) state that there is no clear evidence to suggest that this approach is more helpful with a heterogeneous group than it is with homogenous groups and suggest that it is instead more helpful to use problem-solving. A strengths perspective emphasis is taught as an aspect of the problem-solving approach in each social work course at Mansfield University. Perhaps these two concepts should be taught separately and then combined to clarify the distinctions between them. The problem-solving approach and a strengths perspective are essential social work treatment strategies.

The third concept not clearly demonstrated is *termination.* Group facilitators did not routinely summarize and terminate each session and usually ran out of time, ending the session abruptly. These endings interrupted the flow of the group, causing confusion among members. Summarizing would have cemented the concepts and ideas portrayed in each stage. The absence of summarizing could, in a real-life setting, leave the members with many questions about group purpose, group participation, and identifying and achieving the group goals. Additionally, by not summarizing in the videos, each stage often appeared choppy and disjointed due to not allowing members to reflect on the work accomplished. Ending a session without a clear assessment and summary leaves members with an unclear perspective as to what has occurred. As a result, the instructor plans to utilize more in-class role-plays to promote more effective termination skills in students.

Finally, the groups rarely portrayed a *pre-group phase*. The decision of various students to exclude this stage must be addressed. Many social work educators and practitioners emphasize the importance of a pre-group stage (Toseland & Rivas, 2005; Berman-Rossi, 1992; Garvin, 1997; Rose, 1989). The Association of the Advancement of Social Work with Groups (1998) clearly emphasizes a pre-group phase. When the pre-group stage was ignored in the videos, the groups did not appear to establish group purpose, which rendered the videos hard-to-follow. This negatively impacted the groups' ability to establish clear and concise goals. Therefore, pre-group tasks are essential to the overall group process. The instructor must respond to this issue and in future classes, the importance of the pre-group stage will be emphasized by using role-plays. Additionally, the instructor will require for each video a pre-group stage. It will be interesting to see how this emphasis will affect future videos.

Summary

In order to be an effective and confident group facilitator, it is imperative that the student have a clear understanding of the theories and skills necessary to do group work. However, it is not enough to merely possess the knowledge or skill; group social workers must be able to incorporate these theories and skills into their practice in order to be successful. This can be accomplished in several ways. First, group workers can facilitate a mutual understanding about the purpose of the group as a whole and how it relates to each of the members. Second, group workers can state goals that are clear, achievable and measurable. Third, group workers can recognize and address conflict. Finally, group workers can summarize each group session to facilitate smooth transitions to subsequent sessions as well as endings that are meaningful to each member.

Mastering these practice skills, learned through video-taped assignments, allows students to not only increase their future professional marketability, but also improve client treatment outcomes once the students are professional social work practitioners. Social work educators have a responsibility to ensure that students are prepared to meet the needs of the profession and the needs of those who would seek a social worker's assistance. This project and analysis contribute to the information social work educators need to facilitate that preparedness.

References

Association for the Advancement of Social Work with Groups. (1998). *Standards for social work practice with groups.* Akron, OH: AASWG.

Berger, R. (1996). A comparative analysis of different methods of teaching group work. *Social Work with Groups, 19,* 79-89.

Berman-Rossi, T. (1992). Empowering groups through understanding stages of group development, *Social Work with Groups, 15*(2/3), 239-256.

Cohen, M. B., & Garrett, K. J. (1995). Helping field instructors become more effective group work educators. *Social Work with Groups, 18*(2/3), 135-148.

Garvin, C.D. (1997). *Contemporary Group Work* (3rd ed.). Allyn & Bacon: Needham Heights, MA.

Gitterman, A. (1988). Teaching students to connect theory and practice. *Social Work with Groups, 11*(1), 33-41.

Goldberg, T., & Lamont, A. (1986). Do group work standards work? Results form an empirical exploration. *Social Work with Groups, 9*(3), 89-109.

Kurland, R., & Salmon, R. (1999). *Teaching a Methods Course in Social Work with Groups.* Alexandria, VA: Council on Social Work Education.

Manor, O. (1988). The monitoring of a co-active learning in social group work: A pilot study. *Social Work with Groups, 11,* 53-75.

Parry, J. (1988). Organizing principles for developing a foundation group work practice course. *Social Work with Groups, 11,* 77-85.

Rose, S. (1989). *Working with Adults in Groups: Integrating Cognitive-Behavioral and Small-Group Strategies.* San Francisco: Jossey-Bass.

Toseland, R., & Rivas, R. (2005). The ending stage. In *An Introduction to Group Work Practice.* (pp. 401-429). Needham Heights, MA: Pearson Education Company.

Wayne, J., & Garland, J. (1990). Group work education in the field: The state of the art. *Social Work with Groups, 13,* 95-109.

Wilson, G. (1976). From practice to theory: A personalized history. In *Theories of Social Work with Groups.* (pp. 1-44). New York: Columbia University Press.

History
Based on a presentation at the XXVII AASWG Symposium, Minnesota, MN, 2005. First published in the Proceedings series in: Kuechler , C.F. (Ed.) (2011) *Group Work: Building bridges of hope.* London: Whiting & Birch (pp.103-115)

Notes on authors (at time of first publication)
Patrick Hull, BSW Student, Mansfield University of Pennsylvania. At publication (2009), BSW, Blended Case Manager, Clinical Services, Tioga County Department of Human Services, Pennsylvania.

John Mansfield, PhD (Barry University), Associate Professor, Mansfield University of Pennsylvania, Associate Professor Social Work, Anthropology and Sociology.

More than ice breakers: Teaching social work students how to effectively use activity in the group

Preface to the 2021 reprint

The initial design of the manual described in this paper came about in response to feedback provided to the authors from upper-level undergraduate social work students, entry-level social work practitioners and social work agency representatives. Although the feedback was uniquely different from each cohort, a common theme emerged, which was an increasing need for students and practitioners to facilitate activity-based groups. The challenge was for the Undergraduate BSW students to understand the role of mutual aid while still providing an opportunity to engage the group members in a curriculum. Throughout the student's undergraduate experience, we as educators and practitioners consistently require, encourage, and expect students to participate in experiential-based groups, support groups, task-oriented groups, social groups and so forth. Within many of these groups the use of activities are key to developing relationships, team building, ice-breaking, and application of concepts/major points discussed.

Our desire in creating the manual entitled *"Effective Activity-Based Group Work"* and then presenting our work at the Montreal IASWG (formerly AASWG) Annual Symposium, was to equip students with a tool/manual that would help bridge the gap between the classroom and the field. Moreover, entry level practitioners and agency representatives shared the realities of needing graduates who were competent in conducting group work and using activities in such places as partial hospitalization programs, community residential rehabilitation programs, in-patient settings, drug and alcohol treatment centers, senior centers and alternative educational programs.

Since the publication of this original presentation, the manual was developed and shared with students in the BSW program. In addition, the manual has been shared with other programs since the original presentation at Montreal. Students continue to use the manual in their final field practicum placements with additional feedback given by agency field instructors.

Jennifer A. Clements and Samuel R. Benbow

Jennifer A. Clements, PhD, LCSW, is a Professor of Social Work at Shippensburg University Department of Social Work and Gerontology

Dr. Samuel R. Benbow is an Associate Professor at Shippensburg University Department of Social Work and Gerontology

More than ice breakers: Teaching social work students how to effectively use activity in the group

Jennifer A. Clements and Samuel R. Benbow

Social work educators are continuously challenged with the difficult task of preparing entry level practitioners to apply theories, skills and techniques learned and practiced in class, to that of the real world of work. One way to bridge the gap between classroom knowledge and the demands of social workers conducting group work is the utilization of experiential-based activities. Without question, the classroom setting provides an ideal developmental practice environment for students to serve as group members, facilitators and an informal peer support system in a safe and controlled setting. The experiential-based, five-sectioned manual entitled Effective Activity-Based Group Work was developed for social work students seeking to use activity as a supplement to course requirements and has been well received by students.

One of the primary challenges facing entry level as well as experienced social work practitioners is the ability to effectively create working relationships with groups in a very short period of time. Certainly there was a period in social group work where the use of activity in the group setting was discouraged. Ruth Middleman (1980) discussed this loss as 'a flight from activity in favor of talk'. In part due to Middleman and many others writing and teaching during this time period, a resurgence and belief of activity in the group was born. Beginning practitioners and students are often eager to use activity-based group work. The challenge is that activity-based group work has great potential when activities are chosen to deepen relationships as well as provide purpose and meaning for the interaction instead of to fill silence (Doel & Swanson, 1999). The importance of teaching social work students how to use activity in the group and make educated decisions about activity cannot be stressed enough.

Experiential-based group activities in a classroom setting attempt to close the gaps between theory, practice, and the preparations needed to meet the expectations and demands of social group workers and those who seek services (Frumpkin & Lloyd, 1995; Goldstein. 2001). Shulman (2009) refers to this concept as 'a mixed transactional model'. Dennison (2005) describes this as an opportunity for educators and students to learn about experiential-based group activities designed to link classroom learning with real life experiences. Thus the classroom begins to develop the skills needed in the group. Further review of the literature suggests that social service agencies are looking more towards the use of group work. Whether from a cost cutting/dollar maximizing perspective or a greater understanding of the benefits of mutual aid, agencies are recognizing the benefit of groups over individual and family treatment (Daley & Koppenaal, 1989; Garland, 1992; Strom & Gingerich, 1993). The classroom setting serves as a developmental practice environment to methodically identify the when, where, and how to implement group activities as well as assess their effectiveness. Social work students are provided with the opportunity to serve as members, facilitators and most importantly empowering support systems for each other in a safe and controlled environment. The experiential activities must be carefully selected so that they can offer comfort, support and a means of coping at the various stages within the group process (Redmann, 2006). To the contrary, social workers who fail to consider the nuances of the client population being served, fail to understand how to use activity effectively as a therapeutic intervention and/or fail to consider member characteristics, skills and abilities will most likely be a determent to agency and those being served.

The vast majority of the core undergraduate social work courses require small group work and or team-oriented activity as a crucial supplement to the course content. Repeatedly, it has been demonstrated that experiential-based activity serves as an invaluable tool to draw the necessary connections for students in and between textbook knowledge, classroom discussion, and real-life application. The objectives of the classroom-based group sessions are to address the challenges of effectively establishing and maintaining working relationships in a shortened period of time with clients through activity-based group work as a solution to assisting those hard to reach clients. In addition, the course instructors wanted to teach students how to select group activities that are appropriate to the population they intend to served as well as understand how to use activity effectively as a therapeutic intervention.

There was and continues to be the need to develop a manual that provided individual and small group activities for which program students could draw upon at different stages in the group development process to enhance the work within the group session. Curricula-based manuals have been historically developed and utilized to provide 'a means of systematizing practice, so that practice standards may be consistently met across a variety of workers' (Galinsky, Terizan & Fraser, 2006). The manual developed by the course instructors entitled 'Effective activity-based group work' was developed with the objectives of: 1) addressing the challenges of group work and offer activity-based group work as a solution for those hard to reach clients; 2) learning how to select group activities that are appropriate to the population being served; 3) understanding how to use activity effectively as a therapeutic intervention; and 4) learning numerous group-based activities that participants use in their own group practice. The objectives assist in ensuring that the manual used the most current evidenced-based practices, took into account the realities of implementation by novice/entry level practitioners, provided information regarding the unique dynamics of group processes, while reinforcing the need for constant mindfulness of group culture (Galinsky, Terizan & Fraser, 2006) .

The manual was designed in five sections which provide specific activities or, as coined by Doel and Sawdon (1999), "action techniques" tailored towards the stages of group development to include beginning, middle and ending phases of therapeutic-based group work, team building exercises for non-therapeutic-based group work, and a planning as well as check sheet of considerations prior to and after selection and implementation of an activity. As activities were shared and practiced, the instructors, using a model discussed by Toseland and Rivas (2005), processed questions to include: 1) at what stage of group development would this activity be useful and why?; 2) how would member characteristics, skills, and abilities influence the way you would modify the activity?; and 3) how would you evaluate the usefulness and impact of this activity on the group and its members? This process has been proven to be an essential component in the student's learning, as it reinforces the need for flexibility in planning to account for the inevitability that an activity may not go as planned (Doel & Sawdon, 1999).

An example of one type of activity in the manual involves members using a basic sentence completion activity about human needs. This activity is placed in the work phase section of the manual since it involves some group member reflection of each other. Each group member completes a 'Need Pie' where slices of the pie are symbolic of types of needs (spiritual, cultural, emotional, physical, etc). Once the individual member completes their pie, they share the sentence completion of 'One need I have that is not getting met is____?' and 'One need I see (insert group member name) has that is not getting met is'. This then begins a process of group discussion, confrontation and processing of observations of each member of the group.

The next step in the student's continued learning was a specific assignment to use activity effectively in a particular stage of group work. Students signed up to facilitate a group at either the beginning, middle or end stage of the group. This was done though a simulated group session in the classroom. As students practiced using activity in their simulated sessions, the classroom professor and the observing classmates would evaluate how effective the student was in their facilitation. Instructors also sought feedback from group participants by requiring them to provide verbal and or written feedback regarding: 1) the effectiveness of the session based on the intended goal and purpose; 2) the appropriateness of the activity for the session; 3) the facilitator's ability to plan, implement and end the activity; and 4) what more could the facilitator have done to enhance the activity.

Students reported that the process for them was extremely helpful. When it came time to develop their group skills in the groups they facilitated in both the field and the classroom simulations, they were better prepared to use activities appropriately. After completion of a consent form defining the confidential nature of the feedback, written and verbal evaluations were completed at the conclusion of the group work course. In order to maintain confidentiality, verbal feedback was given directly to a graduate research assistant. One student shared:

> *... at first I was excited to get some ideas, trying to figure out what to do in an hour group seemed hard. But thinking through even just an ice breaker as a way to really get people talking was awesome.*

Another shared:

> *I did one activity, just one and then the people in the group started talking and sharing about what came up for them. I was glad I used something from the middle stage since it made people really think about what they wanted out of the group at a time when we were struggling.*

As part of the evaluation process, students were highly encouraged to add to the manual content as they further developed their skills and practice experience as entry-level practitioners to address what Galinsky, Terizan and Fraser (2006) identify as the 'cultural characteristics' (p.20) which are ever-changing in group work. The process was developed on-line using web-based software where students could post an activity along with suggestions of how best to implement the activity. They were to indicate the stage of group development the activity was most suited to, as well as any additional information that a group worker would need to implement the activity in a group.

Activity in group work can initially be attractive to a novice group worker. A lack of understanding of the importance and complexity of activity-based group work is a common error in mutual-aid-based groups. By understanding how activity-based group work can enhance mutual aid and deepen intimacy of group members, group facilitators will be better prepared to use these skills in their groups. The classroom becomes the perfect learning lab where students are able to practice activity using the framework from a manual developed out of a group work course. Students walk away from the course more prepared, less likely to want to control the group and, hopefully, more effective mutual-aid-based group workers. This process has been evaluated by the course instructors following video-taped sessions, simulation group sessions in the classroom and feedback given by the students at the end of the course. Due to the way the manual was developed, it is not a published work of any one individual. Similar to great stories that are shared through the years, the manual has become an activity-based story that students carry with them as they leave our program. Interested readers can contact the authors for a digital copy.

References

Daley, B. & Koppenaal, G. (1989). Training mental health clinicians to lead short-term psychotherapy groups in an HMO. *Journal of Independent Social Work, 3*(4), 111-124.

Dennison, S. (2005). Enhancing the integration of group theory with practice: A five-part teaching strategy. *The Journal of Baccalaureate Social Work, 10*(2), 1-17.

Doel, M. & Sawdon, C. (1999). *The essential groupworker: Teaching and learning creative groupwork.* London, Eng: Kingsley Publishers.

Frumpkin, M. & Lloyd, G.A. (1995). Social work education. In *Encyclopedia of social work* (3), 2238-2247. Washington, DC: NASW Press.

Galinsky, M.J., Terzian, M.A. & Fraser, M.W.(2006). The art of group work practice with manualized curricula. *Social Work with Groups, 29*(1), 11-26.

Garland, J. (1992). Developing and sustaining group work services: A systemic and systematic view. *Social Work with Groups, 15*(4), 89-90.

Goldstein, H. (2001). *Experiential learning: A foundation for social work education and practice.* Washington, DC: Council on Social Work Education

Middleman, R. (1983). Activities and Action in Group Work. *Social Work with Groups, 6*(1), 3-7.

Redmann, H. (2006). Warning: There a lot of yelling in knitting: The impact of parallel process on empowerment in a group setting. *Journal of Social Work with Groups, 29*(4).

Shulman, L. (2009). *The skills of helping individuals, families and groups.* (4th ed.) Itasca, IL: Peacock Publishers.

Strom, K. & Gingerich, W. (1993). Educating students for new market realities. *Journal of Social Work Education, 29*, 78-97.

Toseland, R. & Rivas, R. (2005). *An introduction to group work practice.* (4th ed.) Boston, MA: Allyn and Bacon.

History
Based on a presentation at the XXXI AASWG Symposium, Chicago, IL, 2009. First published in the Proceedings series in: Bergart, A.M., Simon, S.R., and Mark Doel, M. (Eds.) (2012) *Group Work: Honoring our roots, nurturing our growth.* London:Whiting & Birch (pp.242-247)

Notes on authors (at time of first publication)
Jennifer A. Clements, PhD, LCSW, is Associate Professor, Shippensburg University Department of Social Work and Gerontology. She currently serves on the Executive Committee and is a Board member of AASWG. She enjoys teaching group work at the BSW and MSW levels.

Samuel R. Benbow, D.Ed., M.S. is an Assistant Professor, Shippensburg University Department of Social Work & Gerontology. He is a member of the Association of the Advancement of Social Work with Groups. He enjoys facilitating psychodynamically-based groups with teens and young adults.

Increasing diversity competence in social work students through group research projects

Preface to the 2021 reprint

Stephen Yanca, PhD, MSW, LMSW, ACSW, LMFT was a faculty member in Social Work at Saginaw Valley State University, Michigan, from 1991 until his death in June 2012. He had co-authored (with Louise Johnson) several textbooks related to practice, including *Generalist Social Work Practice with Groups, Generalist social work practice with families,* and *Social work practice: A generalist approach* (Allyn & Bacon). As Dr. Yanca describes in this paper, the theme of diversity-competent practice is prevalent across his writings. This paper provides a good example of how group work can be used to build what he calls diversity competence, a topic needed more than ever today.

Yanca's introduction, published in 2010, hails the election of President Barak Obama in the United States (U.S.), an event that Yanca said represented "a watershed moment that marks the power of people of color in the American electorate." After two terms and putting in place many policies supporting social justice, President Obama was succeeded by a president with very different views. Today, Yanca's discussion of settlement houses is highly relevant, highlighting how workers were involved in helping immigrants adjust to life in America, despite exploitation by employers, landlords, and business people. Settlement workers were dedicated to "advocacy and the ability to organize to overcome exploitation." As Yanca notes, "they were caring, empathetic, genuine, and accepting. In many ways they were the prototypes for modern diversity competent social workers." More than ever, we need group workers educated in the spirit and practice of the settlement house, to prevent exploitation and discrimination and to advocate for human rights, especially for persons leaving their countries or origin to settle in the relative safety of the U.S.

Yanca's chapter offers an approach that helps students develop competence in working with marginalized populations experiencing prejudice, discrimination, and oppression. As part of making a difference in today's world, this chapter offers a practical approach to improving diversity competence through group work.

This preface was written by the Editors, Mark J. Macgowan and Carol S. Cohen due to the death of Stephen J. Yanka in 2012

Increasing diversity competence in social work students through group research projects

Stephen J. Yanca

Introduction

The U.S. is experiencing major demographic changes that will inevitably lead to all races becoming a minority some time around the middle of this century. These changes are evident in the election of Barak Obama as the first African American President. His election represents a watershed moment that marks the power of people of color in the American electorate. However, while some have hailed this event as signaling the beginning of the post-racial era, the rise in racial hatred and hate groups and hate crimes indicate otherwise. The fact is that a majority of white voters did not vote for President Obama, but this was overcome by a huge majority of nonwhite voters.

By the middle of this century, projections indicate that more than half of American high school graduates will be children of color, as well as half of working-age adults. In the U.S., the majority of social workers are white middle and working class females. However, significant numbers of social work clients are not members of this demographic group. There is a great likelihood that social workers and other human service providers will be working cross-racially, cross-culturally, cross-gender, or cross-diversity. Thus, it is imperative that professional social workers become competent in working with clients from diverse backgrounds.

This paper will discuss the concept of diversity competence, the use of groups to increase diversity competence, a model for doing so, and examples of student papers that demonstrate the results of using research groups to study diverse populations.

Diversity competence

At one time, diversity was seen as a barrier to be overcome. During the 1960s when the Civil Rights Movement was at its peak, there was a belief that one should be 'color blind.' However, it is not enough to be 'color-blind' or 'culture blind' or 'diversity blind.' Professing tolerance for diversity can easily be interpreted as being insensitive. Assertions of tolerance may not lead to developing trust in clients who are diverse. In fact, it is more likely to lead to mistrust. Clients may interpret this as diversity does not matter when they know that it does (Johnson & Yanca, 2010). Obviously it should not, but reality is that members of diverse populations have continued to face prejudice, discrimination, and oppression despite the fact that it is now against the law.

Next came the development of ethnic sensitive practice in which the worker respected and valued the ethnicity and culture of the client. However, being sensitive does not mean that the worker would make substantial changes to the way in which services were delivered. Typically it meant that the worker would continue to deliver services in a manner with which he felt comfortable, but he would be sensitive to the differences between himself and his client.

The next step in this evolution has been to develop the concept of cultural competence. This calls for the worker to practice in ways that are consistent with expectations for giving and receiving services or help within the client's culture. This is a very significant and qualitative change in working with diverse cultural groups. In a sense, it calls on the worker to be the one who is likely to feel uncomfortable, not the client. Of course this is really how it should be since the worker is the professional and should be more capable of handling the discomfort involved with the situation. In many respects this approach can serve as the great equalizer in balancing the relationship between helper and the person receiving help.

In the last three editions of *Social work practice: A generalist approach* (8th, 2003; 9th, 2007; and 10th, 2010) and in two other texts that form a trilogy that covers the entire generalist practice curriculum [*Generalist social work practice with families* (2008) and *Generalist social work practice with groups* (2009a)], Louise C. Johnson and this author take this evolution a step further by developing what is called diversity competent practice. This takes the concept of cultural competence and extends it to all forms of diversity. The term diversity may include differences related to age, class, gender, color, culture, disability, ethnicity, marital status, family structure, race, national origin, religion, sex, sexual orientation, or any other distinctive feature or trait. Diversity competent practice is a more descriptive term than cultural competence. The list of populations extends well beyond culture and recognizes that people can be different from each other in many ways, and in multiple ways, as well.

Often students have difficulty in identifying their own diversity. Nichols (unpublished paper cited in Dewees, 2001) found that

> ...many students from White, dominant, middle-class status, particularly in geographical areas with limited racial diversity, regard themselves as having no culture or ethnicity.

This is consistent with the author's experiences teaching BSW students. Some of the lack of cultural identity may be a consequence of the mixing of cultures and ethnic groups in the U.S. Unfortunately, the inability to identify one's own culture or ethnicity does not mean that cultural or ethnic influences do not exist. It merely means that one is not aware of these influences. The author has frequently observed that many young female students have difficulty in recognizing discrimination toward women. This tends to change when the discussion shifts to male privilege especially who did what around the house when they were growing up or in their current living situations (Johnson & Yanca, 2010).

The problem is that the social worker is not likely to recognize or be open to the effects of diversity on his relationships with his diverse clients and will not be prepared to deal with issues his clients' experience related to their diversity. The competent professional social worker must include being 'diversity competent,' or competent in working with diverse clients, especially those who are different from him. Diversity competence begins with becoming aware of one's own diversity, experiences with diversity (direct and vicarious), and the effect that diversity has in one's personal life. Leigh (1998) proposed that knowing one's own cultural influences is critical to developing cultural competence and that everyone has unconscious cultural influences that either are directly prejudicial toward certain other cultures or that lead in that direction. Okum, Fried and Okum (1999) discussed the need to develop self-awareness regarding diversity before being able to develop an awareness of the diversity of others. Lum (1999) cited sources that reinforce the need for self-awareness. According to Diller (1999), one cannot appreciate the effects of culture on others, especially clients, if one is not aware of one's own cultural background. Lu, Lum and Chen (2001) developed a conceptual framework for cultural competence that begins with becoming aware of cultural and ethnic experiences, both personal and professional. They included racism, sexism, homophobia, and other forms of prejudice/discrimination. Two out of four steps proposed by Dewees (2001) for cultural competence with families are related to the need to identify one's own cultural influences (Johnson & Yanca, 2010).

Thus, to become diversity competent, the social worker must begin with an examination of her own diversity, along with examining how her experiences have shaped her attitudes toward her own diversity and the diversity of others. Cultural influences play a major role in this process. The authors cited above indicate that the social worker needs to obtain knowledge about the culture of the client and skills in working within the client's cultural system (Johnson & Yanca, 2010).

Using groups to increase diversity competence

The author was not able to find much research on the effects of using groups to develop diversity or cultural competence. In particular, it appears that little is known about the effects of working together in a research group on the attitudes and beliefs of group members toward diversity. It is suspected that this method may be much more widely used than would be indicated by the paucity of literature. Educators may be using groups to enhance diversity competence, but there does not seem to be actual research or publication regarding the effectiveness of this method.

The research that was found on group work and diversity was focused on the direct interaction among diverse group members. DeLois and Cohen (2000) developed an educational support group in a seminar format to share experiences and study topics by and about people who are GLBT. The article included research activities, but it was clear that the authors saw the interactions among group members as the most salient features of this experience. Nagda, Kim and Truelove (2004) looked at combining classroom learning and intergroup learning to teach about diversity. Teasley, Gourdine and Canfield (2010) found that school social workers identified collaborative practice and increasing knowledge as major facilitators in developing culturally competent practice. In each of these, the concept of collective learning was used, but not with a focus on using research groups. Instead, it was the interaction with diverse members that facilitated the development of diversity competence and not the research activities by the group.

All modern group work texts include a consideration of diversity, but this is focused on diversity within the group as opposed to the use of groups to research and increase diversity competence. However, some potential for the latter is implied by Toseland and Rivas (2005, p.8) when they identify one of four key values: '. . . We value the ability of groups to help enrich members by acquainting them to people from other backgrounds. . .' While this refers to direct interaction with those from diverse backgrounds, it could also be applied to group experiences in which members develop an appreciation for diversity by studying diverse groups.

Considering the development of group work in the early settlement houses can lead one to surmise that attitudes and beliefs among group members can at least be reinforced if not changed by the group experience. The people who were served in the early settlements were immigrants, mainly from Europe. In the larger society, these immigrant groups were looked down on and their status in American society was quite low. This led to prejudice and discrimination. Many of these groups were portrayed in very derogatory ways by the media and others. Most were from countries where autocratic rule and the use of the police and authority against them were the norm. These immigrants were easily exploited by employers, landlords, businessmen, and the like. They needed assistance in making the adjustments necessary to be successful in America. They needed advocacy and the ability to organize to overcome exploitation.

Settlement workers devoted their time and energy to this cause in ways that established what would later become the core of professional social work practice. That is, they were caring, empathetic, genuine, and accepting. In many ways they were the prototypes for modern diversity competent social workers. One might assume that this was planned, but it may not have been. In reality, the settlers had little choice if they were going to be successful in helping the populations they sought to serve. Without these traits, they would have had difficulty in attracting the immigrants to the settlements. After all, their clients were voluntary and the settlers had no real hold on them. On the other hand, caseworkers from charity organization societies (COS) were focused on establishing eligibility for charity. They frequently went out on home visits in doing this. Clients could refuse to let them in, but then that would mean a loss of any benefits. The truth is that COS workers did not need to be caring, empathetic, and accepting. That is not to say that they were not, but there is something coercive and judgmental about establishing eligibility for assistance or for services. In the settlement movement there was a considerable focus on the democratic way of functioning. Jane Addams saw groups as epitomizing the democratic way and allowing group members to experience democracy as part of life and not just a concept or a distant political process (Yanca & Johnson, 2009b).

Gertrude Wilson (1976) made an interesting observation on the development of group work. She indicated that the settlers did not set out to use group work as a means of delivering services. They did so because people frequently came to the settlement with friends, neighbors, and family members (pp.3-4). They might come alone but often they came in groups. Settlement social workers served people in whatever way they presented themselves. As groups were formed, others joined in and social work with groups began. What is particularly important is that groups were generated by the participants. The settlement workers' response represented an early version of 'starting where the client is,' a fundamental principle of social work practice. Allowing the situation to dictate the type of client system (individual, group, family, organization, or community) is a basic principle of generalist social work practice which began with settlement social workers. Of course the principle 'starting where the client is' is also fundamental to diversity competent practice (Yanca & Johnson, 2009b).

The author was not able to uncover any research or consideration of the extent to which settlement workers developed anything resembling diversity competent practice as such. It would seem that at some level, they were cognizant of the need to accept participants as they were before offering them opportunities to learn how to survive and prosper in their new environment. It would seem that developing a culture of caring and acceptance within the settlement house was essential for success. Some settlers lived in the settlement house. Others lived in the community, but would spend time at the settlement house. It would seem that working together collectively was probably some of the attraction for this kind of work. There is also the sense of being part of a movement. However, as accepting as settlers were, early settlements were segregated by race. It is questionable whether settlements could have survived if they were integrated given the intense racism that existed in the U.S. at the time. It is unlikely that whites and blacks would have been comfortable mixing when the larger society was invested in maintaining separation between the races.

The larger society looked down on immigrants who were served by settlers and some looked down on settlers themselves as well, along with their work. To counteract the effects of these negative attitudes, the settlers created a haven from it. They created what might be called a counterculture. Indeed, later counterculture groups formed communes and communities where they lived collectively. It would seem that collective identity and commitment are necessary ingredients to developing and maintaining a counterculture. This serves as part of the rationale for using groups to increase diversity competence. The ability of groups and group behavior to influence individual attitudes and beliefs can be applied to efforts to establish alternative attitudes and beliefs that are different from those that society at large might hold.

Another aspect to consider is the source of negative attitudes and beliefs about various populations that are or might be the objects of prejudice and discrimination. It is proposed that much of this is born out of messages from members of one's family and later from peers and others who hold negative attitudes and beliefs. As a result, it makes sense that some form of collective experience may be necessary to overcome negative attitudes and stereotypes.

In addition to the collective nature of the establishment of negative attitudes, beliefs, and stereotypes, most people who hold these typically have little if any contact with the populations that are the objects of them. Thus, there are few if any opportunities to examine or refute misperceptions. In the absence of support for changing erroneous perceptions, most people will hold on to what they know, especially when those perceptions are supported by both their nurturing and their sustaining environments (Norton, 1978).

Thus, overcoming negative attitudes and stereotypes requires exposure to and information about the objects of these attitudes and stereotypes. To some extent it would seem that this needs to be done in an environment that supports change. It is proposed that such an environment needs to provide collective or group experiences in order to provide the support necessary to overcome the effects of prolonged collective reinforcement that supports entrenched negative attitudes and stereotypes. Thus, it is proposed that negative attitudes and stereotypes toward various populations are primarily formulated through collective experiences (family, peers, society, etc.). If this is accurate, then it is logical to assume that having collective experiences that refute these negative attitudes and beliefs and that support more positive views can lead to changes in attitudes and beliefs about diverse groups. This is the primary rationale behind using group research experiences to study diversity competent practice.

It is interesting to note that experiences in teaching diversity competence in other classes seem different when the teaching comes primarily from the professor. For example, the author's African American colleagues are often seen by students as pushing a personal agenda when they discuss discrimination toward African Americans. Gay and lesbian colleagues are often seen in a similar way when discussing sexual minorities. However, when research is conducted and presented by fellow students and discussed in class, little if any of these perceptions have been evident.

A model for using group research projects to increase diversity competence

For the past decade or so research groups have been used to increase diversity competence in BSW students at Saginaw Valley State University (SVSU) located in the Great Lakes Bay Region of Michigan. Diversity awareness and diversity competence is infused throughout the curriculum. In addition, there is a concentrated study of diversity and privilege in the Human Behavior and the Social Environment II course. In a Social Work Practice I course during junior year, there is a study of an ecosystems strengths based change process with a focus on individuals and on developing diversity competent practice. Students are asked to identify various populations who have experienced prejudice, discrimination, and oppression. Inevitably this process includes women, African Americans, Hispanic/Latinos, sexual minorities, and people who are mentally or physically disabled. These are the major groups with whom social workers are likely to practice in the Great Lakes Bay Region of Michigan. Other groups typically identified are people who are older, children, Native Americans, Asians, and similar populations. If there are sufficient numbers of students, additional groups will typically study people who are older and possibly children. It is pointed out that these groups comprise probably 75-80% of the population of the U.S. In addition, members of these groups have no choice regarding their race, gender, ethnicity, sexual orientation or the like. This makes their treatment even more insidious and blatantly unfair.

Students are given a choice about how to form groups of three or four. One option is to select populations they would like to study and then form groups around these. The other option is to do the opposite, form groups and then choose populations. Most choose to form groups which is actually preferred because they tend to form groups around acquaintanceship. It is hoped that this might make the experience more intense. Groups of strangers might allow participants to dismiss findings or attitudes that are different from their own. This is more difficult when they are in groups consisting of friends and acquaintances. Of course there is a risk that a group might reinforce negative attitudes and stereotypes, but the structure of the assignment makes this difficult.

Groups are asked to choose their top three populations they would like to study. They are encouraged to include groups that are unfamiliar or might present challenges. Preference is given to their first choice followed by second and third. During the semester, time is set aside in class for groups to meet and discuss their work and they also do so outside class. The professor visits groups to assist in focusing on important issues or approaches to be considered. During the last four weeks of the semester, groups give Power Point presentations on their population followed by a discussion of diversity competent practice with that population. The assignment as it appears in the syllabus is as follows:

Research/Focus Group on Diversity Competence
Research/Focus Groups will research diversity competent practice with a diverse and disadvantaged and/or oppressed population. Diversity competent practice involves developing knowledge, values and skills that will allow the social worker to serve that population in a manner that is comfortable for the client. The main areas that will be covered by each group will include: 1) Describe the history of the population, especially in the U.S., its strengths, and the primary characteristics by which members are identified. Describe formal and informal mechanisms in American society that cause or reinforce discrimination and/or oppression (past and present). Describe attitudes and stereotypes (current and historical) of the dominant culture toward the population and the impact of these attitudes on the population (psychological, physical, political, economic, social, etc.); 2) Describe privileges and advantages that dominant groups have over the population (male privilege, white privilege, heterosexual privilege, wealth or class privilege, etc.). Identify personal and professional values and beliefs held by most social workers, values and beliefs held by the population and values and beliefs of the dominant culture that are relevant in becoming diversity competent. Describe how these values and beliefs are similar, different, and/or in conflict with each other. Describe how privilege and

these differences or conflicts in values or beliefs might influence the helping process; 3) Identify knowledge and skills regarding relationship building, assessment, planning, actions, evaluation and termination that are necessary to become diversity competent; and 4) Identify at least two direct and two indirect intervention methods that should be used with your population and describe how these would be used to serve them in a diversity competent manner. These areas should be divided by each group in an equitable manner according to the number of students. Each student is responsible for writing a research paper on their portion of the study and will participate in a group presentation. At least 5 professional sources must be used for your report. At least 3 of those sources must be articles from professional journals or historic chronicles. In addition, you may include interviews with people who have expertise with the population being studied. Each group will facilitate a class discussion regarding their population. The purposes of this assignment are: 1) to learn about diversity competent practice with a diverse population; 2) to learn how to conduct research about diversity competent practice with a diverse population; 3) to learn how to write a college level research paper; 4) to begin developing a professional identity that includes sharing knowledge with others; and 5) to use this class project as a means of enhancing cultural and diversity competence. (Yanca & Johnson, 2010)

During their senior year, students develop a portfolio in which they analyze their experiences in each course. Many identify their diversity research groups as the most significant learning experience in Practice I. Some identify this experience as life changing or attitude changing. The two populations that seem to generate this change most often are women and sexual minorities. Many female students were not aware of the history or the pervasiveness of discrimination toward women. For those studying sexual minorities, some students who have strong religious backgrounds have actually changed their attitudes and beliefs entirely. Others have moderated their positions sufficiently to allow them to be much less judgmental and more open to serving members of these populations while setting aside their religious teachings or beliefs.

It is proposed that the success of this activity lies in part in the use of small groups to form what DeLois and Cohen (2000) called 'an educational support group.' In addition, the use of a structured research assignment creates a context that influences the groups to study aspects of diversity that may not be well known and are almost certainly not the basis for the negative attitudes and stereotypes to which group members have been subjected. In addition, group presentations to the class can create a larger educational support group to support the development of diversity competent practice skills.

The combination of a structured group research project along with a group experience of studying and presenting information on diverse populations can enhance the development of diversity competence. This model is an example of how this can be accomplished. It may be that small group learning activities are a more powerful approach than instruction from teachers regarding topics that relate to attitudes and beliefs. Further study is needed to support this.

Examples of diversity research group projects

Nowhere is the transition to greater diversity awareness and competence more apparent than in some of the writings that are produced by students who have participated in the group research project in Social Work Practice I. The following are some excerpts from a sample of those papers. The first is by Autumn Ward (2009), a 20-something year-old female student who wrote the following to describe the connection between *The Bible*, European history, and the attitudes and treatment of women in early America:

The notion that women were meant by God to serve mankind began the treatment of women as inferior beings without a voice. This led to the denial of a woman's right to vote, own property, work outside the home in many professions, go to college, bring suit to court, or even choose what to do with her own body (Rowland, 2004). As far back as the Middle Ages, women were valued solely for their procreative abilities, in other words, the ability to produce heirs so that their husbands could gain status in society (Rowbotham, 1997). This idea that women were only valued for their ability to bear children did not stop in the Middle Ages, this notion was passed down through generations. Early American society deemed women as dependents of their men folk, who would speak for them in economic, political, and legal affairs. When America was first founded, the leaders ... adopted the same rules regarding women that had worked so well in Europe ... to keep women submissive to their husbands, fathers, and masters. When a woman married a man, all of her moveable property she had owned previous to marriage became her husband's to sell, keep, or give away as he pleased, leaving women nothing to call their own (Rowland, 2004).

Ward (2009) pointed out the strong connection between reproduction and the oppression of women as she cited sources that described how attitudes toward bearing children were used to justify this.

A woman's destiny ... was to bear children. In early American society, a single female – one devoid of maternal instincts, or one who refused to have children – was a so called threat to society, as dangerous as terrorism, viral and contagious, and downright unpatriotic (Rowbotham, 1997). ... Women were not allowed to take contraceptives, or even look at information regarding any type of birth control. Birth control information was not to be distributed, and doctors could not even prescribe it. Anthony Comstock('s) ... efforts against contraceptives gave way to a law forbidding the use of the postal system to distribute any type of contraceptive paraphernalia. Women were not allowed to choose whether or not they would like to bear children, they were basically told they had to (Rowland, 2004). This idea that women should not have the right to choose to be a mother paved the way for thousands of botched abortions, deaths from childbirth, and suicides (Cook & Howard, 2007). So women did have a choice, they could choose not have children and die, or choose to have children and die anyway.

Ward (2009) concluded her paper as follows:

In conclusion, women have endured everything from being deemed a genetic flaw, to having leeches 'cure' her so called female diseases. Women have battled with discrimination for centuries, and finally put up a fight for their freedom from the role of submissive housewife. Women are strong, capable, intelligent, and contrary to what they have been told in the past, they are very useful in so many more ways than just to bear children. Although women have fought a few battles of inequality, and came out victorious, the war is yet to be won.

A second paper by Kelsey Clark (2010), a Caucasian female in her 20s, discussed the use of a feminist approach in the change process consisting of engagement, assessment, planning, action, and evaluation and termination:

... To build a successful relationship with a client who is a woman, it is important to understand that culture uses woman-blaming themes quite often. It is this type of problem that leads to and encourages gender oppression. Also, in many stories women are considered responsible for men's behavior (Hare-Mustin, 1994, as cited in Wood & Roche, 2001).

Clark (2010) added the following:

Women are often taught by society to internalize problems. From the time they are little girls, society creates the idea that many of the issues women deal with are caused by themselves, not those around them. It is this internalizing that needs to be addressed when working with a female client. Teaching a female client to externalize is very important. Externalizing is a process that separates a problem from the client who is dealing with it and makes it a separate entity. Teaching this to a client can help them to stand with the client and against the separate problem (Wood & Roche, 2001).

Clark (2010) concludes with the following summary:

... During the time the worker spends with the client he should continue to engage in radical listening, which includes listening attentively, listening to bear witness, deconstructive listening, and also listening with planned emptiness. . . The social worker should also continue to undermine the oppressive beliefs that the client has. This means the worker should help the client externalize issues. The worker should use deconstructive questioning with the client and seek resistant and defiant ideas and responses from the client. This will help to remind the client of times when she has resisted the oppression placed on her. Finally, the social worker should apply the principle of co-creating a revisioned self-story. By doing this the worker will bring about the process of honoring heroism and courage ... (Wood & Roche, 2001).

A third research paper is by Jennifer Miller (2009), a Caucasian female in her 20s as well. She wrote about using the change process with people who are members of sexual minorities:

... While individuals differ in the diversity groups they are most uncomfortable with, it is not uncommon for social work students to be uncomfortable when talking about working with clients who are not heterosexual. ... it was found that students with limited knowledge of these groups tend to distance themselves from these clients, potentially affecting the services that are provided. ... social workers are often unaware of relevant issues affecting this population and not adequately prepared to serve clients who are not heterosexual. Forty-two per cent of interviewed social work students reported feeling as though they lacked essential knowledge about the issues and challenges faced by gay, lesbian, bisexual, and transgendered individuals. It was mentioned that tolerance or sensitivity do not equal competence ... (Logie, Bridge & Bridge, 2007). Attempting to avoid work with clients is not effective, because it is inevitable that at some point, homophobic attitudes of the worker, if present, will need to be addressed.

Miller (2009) made the following observations:

Living with societal hatred and dealing with homophobic reactions by those in the client's environment are two issues that must be addressed. ... The worker must be comfortable discussing such issues and knowledgeable of the ways that individuals who are gay, lesbian, bisexual, or transgendered are affected by prejudices. One factor ... is the individual's religious affiliation. Belonging to a religion that condemns homosexuality adds psychological stress to the client, because he or she is believed to be immoral by those in the religious community. One study ... found that the more religious people claim to be, the more likely they are to possess homophobic attitudes toward the GLBT population (Rowatt, *et al.*, 2006). Significant differences have been found among religious groups concerning the level of homophobia present, with Protestant individuals reporting more negative attitudes than Catholic respondents (Logie, Bridge & Bridge, 2007). While these religions teach the principle of loving one's neighbor and stress the importance of brotherhood, divisive attitudes directed at people who do not fit the dominant group cause GLBT individuals to become further stigmatized. Being aware of these beliefs and the exclusion of homosexuals from many religious institutions will allow the worker to understand that even if the client is interested in practicing a religion, it may not be as easy for him or her to feel accepted and part of a church family as it is for a heterosexual individual. Even if the individual is accepted, they may be viewed as sinner and the client may hear messages against homosexuality, and the need to seek forgiveness for being homosexual. The client may not feel understood by the other members because it is assumed that he or she can change their 'sinful behavior'. It is assumed that they have chosen homosexuality over heterosexuality. This plays a role in the previously mentioned lack of support system for individuals in the GLBT community. A lack of spiritual institutions that accept individuals in this population further limits the support system that is available.

These excerpts from student research papers are presented to illustrate the quality of work and the insight that has been generated from their group research project experiences and evidence of advanced understanding of the concept of diversity competent practice. These are from young junior level BSW students.

Conclusion

In conclusion, modern social workers are expected to develop competence in working with diverse populations. These populations are at risk of being disadvantaged along with experiencing prejudice, discrimination, and oppression. Students need to be aware of their own attitudes, beliefs, and stereotypes toward these groups as well as the source of these misconceptions.

This paper accompanied a workshop on increasing diversity competence in students by using a group research project. It examined how altitudes toward diversity on the part of settlement workers may have been influenced by the collective experiences of living and working with each other and with the immigrants whom they served. It proposed that collective activities probably gave considerable support for having and acting on attitudes and beliefs toward those immigrants that were different from the larger society. Support from groups can be quite powerful in changing and sustaining attitudes and beliefs. This proposition has been applied to increasing diversity competence in social work students through the use of group research projects by the Social Work Department at Saginaw Valley State University. The paper presents a group research assignment along with examples from student papers.

More research is needed regarding the use of research groups to increase diversity competence and the effects of group research experiences on changing and shaping attitudes and beliefs about diverse populations. It is proposed that the use of groups can be a powerful tool in increasing diversity competent practice.

References

Cook, R. & Howard, S. (2007). Accommodating women's differences under the women's anti-discrimination convention. *Emory Law Journal, 56*, 1039-1092.

Clark, K. (2010, unpublished paper). Women and diversity. Submitted Winter 2009, Saginaw Valley State University, University Center, MI (SVSU). Quoted with permission.

DeLois, K. & Cohen, M. (2001). A queer idea: Using group work principles to strengthen learning in a sexual minorities seminar. *Social Work with Groups, 23*(3), 53-67

Dewees, M. (2001). Building cultural competence for working with diverse families: Strategies from the privileged side. *Ethnic & Cultural Diversity in Social Work, 9*(3), 33–51.

Diller, J. (1999). *Cultural diversity: A primer for the human services* (p.14). Belmont, CA: Brooks/Cole & Wadsworth.

Hare-Mustin, R. (1994). Discourses in the mirrored room: A postmodern analysis of therapy. *Family Process, 33*, 19-35.

Johnson, L. & Yanca, S. (2010). *Social work practice: A generalist approach* (10th edn.). Boston, Massachusetts: Allyn & Bacon.

Leigh, J. (1998). *Communicating for cultural competence* (pp.31–33). Boston: Allyn & Bacon.

Logie, C., Bridge, T.J. & Bridge, P.D. (2007). Evaluating the phobias, attitudes, and cultural competence of Master of Social Work students toward the LGBT populations. *Journal of Homosexuality, 53*(4), 201-221.

Lu, Y., Lum, D. & Sheying Chen, S. (2001). Cultural competency and achieving styles in clinical social work: A conceptual and empirical exploration. *Ethnic & Cultural Diversity in Social Work, 9*(3/4), 6.

Lum, D. (1999). *Culturally competent practice: A framework for understanding diverse groups and justice issues.* Pacific Grove, CA: Brooks/Cole.

Miller, J. (2009, unpublished paper). Social work with the GLBT community: A walk through the change process. Submitted Winter 2009, SVSU. Quoted with permission.

Nagda, B., Kim, C. & Truelove, Y. (2004). Learning about difference, learning with others, learning to transgress. *Social Issues, 60*(1), 195-214

Nichols, W. (2001). 'Portfolio,' unpublished paper (University of Vermont, Burlington), as cited by Marty Dewees in: Building cultural competence for working with diverse families: Strategies from the privileged side. *Ethnic & Cultural Diversity in Social Work, 9*(3), 41.

Norton, D. (1978). *The dual perspective.* New York: Council on Social Work Education.

Okum, B., Fried, J. & Okum, M. (1999). *Understanding diversity: A learning-as-practice primer* (chaps. 2 & 3). Pacific Grove, CA: Brooks/Cole.

Rowatt, W., Tsang, J., Kelly, J., LaMartina, B., McCullers, M. & McKinley, A. (2006). Associations between religious personality dimensions and implicit homosexual prejudice. *Journal for the Scientific Study of Religion, 45*(3), 397-406.

Rowbotham, S. (1997). *A century of women.* New York: Penguin Books.

Rowland, D. (2004). *The boundaries of her body: The troubling history of women's rights in America.* Naperville: Sphinx Publishing.

Toseland, R. & Rivas, R. (2005). *An introduction to group work practice* (5th edn.). Boston: Allyn & Bacon

Ward, A. (2009, unpublished paper). Living with discrimination: A history of women's fight for rights. Submitted Winter 2009, SVSU. Quoted with permission.

Wilson, G. (1976). From practice to theory: A personalized history. In R. Roberts & H. Northern (Eds.), *Theories of social work with groups.* New York: Columbia Press.

Wood, G. & Roche, S. (2001). An emancipatory principle for social work with survivors of male violence. *Affilia, 16*(1), 66-79.

Yanca, S. & Johnson, L. (2008). *Generalist social work practice with families.* Boston: Allyn & Bacon.

Yanca, S. & Johnson, L. (2009a). *Generalist social work practice with groups.* Boston: Allyn & Bacon.

Yanca, S. & Johnson, L. (2009b). Generalist social work practice with groups: Sharing the past, present, and future. Paper presented at 31st International Symposium on Social Work with Groups, Chicago, June, 2009.

Yanca, S. & Johnson, L. (2010). *Instructors manual and test bank for social work practice: A generalist approach* (10th edn.). Boston: Allyn & Bacon: Sample Syllabus.

History

Based on a presentation at the XXXII AASWG Symposium, Montréal. Québec, 2010. First published in the Proceedings series in: Roy, V., Berteau, G., and Genest-Dufault, S. (Eds.) (2014) *Strengthening Social Solidarity through Group Work: Research and creative practice.* London: Whiting & Birch (pp.91-108)

Notes on authors (at time of first publication)

Stephen J. Yanca, PhD, DIPLO, ACSW, LMSW, LMFT, was Professor of Social Work at Saginaw Valley State University. Prior to his recent passing, he was a productive university scholar and an active member of IASWG. He received an MSW from Wayne State University, and a Ph.D. from Michigan State University. He had experience in counseling, group work, child welfare, juvenile corrections, community mental health, supervision, and administration. He was the co-author of three social work texts, and his life and contributions are still cherished by his former students and colleagues.

The 'Rainbow Nation' way of teaching sensitivity to diversity for social work with groups

Preface to the 2021 reprint

Eight years since this paper was originally presented, the "Rainbow Nation", a term coined by Archbishop Desmond Tutu to reflect the unique diversity of South Africa is still used 23 years into democracy after the positive political changes in 1994. Although one would want to see the rainbow as a unit, it is both impossible and insensitive to disregard the diversity and the differences. Diversity does not only refer to race, culture and class differences. It includes characteristics that make people unique and provide an identity (Reynecke, 2017). Divides, discrimination and racial confrontations in South Africa continue (Swartz et al, 2014). Considering diversity, discrimination and multicultural contexts, this is not unique to the South African context. Racial tension and confrontations occur worldwide. Teaching sensitivity to diversity and cultural competence as teaching practices that are offered but one time to make people aware and particularly social work students in preparation for their contexts, would however not be sufficient in establishing cultural competency.

Diversity training and attempts to understand, accommodate and embrace human differences are vital to aid in becoming effective citizens and professionals (Bozalek & Biersteker, 2010; Kerelian 2017; Reyneke, 2017; Williams 2017). However, lived experiences are crucial in the process of becoming sensitive to differences and acknowledging diversity (Cross & Naidoo 2012; Kerelian 2017; Prinsloo et al, 2017; Williams 2017). Exposure to and experience of differences contribute to acknowledging, respecting and familiarizing oneself with the contexts of other human beings. Experiences contribute to learning, thus having an influence on cognitive, social and emotional spheres

(Prinsloo, 2014; Reyneke, 2017). Safe spaces and imaginary experiences prove valuable in diversity training, with an emphasis on positive experiences to learn and unlearn (Cross & Naidoo, 2012). Kerelian (2017) emphasizes that diversity, often asking for a confrontational approach provides a rich opportunity, yet not only in the form of training but through lived experiences. Confrontation, discomfort and criticism are key elements in working towards sensitivity to diversity (Cross & Naidoo 2012; Swartz et al, 2014; Williams 2017).

Since the paper was written, the author has presented different experiential programs in teaching sensitivity to diversity in social work with groups (Prinsloo, 2014; Prinsloo et al, 2017). Feedback from students continuously emphasise the value of opening issues of differences, sharing lived experiences and knowledge and critically engaging with diversity as beneficial in creating understanding, tolerance, respect and acceptance. Involving people, and in the case of this article social work students in programs where they can feel, talk, live and share their differences, create pathways for growth.

Reineth Prinsloo

Reineth Prinsloo is an Associate Professor in the Department of Social Work and Criminology at the University of Pretoria in South Africa

References

Bozalek, V. & Biersteker, L. (2010) Exploring power and privilege using participatory learning and action techniques. *Social Work Education*, 29, 551–572

Cross, M. and Naidoo, D. (2012) Race, Diversity Pedagogy: mediated learning experience for transforming racist habitus and predispositions. *Review of Education, Pedagogy, and Cultural Studies*, 34, 5, 227-244

Kerelian, N.N. (2017) Placing diversity: graduate encounters with group work. *Social Work with Groups*, 40, 1-2, 107-112

Prinsloo, R. (2014) Social work values and principles: students' experiences in intervention with children and youths in detention. *Journal of Social*

Work Practice: Psychotherapeutic Approaches in Health, Welfare and the Community, 28, 4, 445-460

Prinsloo, R., Botha, J., Human, L., Maphalala, L., Masuku, T., Tshapela, Z. and Van den Berg. E. (2017) Flowers and a garden, children and games, laughter and fun: unity in diversity. *Social Work with Groups*, 40, 1-2, 129-136

Reyneke, R.P. (2017) Apples and Pears: engaging social work students in social dialogue. *Research on Social Work Practice*, 27, 2, 239-247 [Accessed 6 January 2018 at http://journals.sagepub.com/toc/rswa/27/2]

Swartz, S., Arogundade, E. and Davis, D. (2014) Unpacking (white) privilege in a South African university classroom: A neglected element in multicultural educational contexts. *Journal of Moral Education*, 43, 3, 345–361

Williams, N.J. (2017) When the trainer got trained: seven things I learned about delivering diversity trainings. *Social Work with Groups*, 40, 1-2, 3-9

The 'Rainbow Nation' way of teaching sensitivity to diversity for social work with groups

Reineth Prinsloo

Because social work clients are often members of oppressed, vulnerable and disempowered groups, teaching sensitivity to diversity and empowering social work students to be culturally competent is of the utmost importance. South Africa's history of *apartheid* has had detrimental effects on personal, social, economic, and political development. A department of social work at a university in South Africa introduced specific study units within its BSW programme to address the influence of this particularly vicious form of discrimination. The units help students to confront their own prejudices, enhance their self-awareness, and obtain knowledge of and exposure to diverse client populations. This paper discusses the need for coursework in this area, and describes the process of teaching these study units.

'I am glad for the word *apartheid*'. The audience falls silent. How is it possible for a white South African woman to state this at an international symposium in the United States of America?

The liberation of South Africa from apartheid in 1994 has resulted in changes which have forced the people of this 'Rainbow Nation' towards greater tolerance and accommodation. It is the author's opinion that by openly *naming*, discussing, criticizing, judging, and eventually addressing apartheid, discrimination and insensitivity to cultural diversity are finally being confronted in South African society.

South Africa has eleven official languages and as many and more different cultural groups. This diversity creates many wonderful opportunities to learn about other cultures and overcome conscious or unconscious discrimination. This paper describes the specific study units developed by a department of social work at a university in South Africa to prepare their BSW students to address the influence of apartheid.

63

The effects of apartheid

The former National Party of South Africa, consisting mainly of white South Africans, implemented and maintained a system referred to as 'apartheid' – an extreme form of discrimination and insensitivity to diversity – from 1948 until 1994. This political party used their immense power to influence people and decide on the distribution of resources. As Mamphiswana and Noyoo (2000, p.31) emphasize, apartheid was a brutal form of colonial domination that sapped the energies of the people and eroded their self-worth. Apartheid had detrimental effects on personal, social, economic, and political development. Poverty and inequality in South Africa result from centuries of colonialism and apartheid during which indigenous populations were oppressed and their lands, productive assets, cultural heritage and self-respect severely impacted (Hölscher, 2008, pp.120-121).

South Africa has been faced with many challenges with regard to a 'new' way of functioning since the democratization in 1994. All spheres of life and social relations have been affected. While the nation has reached higher levels of liberation from apartheid since 1994, poverty, structural oppression, and power imbalances continue (Smith, 2008, p.371).

Sensitivity to diversity in social work

Cultural diversity refers to the variety in human society and culture in a specific region – seen in aspects such as language, dress, tradition and the way people interact with their environment. Unfortunately, human beings often respond to diversity with conscious or unconscious discrimination. Discrimination and abuse of power are worldwide phenomena. As defined by Zastrow (2009, p.198), discrimination means taking action against people because they belong to a specific category of people. Such behaviour is unethical. Although there are different views about specific social work values and principles, most reflect the acceptance and positive evaluation of diverse ways of life (Wilson et al., 2008, p.83).

Failing to recognise the reality of all people, but especially a disadvantaged or socially excluded person, may in itself be regarded as oppression (Wilson *et al.*, 2008, p.83). Miley *et al.* (2009, p.94) regard oppression as the injustice that results from domination and control of resources by favoured groups. Social work deals with clients that are oppressed, disempowered and vulnerable. This necessitates that social workers should confront the multiple dimensions of oppression (Miley *et al.*, 2009, pp.95-96), understand the world of the powerless, and not contribute to oppression in any way.

Populations served by social workers cut across diverse socio-cultural contexts. Social workers need a depth of knowledge and skills to intervene with sensitivity (Carter-Black, 2007). Cultural competence and a practical familiarity are of the utmost importance to maintain high standards in service delivery (Corey & Corey, 1996, p.28; Carter-Black, 2007, p.31; Allen-Meares, 2007, p.83). Social workers with a culturally sensitive approach appreciate clients' uniqueness (Miley *et al.*, 2009, p.70). Acceptance of and respect for this uniqueness are necessary for competence.

Sensitivity to diversity in group work

Konopka (1983) suggests that the following values related to diversity are important in group work practice:
1. positive relations and participation among people of different colour, creed, age, national origin and social class;
2. a high degree of individualization so that every member's unique concerns are addressed.

Group leaders often work with group members from diverse backgrounds. The *Standards for social work practice with groups*, developed by the Association for the Advancement of Social Work with Groups, Inc. (1998) emphasizes that a core value of group work practice is respect for persons and their autonomy. Group workers must place a high value on respect for diversity in all its dimensions, including culture, ethnicity, gender, sexual orientation, physical and mental abilities, and age (Johnson & Johnson, 2003, p.479). They should appreciate and understand the differences among members, and between members and the group worker, that may influence practice.

Effective group work practice calls for cultural competence.

No matter how stigmatized group members may be by society, they deserve to be treated with respect and dignity. Group work should facilitate understanding and camaraderie among people from diverse backgrounds (Toseland & Rivas, 2009, p.8). Effective counsellors learn how to recognize diversity and shape their intervention according to the world of a group member. Lordan and Wilson (2002, p.11) emphasize the importance of naming differences as a first step to understanding them. Identifying and engaging differences from the beginning of the group create opportunities for better understanding and intervention. Doel (2006, p.143) emphasizes that it is likely that there will be different values within every group and that denying or suppressing differences will not make them disappear.

Not only should group workers help members to recognize differences and understand them, but they should also recognize and understand their own values and differences. As Marsiglia (2003, p.84) points out, group workers' world views, beliefs and values influence their practice. A group worker has to be clear about his or her own values and perceptions before attempting to engage with others.

Culturally skilled group workers will move away from their own values and prejudices to understand the world of their group members. It is, however, not possible to do so without understanding their own cultural conditioning and family of origin beliefs, as well as the socio-political systems that they are part of. Family of origin provides the foundation of culture, gender expectations, and general perceptions of society (Waldegrave, 2009, p.86). For example, the political system in South Africa dictated and ascribed certain values and prejudices to different groups, regardless of individual differences, and this was conveyed in the context of the family of origin.

If group workers are not aware of their own values, they will have difficulty when faced with value-laden situations. Exercises to clarify values can help group workers to identify personal and professional values that may influence their group work practice. Supervision can also help group workers to become aware of their own values, and to modify or change values that are neither consistent with the values of the social work profession nor helpful in their group work practice.

Members who reflect on and recognise their own culture are more likely to participate and to benefit from intervention (Marsiglia, 2003, p.85). Group workers should be aware of the cultural backgrounds of group members, and how their backgrounds affect their attitudes about sharing personal information with persons outside the family or their culture (Henry, 1992). Group workers also need to be sensitive to the effects that cultural diversity have on valued behaviour in the group. Culture influences beliefs about social distance, the appropriate way to speak, the proper treatment of persons in authority positions and certain age groups, and the correct way to address persons from other cultural or age groups.

Sensitivity to all of these factors requires knowledge with regard to the values of different cultural groups. A group leader should understand the different cultures of group members as well as how these cultures affect participation in group contexts (Jacobs *et al.*, 2009, p.140; Zastrow, 2009, p.215).

The role of social work education

Preparing social work students to conduct their practice with respect for diversity and sensitivity to discrimination has been a long-standing objective of social work education. Social work programs across the globe have a responsibility to teach sensitivity to diversity in order to prepare social workers to address inequality and help vulnerable groups affected by skewed power and racism. This holds especially true for teaching social work in post-apartheid South Africa.

Collective social responsibility is necessary in order to overcome the legacy of apartheid. Social work holds an excellent position in such collective efforts.

> Social work has ... a major role in rejuvenating the spirit of self-worth, especially amongst the African communities who were brutalized both physically and mentally by apartheid for many years (Mamphiswana & Noyoo, 2000, p.31).

Erasmus (2006) in Leibowitz *et al.* (2007, p.703) argues that race, as well as identity based on racial perceptions, influences the lives of South African students. Since social work students enter the field of study from a specific historical and rational context of racial discrimination, it is imperative that social work teachers stimulate the process of critical reflection (Smith, 2008, p.374).

The department of social work in a university in South Africa has developed a program to teach sensitivity to diversity. The department has a diverse student population, including individuals from the different cultural and ethnic groups. These students are exposed to equally diverse client groups in their social work practice. Cultural sensitivity is thus of the utmost importance.

Teaching diversity in a South African BSW programme

This paper describes the activities used for teaching sensitivity to diversity in a BSW programme within a department of social work in a South African university.

The first year practice module aims to enhance understanding and sensitivity to diversity. In order to accomplish this goal, lecturers purposefully divide students into small groups, based on gender and cultural/ethnic diversity. They attempt to ensure that practice groups include both male and female students from different ethnic backgrounds. Within these groups, students identify and discuss their individual cultural practices, with an emphasis on being sensitive and respectful to fellow learners. The importance of cultural sensitivity in social work practice is discussed.

Social work students receive the opportunity to gain knowledge in group supervision and discussion classes when talking about rituals and practices in their cultures. Dating and mating rituals, wedding practices, funeral rituals and methods of communication are discussed. Students become aware of dowry practices in modern times; the management of marital conflict in traditional families; extended family practices; the use of eyes in communication to reflect respect; and norms for addressing someone older than oneself.

A handshake is very important in African greetings and is done in a specific way. Students unfamiliar with the handshake learn how to greet in the appropriate way, while the students teaching their peers feel privileged to do so. Greetings in the different languages are practiced. This exercise results in laughter and bonding at the same time, as students struggle to pronounce the words correctly. Students are encouraged to greet each other in the different languages outside the classroom setting. It is clear that they enjoy learning how to greet in a different language, but what is even more important is that the students being greeted in their own language feel valued and understood. Students are also encouraged to enquire about the origin and meaning of each other's names. Showing interest in another's name makes a person feel respected and valued.

Animals have many meanings in Africa, and certain animals signify certain character qualities. Some cultures view owls as bad omens, rather than as embodiments of wisdom and intelligence. A baboon may be regarded as an evil spirit and even be linked to witchcraft. A chameleon may be associated with witchcraft because of its ability to change colour. Students need to have knowledge of these meanings in order to intervene in a sensitive way. In conversations, exercises, and classroom discussions they learn to be sensitive to the use of animal metaphors.

Exercises to discuss the above cultural practices and meanings are included in the study units. Experiences are reflected in narrative reports and, where necessary, discussed in supervision. Students openly admit their ignorance about other cultures and aspects of diversity and are excited to learn about each other's cultures.

Feedback from students includes the following comments:

1. 'I now understand the emphasis on getting engaged and having an engagement ring. I thought it was just to show off and never knew that it was an expectation.'
2. 'I am glad that I do not have to be present when the bridegroom slaughters a cow but now understand that it is a cultural ritual. The colourful wedding process to incorporate western and traditional practices amazes me. I wish that I can have the opportunity to be invited to such a wedding.'

Teaching sensitivity to diversity intensifies in the second year of the programme and focuses on self-development. Within small groups, students further identify diverse cultural practices amongst themselves and in the community. These groups are again purposefully composed to be culturally/ethnically diverse. Students are asked to confront their own personal stereotypes and prejudices. Lecturers facilitate the development of awareness and mutual understanding of group members' cultural practices.

Class exercises to clarify values can help students to identify personal and professional values that may influence their practice. They examine their own personal backgrounds and socialization experiences, consider personal manifestations of prejudice, and then list ways to overcome their prejudices.

Students discuss specific scenarios where cultural and religious diversity are prominent. An example of such a scenario is one in which a black farm worker is killed by both a white and a black man and then fed to a lion on the farm. What do students see when they first read the headline? A white man killed a black man? A white man and a black man committed murder? Just a brutal murder?

A second example involves a single sex white couple wanting to adopt a black AIDS orphan. Do students first see that this couple is single sex? Do they see a white couple wanting to adopt a black baby? Do they see the selfless act of providing a home to an orphan?

In response to these scenarios students, within two-hour classes, identify and reflect upon their own prejudices and identify areas for change and growth. Their responses include:

1. 'When I first read the scenario I saw a black farm worker killed by a white man. When I read it again and we discussed it in class I realised that it was murder and had nothing to do with race. I realise that my family background and the way I was raised make me to sometimes respond with the looking glass of prejudice, induced by my family that suffered because of apartheid. I have to change my own way of thinking. I cannot react this way as a social worker.'
2. 'Perhaps the white man used the black man to do his dirty work. No, they both killed a man. This has nothing to do with skin colour and I may not think this way. Murder is wrong!'
3. 'HIV/AIDS is such an enormous problem and children do not ask to be influenced. Anyone that can provide a home, love and care should do so. Sexual preferences and ethnic group play no role.'
4. 'I will gladly assist in facilitating adoption of orphans because of the pandemic, regardless of diversity.'
5. 'How can I be so stuck on skin colour? Are we not all the same human beings with similar feelings? Apartheid was so wrong.'

Students indicate that confronting and discussing these scenarios, although disturbing, forces introspection and change. They report enhanced awareness of their own beliefs, prejudices, and values.

Each second year student is required to conduct and record an interview with a person who has a sexual, cultural or religious orientation, which is different from his or her own. Lecturers assess the contribution of the interview to the student's own sensitivity to diversity. Student comments include: 'I have never thought that a person of that religion experienced so much stigmatization, even here on campus. The interview made me realise that I should not do the same and never judge. I have to respect people's preferences' and 'The person from the interview could not thank me enough for asking and showing interest. He thinks that everyone should be willing to gain knowledge to understand and not to judge without knowing.'

During the second year, students reflect on their self-development in reports of their growing awareness, insight, and self-confidence. They are also expected to demonstrate the ability to internalise their new skills and knowledge in everyday practice and in professional conduct during class exercises.

The theory module for social work intervention with groups provides the basis for the practice training which follows. Students work in task groups and discuss approaches to multi-cultural group work, as well as ways for the group worker to intervene with sensitivity to issues of diversity in the group. All students in the task groups, in turn, discuss their ethnic backgrounds. They discuss how their heritage might influence participation in a group. They also discuss how demographic variables such as age, gender, education, or socio-economic status influence the behaviour of group members. A volunteer within the task group discusses an incident in which he/she experienced prejudice or discrimination (prejudice could occur because of many characteristics, such as age, race, gender, or disability).

The study unit on self-development comes together in a practice experience in which students demonstrate their sensitivity to diversity by conducting life-skills groups with first year students from diverse backgrounds.

Finally, students complete an assignment involving sketching a possible diversity scenario for a treatment group. They are required to discuss one of the eight ways proposed by Toseland and Rivas (2009, pp.139-146) in which the group leader can intervene with *sensitivity to issues of diversity* in the group:

1. Using social work values and skills
2. Using a strength perspective
3. Exploring common and different experiences among group members
4. Exploring meanings and language
5. Challenging prejudice and discrimination

6. Advocating for members
7. Empowering members
8. Using culturally appropriate techniques and program activities

This final assignment contributes to students' ability to make connections between theory and their practice experience. Second year social work students consistently reflect that the learning modules just described empower them to broaden their frame of reference and knowledge base.

Conclusion

Diversity provides many opportunities for the enrichment of society, but we can only take advantage of these opportunities if we embrace it with sensitivity and respect. In every society, social work plays a major role in contributing to an environment that works toward this goal. The study modules discussed in this paper are one attempt to address the need to prepare social work students in South Africa to address the critical issues of diversity in a post-apartheid society. In an increasingly global world, it is imperative that we share our strategies for teaching this critical aspect of social work and group work practice with the next generation. If we embrace diversity with the necessary sensitivity and respect and humbly acknowledge our differences, we realise that these differences create a unique rainbow.

References

Allen-Meares, P. (2007). Cultural competence: An ethical requirement. *Journal of Ethnic and Cultural Diversity in Social Work, 16*(3), 83-92.

Association for the Advancement of Social Work with Groups. (1998). *Standards for social work practice with groups.* Akron, OH: AASWG.

Carter-Black, J. (2007). Teaching cultural competence: An innovative strategy grounded in the universality of storytelling as depicted in African and African American storytelling traditions. *Journal of Social Work Education, 43*(1), Winter 2007, 31-50.

Corey, M.S. & Corey, G. (2006). *Groups. Process and practice.* USA: Brooks/ Cole.

Doel, M. (2006). *Using groupwork.* London: Routledge.

Henry, S. (1992). *Group skills in social work. A four-dimensional approach.* (2nd ed.) Pacific Grove: Brooks/Cole.

Hölscher, D. (2008). The Emperor's new clothes: South Africa's attempted transition to developmental social welfare and social work. *International Journal of Social Welfare, 17,* 114–123.

Jacobs, E.E., Masson, R.L. & Harvill, R.L. (2009). *Group counselling. Strategies and skills.* (6th ed.) Belmont: Thomson Brooks/Cole.

Johnson, D.W. & Johnson, F.P. (2003). *Joining together. Group theory and group skills.* (8th ed.) Boston: Allyn & Bacon.

Konopka, G. (1983). *Social group work: A helping process,* (3rd edn). Englewood Cliffs, NJ: Prentice-Hall.

Leibowitz, B., Rohleder, P., Bozalek, V., Carolissen, R. & Swartz, L. (2007). 'It doesn't matter who or what we are, we are still just people': Strategies used by university students to negotiate difference. *South African Journal of Psychology, 37*(4), 702–719.

Lordan, N. and Wilson, M. (2002). Groupwork in Europe: tools to combat social exclusion in a multicultural environment. In S. Henry, J. East, & C. Schmitz, (Eds.), *Social work with groups. Mining the gold.* New York: Haworth Press, 9-30.

Mamphiswana, D. & Noyoo, N. (2000). Social work education in a changing socio-political and economic dispensation. Perspectives from South Africa. *International Social Work, 43*(1), 21–32.

Marsiglia, F.F. (2003). Culturally grounded approaches to social justice through social work with groups. In N. Sullivan, E.S. Mesbur, N.C. Lang, D. Goodman, & L. Mitchell (Eds.), *Social work with groups. Social justice through personal, community, and societal change.* New York: Haworth Press, 79-90.

Miley, K.K., O'Melia, M. & DuBois, B. (2009). *Generalist social work practice. An empowering approach.* (6th ed.) Boston: Pearson Education.

Smith, L. (2008) South African social work education: Critical imperatives for social change in the post-apartheid and post-colonial context. *International Social Work, 51*(3), 371-383.

Toseland, R.W. and Rivas, R.F. (2009). *An introduction to group work practice.* (6th ed.) Boston: Allyn & Bacon.

Waldegrave, C. (2009). Cultural, gender, and socioeconomic contexts in therapeutic and social policy work. *Family Process, 48*(1), 85-101.

Wilson, K., Ruch, G., Lymbery, M. & Cooper, A. (2008). *Social work. An introduction to contemporary practice.* Essex: Pearson Longman.

Zastrow, C.H. (2009). *Social work with groups. A comprehensive workbook.* (7th ed.) Belmont: Thomson Brooks/Cole.

History

Based on a presentation at the XXXI AASWG Symposium, Chicago, IL, 2009. First published in the Proceedings series in: Bergart, A.M., Simon, S.R., and Mark Doel, M. (Eds.) (2012) *Group Work: Honoring our roots, nurturing our growth.* London:Whiting & Birch (pp.128-139)

Notes on authors (at time of first publication)

Reineth (CE) Prinsloo,DPhil, is a senior lecturer at the Department of Social Work and Criminology, University of Pretoria, South Africa. Her fields of specialisation are social work with groups and family development and guidance. She works from a strength perspective and focuses on prevention and enrichment.

Using literature groups to teach diversity

Preface to the 2021 publication

Book clubs and reading groups have become even more popular since the original writing of this piece (Southwood, 2012; Daniels, 2008). They are now a vital element of social culture that crosses all manner of diversity lines including but not limited to gender, sexual orientation, ethnicity, age, religion and social class (Craig, 2016; Pecoskie, 2010; Long, 2004). The reasons for this popularity reflect not only the human need to connect and understand social issues more deeply, but also to create support for actually reading books. Nevertheless, college students report that they don't have time to read literature while they are students. They feel more pressure to keep informed via daily news feeds and social media. Reading for "fun" has taken a back seat to online television, video and movie viewing options that have made "binge watching" the college past time of choice (Binge watching and college students, 2017; Flayelle, Maurage, & Billieux, 2017; Riddle, Peebles, Davis, Xu, & Schroeder, 2017).

Yet, reading literature gives us access into the worlds of others while simultaneously giving us access into our own experiences. And, reading literature does this in a way that reading other kinds of non-fiction (like textbooks), and watching good film and documentaries does not. For starters, when we read we are completely in charge. We are in charge of the images we create, when we pause, how much we can take in at a time, when and where we read. Reading is after all, a completely autonomous and safe experience. Not necessarily limited to absorbing information, reading *can* be a way of involving oneself with others, even fictitious others. The act of reading itself creates a place where solitary and social dimensions connect (Pecoskie, 2010), and finding this "place" or space is essential in diversity education.

Without personal self-involvement, conversations tend to stay at superficial levels, shutting down when we feel threatened, anxious or inadequate. This is especially apparent in dealing with racially charged topics like white identity (DiAngelo, 2016; Irving, 2014), white supremacy (Coates, 2017; Shin, 2016; Coates), and politically charged topics evoking implicit ideological and/or religious assumptions that have been especially polarizing in recent years (Bruni, 2017; Graham, 2016). To make readings and discussions of privilege in its many forms more than an academic exercise, we need to "catch" *ourselves*, and using literature groups can help both teachers and students do this.

Reading fiction (or memoirs that read like fiction) can take us "under the radar" of our conscious awareness because we need to suspend external expectations in order to figure out our particular path for "entering" a creative work. Contrast this with the experience of consciously looking for "answers" or whatever we imagine the teacher wants us to learn from a textbook or journal article. Outcome-motivated reading of this sort doesn't require us to access our emotions or lived experiences; we read just enough to satisfy ourselves that we have met expectations, avoiding personal triggers, and having little (if any) awareness of what we have filtered *out*. But reading fiction doesn't let us off the hook as easily-- if we succeed in getting "into" a novel, for example. We develop relationships with characters even though we know they are not real. More importantly, we have at least some awareness that we are participating in the drama that we are co-creating *with* the writer *as* we read.

My aim in using literature in the classroom is to heighten these awarenesses. In fact, the most significant update to this piece is that teachers make these purposes as explicit as we can, modeling the kind of vulnerability we hope students will permit themselves. Teachers need to be willing to go *there* in order to model an authentic encounter with difference—to show just how challenging and exhilarating it is—and, that there is no shortcut to getting *there*. I encourage you to choose works of literature that are evocative for *you,* letting students know why and how *up front,* as a way of modeling that sensitivity and responsiveness to diversity aren't merely techniques; they require an ongoing, dynamic relationship with *oneself.*

Mari Ann Graham

Mari Ann Graham is MSW Program Director, and Associate Professor, St Catherine University

References

Binge watching and college students: Motivations and outcomes. (2017). *Young Consumers,*18(4), 425-438.

Bruni, F. (2017). An abomination. A monster. That's me? *New York Times*, 10 December, Op Ed section, p.3.

Coates, T. (2017). *We were eight years in power.* New York: One World.

Craig, C. (2016). Exploring gendered sexuality through American and Irish women's book clubs. *Sexuality & Culture,* 20(2), 316-335.

Daniels, H. (2008). *Looking into literature circles.* Portland, ME: Stenhouse.

DiAngelo, R. (2016). *What does it mean to be white? Developing white racial literacy,* revised edition. New York: Counterpoints.

Flayelle, M., Maurage, P., & Billieux, J. (2017). Toward a qualitative understanding of binge-watching behaviors: A focus group approach, *Journal of Behavioral Addictions,* 6(4), 457-471.

Graham, M. A. (2016). Binding up our nation's wounds, *Bold Moves for Real Change,* CSJ Ministries Foundation, spring issue, 20-21.

Irving, D. (2014). *Waking up white and finding myself in the story of race.* Cambridge, MA: Elephant Room Press.

Long, E. (2004). Literature as a spur to collective action: The diverse perspectives of nineteenth- and twentieth-century reading groups, *Poetics Today,* 25(2), 335-359.

Pecoskie, J. (2010). The solitary, social, and 'grafted spaces' of pleasure reading: Exploring reading practices from the experiences of adult, self-identified lesbian, gay, bisexual, and queer readers and book club members, *ProQuest Dissertations and Theses.*

Riddle, K., Peebles, A., Davis, C., Xu, F., & Schroeder, E. (2017). The addictive potential of television binge watching: Comparing intentional and unintentional binges, *Psychology of Popular Media Culture.*

Shin, S. Y. (2016). *A good time for the truth: Race in Minnesota.* St. Paul: Minnesota Historical Society Press.

Southwood, Sue. (2012). The Joy of Reading Groups, *Adults Learning,* 23(3), 36-37.

Using literature groups
to teach diversity

Mari Ann Graham

I have been using literature groups (otherwise known as reading groups or book groups) to teach diversity for a number of years. Novels and memoirs can help students appreciate the struggles of immigrants adapting to western culture (Fadiman, 1995), become more personally aware of their whiteness and privilege (Lazarre, 1997), get inside the complexities of transgender identity (Feinberg, 1993), and develop empathy for dwarfs and comprehend the many ways that people get caught in systemic oppression (Hegi, 1994). Using literature has been an engaging way to teach the *realities of diversity*, as opposed to merely talking intellectually *about* it. Experiences with these reading groups are among my most rewarding moments in the classroom. I would like to begin by first articulating a rationale for using *literature* (as opposed to conventional texts), moving to a rationale for using literature *groups*. This will be followed by a brief description of structure and format that I have used for these groups, and a few general recommendations for those who want to use groups of this nature. I will conclude with what I have learned from using these groups via actual experiences of students, noting both the rewards and challenges of using this method of instruction.

Why use literature?

OK, I confess – I can't stand textbooks. I know I'm not supposed to say that, but it's true. I'm an educator and I can hardly bear the thought of textbooks each year. Well, that's a little dramatic, I suppose. The truth is, I don't find them particularly engaging. In short, they bore me. And I figure if I'm bored, this doesn't bode well for my students. I think my lack of engagement has to do with the predictability and sterile way in which information is presented. Everything is so orderly – each main point, followed by relevant sub points (A, B and C), with an occasional example tossed in for application or special emphasis. And to the extent that we need to present information in orderly, sequenced ways, textbooks are, of course, the most efficient way to get the job done. But since I am less and less inclined to teach from the traditional paradigm in which it is assumed that teachers have information which can readily be transmitted to students, and since the older I get I am less and less inclined toward efficiency (at least in terms of how it is typically conceived), I find myself tolerating academia's dependence on textbooks, while actively searching for more authentic ways of engaging students (as well as myself) in the learning process.

Use of literature – novels, short stories, poetry – is one such way. Literature, like music or the daily news, is much more like real life. It is full of surprises. It reflects a particular point of view, and requires that the reader temporarily suspend his or her reality in order to enter the frame of the writer. Often, the act of suspending one's own point of view is instructive in and of itself. What we learn about *ourselves* (where our assumptions are, where it is most difficult to 'let go,' where our particular resistances are) can be every bit as important as *what* we are trying to learn. While one might argue correctly that this temporary suspension of one's frame of reference is necessary when reading anything, when reading literature, the point of view of the author is not so readily taken for granted. Writers have the responsibility of actively engaging their readers in their point of view and can't assume that readers will passively receive the so called 'factual' information presumed to be 'true' by textbook authors. Because of this difference, readers of literature are forced to use their imagination and themselves in important ways.

But this more active posture on the part of the reader (and all that goes with it) isn't the only reason for using literature. Literature gets the reader 'inside' other people's stories, in contrast to textbooks, which keep readers at an analytical distance. Good literature makes us feel as well as think, and somehow changes us as a result of the experience. Literature, like other art forms, offers opportunities for vicarious learning that more closely approximates real life. If effective, literature has a way of getting in 'under the radar' of our habitual defenses, engaging even our unconscious selves, and leading us into places we would otherwise never go. That's the power of any art form – to take us *there*. Textbooks by their very nature simply cannot take us *there*.

Since diversity content is infinite, and since the goal in social work education is not the mere transmission of sterile information but rather the development of genuine appreciation for diversity and increased self-awareness of personal bias, using literature (and other art forms) makes good sense. A story can deal simultaneously with many forms of diversity and with multi-layered responses in ways that a textbook cannot. Stories don't so much *tell* as they *evoke*. And I would argue that diversity education that is not evocative is not only useless, it is potentially dangerous. Dangerous because telling students *about* discrimination without helping them see how we are all victims and perpetrators can reinforce the all too common tendency to blame and respond punitively, rather than encouraging them to do the hard work of sorting through the complexities inherent in most diversity issues. Dangerous because setting up unrealistic expectations that lead to professional guilt and/or burnout damages professionals and clients in ways that we still find difficult to articulate. Dangerous because information without transformation is like an accident waiting to happen.

Ironically, however, we use textbooks because they seem 'safer.' They don't evoke much in the moment, and therefore, the implicit dangers are obscured. Evocative teaching methods seem more dangerous because instructors lose a measure of control. Once students are evoked by literature, the instructor has to be willing to follow wherever that might lead. This can be unsettling for teachers who have been conditioned to maintain control as an indicator of their competence. But some loss of control is inherent in the shift toward a more critical, constructivist pedagogy.

Consistent with the movement towards critical/constructivist pedagogy in social work education (Graham, 2003; Graham, 2002; Laird, 1993; Weick, 1993; Jackson & Taylor, 1991; Brigham, 1977), use of literature in the classroom can bring out students' 'lived experience' of diversity, assist them in de-constructing and re-constructing their assumptions and facilitate a genuine appreciation of the ways that perceptions are tied to experiences. Instead of talking 'about' diversity (from a distance), literature brings diversity 'up close and personal.' Literature provides an arena for students to personally experience themselves as 'the other' as well as experiencing others' otherness.

Besides, reading literature is much more enjoyable. Students and faculty alike bemoan not having the time to read the things they would really like to read because they have to do assigned [textbook] readings, write (or grade) papers, and other 'academic' activities that are considered more legitimate, but less fun. Reading for 'fun' has almost become an oxymoron for students. The use of reading groups can encourage and develop the love of reading and lifelong learning. Reading works of literature and taking class time to discuss them (in anything other than literature courses), however, seems to be a luxury that our crowded, professional curricula can't afford. Using literature (as well as other art forms) is likened to classroom entertainment and appears to transgress the implicit mandate for seriousness and rigor in higher education. What this really implies is that serious, rigorous study can't also be fun. But there are those who celebrate a kind of teaching that enables 'movement against and beyond boundaries' because of how it makes 'education the practice of freedom' (hooks, 1994). This transgression alone may be exciting enough for some; for social work educators, there is even more cause for excitement.

Why literature groups?

The popularity of reading groups in general is also well documented in the literature. There are lots of reasons for this popularity. Perhaps the most obvious reason for reading literature in groups is that it is important to be able to talk about what one has read with others who have read the same thing. To be able to talk about what one has read extends the vicarious nature of the learning beyond one's own interpretations and deconstructions. It is both challenging and fun. Challenging because direct experience with other points of view exposes limitations and inherent biases in one's own perspective. Fun, because such exposure, while certainly uncomfortable at times, is also quite liberating. On a very basic level, it is fun to discover what we don't know in the context of what we do know in the company of peers, friends, and people we trust.

In social work education, teaching group process skills is an integral part of the curriculum. Student groups can be used not only as a supplemental method for elaborating and integrating course content, they can also become the subject of learning itself. In other words, small groups, if used deliberately and with some supervision, can become an arena for dis-covering curricular content and for co-creating knowledge. If students and faculty attend to the group's process (as well as to specified group outcomes), reading groups create opportunities for increasing student awareness and skill related to group process, group dynamics, roles they assume as members and as facilitators, while simultaneously providing a forum in which students can bring what they already know to the table and have an active role in shaping curricular content. Rather than passively receiving information, their 'lived experience' of the subject becomes part of a dynamic process of knowledge creation. This is obviously a lot more interesting and 'fun' for both teachers and students. In short, it is exhilarating. It is what makes teaching and learning worth every bit of effort we put into it.

Use of literature groups is also a relevant teaching strategy in social work education because of how literature group dynamics parallel several narrative practice principles. These groups provide opportunities for 'externalizing conversations,' which are all about creating distance between people and their problems so that they do not identify so fully with their problems and thereby become immobilized by 'problem-saturated perceptions' (White, 2007). The extent to which practitioners, for example, have become immobilized by the problem of their lack of cultural competence is significant. Discussing literature does allow students some distance from the subject, so that they don't become 'swallowed up' by a problem that often feels overwhelming and produces high levels of anxiety. Like clients, students need to be able to have 'the conversation' without it feeling like a personal indictment of who they are. Then, they are free to explore problems more fully, with less defensiveness so that they can have 're-authoring conversations' (White, 2007). In narrative practice, these conversations provide opportunities to experience oneself apart from the dominant story line so that one can change patterns of behavior. This, too, is of critical importance for students who not only need to become aware of their biases and insensitivities, but who also need to develop strategies for dealing with them. Reading groups are a wonderful context for beginning these 're-authoring conversations.' When students share what they have learned in their reading groups with the entire class, these 're-authoring conversations' are expanded to include others outside their group.

Since social work educators are mandated to teach diversity content and content related to group work, use of literature groups in the classroom can be a lively way of fulfilling both purposes.

Description of format

Background

In a required foundation level practice course, we have historically included a unit on unintentional discrimination. We used a required text on unintentional racism to identify the dynamics of unintentional racism (Ridley, 1995), extrapolating this content to make application to other forms of unintended discrimination and to begin some dialogue about what social work practitioners can do to minimize unintentional discrimination and more effectively deal with it when it arises. The text, while provocative in many respects and certainly an adequate starting point for this unit, either seemed to go over the heads of students, or else shut many of them down. Conversations on this topic were (and still are) highly sensitized. It was my observation that the text kept conversations at an academic level of abstraction, and was, therefore, too remote and distant from student experience. I tried various ways of making the content more concrete and accessible (with mixed success) and then one year decided to offer several reading options for that unit. In addition to the textbook, I gave students several other options – *Stonebutch Blues* (Feinberg, 1993), *Beyond the Whiteness of Whiteness* (Lazarre, 1997), and *The Spirit Catches You and You Fall Down* (Fadiman, 1997).

Students were required to select one of these, read it, and work in a small group to present what they learned to the whole class. Facilitation of the group was rotated among group members. Interestingly, the textbook drew nearly as much student interest as the others (I gave brief reviews of each book prior to students making their selections, attempting to 'pitch' each as optimistically as I could), and we had four student groups of roughly the same size. Each group agreed to present to the class for roughly an hour and a half. The focus of the presentation was on identifying the dynamics of unintended discrimination (How does it work? How does it happen?) and how social workers can best respond. I encouraged students to be creative and involve the class actively in whatever they do (as opposed to giving a report). The students then (and now) never ceased to amaze me in terms of the creative ways they find to engage their classmates. These class sessions were and are some of the liveliest and most memorable.

Evolution of the format

Since that first year a few things have changed. The presentations have become longer – two to two and a half hours instead of one to one and a half hours. While students are initially intimidated by the length of time suggested, we quickly find that when we really engage the whole class (rather than lecture), the time goes by quickly. Even with the additional time allotted to these presentations, it is often the case that we wish we had even more time to devote to these issues. Students really do want (and need) to process these issues when given a safe format in which to do it.

The original text is still made available as an optional text but after student interest in it declined, I included another option, *Stones From the River* (Hegi, 1994), and students now select from among these four. Almost any work of fiction (or nonfiction) that deals with an issue of diversity can be used. I tend to select nonfiction that is *not* 'textbooky' for the reasons I've already named. Often, students can't wait to read these. Faculty may even select and rotate books that students really want to read (but say they don't have time to read).

This unit on unintentional discrimination happens to be taught during the same time in the semester as a unit on group work. One year when negotiating assignment options with students, they suggested the creation of reading groups as an in-class activity for the group work unit using the text they selected for the unintentional discrimination unit. Many of them had heard about or participated in reading groups and so long as they had to read the books anyway, they asked why not create and use those groups to learn about group work? Their interest was the ever creative effort to 'kill two birds with one stone,' and I admit having been intrigued by the idea. An avid participant in a monthly reading group myself, it never occurred to me to suggest this as an option for *them*! The results of this shift in format have been positive. In contrast to other in-class group activities (fishbowls, role playing of groups, etc.) students appreciate the fact that these are *real* groups, formed on the basis of a common interest in a book. I observed that they did become *real* groups in terms of cohesion and other group dynamics. They appreciate having some class time (I typically allowed 40-45 minutes, once a week for 6 weeks) to discuss their experience of the book with their peers.

The fact that students are required to give a presentation to the entire class at the end of the 6 week period might suggest to some that it is a task group. In fact, it can become a task group quite easily since it is generally less threatening to focus on planning a presentation, than to share personal reactions to readings. But I encourage students to see the group and facilitate it primarily as an educational/support group. I encourage them to see their growth and development as professionals as primary, the task of presenting to the class as secondary. Prior to beginning these in-class group sessions, we cover some foundation group work content (stages of group, group dynamics, leadership issues, planning a group, and beginning a group), and once groups have begun meeting, we continue our review of group work content in the classroom (assessment in groups, treatment group methods, task group methods, evaluating and terminating groups) for the next several weeks. Students seem to 'get' the group work content and experience its immediacy as a result of having this concurrent group experience. There is some predictable anxiety when it is their turn to lead the group, and in dealing with some of the issues that come up in the group. This appears to keep students focused and interested in the group work content discussed in class. Students are still meeting in their in-class reading groups when we shift the classroom focus to another unit of study, and this has not been at all problematic. After groups have ended, students write a group work self-assessment, assessing their roles as member and as leader (drawing on other experiences they have had in groups), identifying their personal strengths and challenges, and discussing what they have learned about group dynamics and process.

I have gravitated to having the group presentations during the last few class sessions because they are often high energy (at a time when all of us need the energy), and also because this also gives students additional time (if they need it) to plan their presentations to the class.

Recommendations

Having used this method now for a number of years, I am confident in recommending its use to any instructor teaching diversity content, as well as to social work educators teaching practice, policy, field or human behavior courses. It can be easily adapted to meet course objectives, but certain things are worth noting, as follows:

- *Allow students some choice in the selection process.*
  I have tended to present students with a menu of options (often based on recommendations/feedback from former students). In this way, they become invested in the process by virtue of their choice and have a common starting point for dialogue with other students who also selected that book. To keep this manageable, instructors will need to limit the number of options, so that their are adequate numbers of students in each group. I have found that groups work well with 5 to 7 students.

- *Use books that are interesting to you and that you suspect will be interesting to your students.*
  Your interest and enthusiasm is an important ingredient in the process, every bit as important as student engagement. Rather than select books that you think social workers *should* read, select books that they (and you) really *want* to read.

- *Provide consultation/supervision to groups.*
  I have found this to be essential in terms of being able to provide assistance to students when they encounter challenging group dynamics and to help them more thoroughly integrate the readings. I recommend having an 'unobtrusive' presence by occasionally sitting in on groups and/or being available for consultation with groups during the times they are meeting. It is also important to the overall success of the model that the instructor stay connected to what is happening in the groups. Dynamics in the large group (class as a whole) may play out in groups and vice versa. Since discussions are often personal and may be emotionally charged, having the instructor present/available contributes to a sense of safety.

- *Allow in-class time for groups.*
  This communicates the importance of the activity, i.e., that it is just as important as instructor's lecture or any other class activity. Allowing class time for groups also minimizes logistical challenges that arise if students are required to meet outside of class for all meetings.

- *Combine the use of these groups with introspective writing.*
  I encourage students to journal about their experiences in their reading group, so that they have plenty of raw material to reflect

upon when writing up their group work self-assessment and also to facilitate dialogue in their groups. If a written self-assessment is not required, I would see this kind of reflective writing as even more critical.

Two illustrations

There are many illustrations I could give to illustrate the quality of student engagement and learning in these groups. But two stand out as examples of what can happen in the process, how supervision is important and how students benefit from these kinds of group experiences.

One of the most dramatic experiences occurred when a student, let's call her Julie, was purchasing Leslie Feinberg's, *Stonebutch Blues* at a local Barnes and Noble bookstore. The year I decided to shift to this format, students were given ample time to order the book of their choice from a local bookstore and begin reading by a certain date. This was no problem since the books were all in print and readily available for purchase. It also simplified book orders (since I had no way of knowing in advance how many student copies of each to order from our book store). When Julie asked about the book, she was directed to the Gay/Lesbian Studies section, and a clerk made a comment to her along the lines of, 'So this is what lesbians look like nowadays.' Julie, not a lesbian, was immediately offended at the remark and told the clerk she was not a lesbian, but was getting the book for a class. Her husband who was browsing nearby came over to see what the problem was. The clerk apologized to Julie and her husband, and the event might have been relatively uneventful had Julie not decided to share the experience in the context of her reading group.

When she shared the experience in the group, she talked about how she was first of all angered at the presumption that she was a lesbian just because she was purchasing the book. This led to some discussion in her small group (and later to discussion with the whole class) about how it feels to have your sexual orientation incorrectly taken for granted – ironically, the experience that lesbians often have in reverse. And this 'ah-ha,' big as it was for this student, was just the beginning. She remembered, and reported to the group, feeling embarrassed, as though everybody was looking at her, and was somewhat 'paranoid,' wondering what they were thinking after the clerk made the comment. This, too, she used to develop an empathic point of reference for understanding the challenges that lesbians and transgender people face in homophobic settings. Finally, and this was the real clincher, she also reported feeling guilty that she felt embarrassed. Her rational mind said, why should I be embarrassed because somebody thought I was a lesbian? I don't think there's anything wrong with being a lesbian. But if I really thought there wasn't anything wrong with being a lesbian, why did I feel guilt and shame? This, of course, led to some very important dialogue around the nature of internalized oppression, and how we are often unaware of the extent to which we have internalized certain values until we have experiences like this that effectively remove our blinders. The whole class was then able to talk about the various blind spots that social workers have and what we are able to do about them. And all of this, from a brief encounter while purchasing a book!

Another, quite vivid experience occurred rather recently when two students who decided to read *Beyond the Whiteness of Whiteness* (Lazarre, 1997) experienced a conflict that 'hooked' the other members of their group in important ways, and became grist for the mill for the rest of the class. Rhonda, a white student, welcomed the opportunity to read the book and hoped it would shed some light on difficulties she had relating to a black female student in our MSW program, having had virtually no contact with blacks prior to beginning the program. She admitted not having thought very much about what it meant to be white all of her life, and very much wanted concrete 'answers' from the book about how to deal with black people. This motivation resulted in her taking experiences from the book and generalizing them to other groups (to white women, for example) in her sincere effort to try and relate to what the author (a white mother of black sons) was talking about. A black female in her group, Shaniqua, took issue with this approach, and articulated her anger that such comparisons 'water down' and undermine the reality of racism against blacks in this country, and was clearly not the intention of the author.

The dialogue in the reading group quickly polarized (as discussions of race often do), and members of the group felt pressured to take sides with either Rhonda or Shaniqua. Since the others (all white females) were social work students, however, this was tricky. Everybody said they could understand Shaniqua's point. They also could see Rhonda's intention. They consulted with me and asked me to sit in on their next group session and help mediate what they saw as a difficult problem.

When I did so, I observed what I just detailed, reflected back to them what I saw, and asked them to consider how their attachment to a 'position' was getting in the way of seeing what was at stake for the other side (a direct reference to another text used in the course, Fisher & Ury's *Getting to Yes*). At this point Shaniqua said that she can appreciate how Rhonda and other white people try to understand the black experience by using their own experiences, but that the comparisons just don't cut it. Rhonda then said something like, 'wow, it must really be frustrating for you to have people like me doing what I just did. I never realized that before now.' The irony, of course, is that Shaniqua's insistence that whites could not 'cross over' in the way Rhonda was attempting to (a point discussed at some length in Lazarre's work) along with Rhonda's persistence, ultimately did result in a 'crossing over.'

Conclusions

In the first scenario, the student scarcely thought the event worth reporting to her group until I (after overhearing her report her incredulity at the arrogance of the clerk to a friend) suggested that there might be value in processing this experience with her group. She subsequently reported to the entire class that this may have been one of her most memorable experiences as a graduate student. And while the second scenario clearly reflects group member awareness of the need for outside consultation because of the discomfort experienced by group members, what both cases reveal is the critical importance of supervision of these groups. This need is not so much one of ensuring that students stay on task or other accountability functions, but in terms of providing students with useful frames within which they can process their own experiences, learn from them and empower themselves and others. I shudder to think of what might have been lost to the individual students involved, to the two student groups, to both classes as a whole, and subsequent groups of students who have only heard about these experiences had these students not been encouraged to process their experiences. And in many ways, these two experiences are not all that unusual or exceptional. What is perhaps unusual and exceptional is having the courage and taking the time to process experiences like this. These are the 'teachable moments' that are almost always there, waiting below the surface for the courageous and caring eye to notice.

These 'teachable moments' are just as scary for teachers as they are for students, which may help us see why using textbooks and other less evocative teaching methods are often preferred. We don't know ahead of time where these experiences will take us or our students. But then, isn't that the whole point of education? The question isn't so much a 'how to' question, how do we engage them, keep their interest, etc., but rather, do *we* have the guts? And, if we have the guts to use literature and other art forms to evoke authentic engagement from students, we need to have the guts to follow the process with them, using all of who we are to help them be all of who they are. This is one of the most important things I have learned over the years. I need to 'show up' for the process if I have any hope that students will. They need to be able to see me go willingly into the darkness, and maybe then, they can trust that they, too, will come out alive.

I've also learned that students are much more resilient than we think. They don't break, and neither will we, which of course leads to a basic tenant of empowering education – transformation is usually painful. Pain and discomfort are part of the process of change. Aversion to the discomfort and avoidance of that which is potentially painful robs students (as well as clients) of empowering opportunities for growth. But once again, the teacher (or therapist) must be willing to go there. The challenges of going there for teachers have to do with dealing with loss of control and the willingness to experience our own discomfort as well as that of students. That discomfort notwithstanding, teaching diversity in this way is ever-fresh, invigorating, and keeps us on our toes. It is worth every bit of the effort involved, and ultimately much more rewarding than conventional content-driven approaches.

References

Brigham, T. (1977). Liberation in social work education: Applications from Paulo Freire. *Journal of Education for Social Work, 13(3)*, 5-11

Feinberg, L. (1993). *Stonebutch blues*. Ithaca, NY: Firebrand Books

Hegi, U. (1994). *Stones from the river*. NY: Simon & Schuster

hooks, b. (1994). *Teaching to transgress: Education as the practice of freedom.* NY: Routledge

Jackson, S. & Taylor, I. (1991, March). *Enquiry and action learning: Modeling community practice in social work education.* Paper presented at conference on social work education, March

Laird, J. (Ed.) (1993). *Revisioning social work education: A social constructivist approach.* Binghampton, NY: Haworth

Lazarre, J. (1997). *Beyond the whiteness of whiteness.* Durham, NC: Duke University Press

Ridley, C. (1995). *Overcoming unintentional racism in counseling and therapy.* Thousand Oaks, CA: Sage

Weick, A. (1993). Reconstructing social work education, *Journal of teaching in social work, 8(1/2)*, 11-30

Weick, A. (1997). Personal communication with the author, November 26

White, M. (2007) *Maps of Narrative Practice.* New York: WW Norton

History
Based on a presentation at the XXV AASWG Symposium, Boston, MA., 2003. First published in the Proceedings series in: Berman-Rossi, L., Cohen, M.B., and Holly Fischer-Engel, H. (Eds.) (2010) *Creating Connections: Celebrating the power of groups.* London: Whiting & Birch (pp.47-60)

Notes on author (as provided at time of first publication)
Mari Ann Graham, Ph.D., MSW. Mari Ann received her Ph. D. from Case Western Reserve University and her MSW from the University of Nebraska at Omaha. She currently directs the MSW Program and is Associate Professor at the College of St. Catherine/University of St. Thomas School of Social Work in St. Paul, Minnesota, where she also teaches practice courses, supervises clinical research projects and directs the Spirituality Institute.

The model, a continuum of connecting the classroom and community: Utilizing group work

Preface to the 2021 reprint

The Model, described in *A continuum of connecting the classroom and community: Uutilizing group work,* continues to be an essential component of undergraduate social work group education in the Ethelyn Strong School of Social Work at Norfolk State University. The authors believe in the power of group work, and have witnessed this model empower students to use group work as an effective method for change in utilizing task and treatment approaches to practice. The continuation of projects has provided a venue for the faculty to continue to incorporate reciprocal relationships with partners in the public housing community. We have experienced an enrichment of students' learning to facilitate the empowerment of housing clients' voices to engage more actively in the community and to enable them with relationship building with social workers outside the traditional client worker engagement. Our main partners continue to be the Norfolk Redevelopment and Housing Authority Community (NRHA), but include multiple coalitions with United Way Agencies, for profit organizations, and community services providers.

Task groups are still one of the most widely utilized forms of group work in social work practice. Yet, they are not always identified as conscious use of group work instead being viewed as "meetings". This model focused on a purposeful use of group work practice skills, a clear understanding of the impact of group dynamics on the task group process, and how an effective group can impact change on the macro level. The focus continues to engage students in experiential learning that increases their awareness and abilities to function in the multisystem approach to plan, develop, and implement interventions that have impact on populations at risk and underserved communities.

Through years of teaching and community engagement, this model's fruitfulness includes an increase in students' confidence and competence in participating in and leading task groups and increased skill in the creation of treatment groups to affect the change process. Weaving the thread of cultural competence to address diversity issues has become increasingly important in the context of our current society. In our Hampton Roads Community we are currently faced with the closure of housing communities that with impact over 2000 households within the next 5 years. The authors continue to have active reciprocal partnerships that provide leadership task groups to foster University involvement in community development of strategies and interventions, as our downtown community prepares for additional revitalization that will impact economic wellbeing and family stability.

One of the overarching themes in this sequential model is creating empowerment. First, the focus is on empowerment of faculty in the School of Social Work to provide expertise to the community with advocacy, policy formation, strategy development and development and provision of interventions. Second, it involves the continued use of task and treatment groups in the provision of the BSWs' educational experiences in mezzo and macro practice in order for them to acquire knowledge, values, and skills, to benefit from multilevel interactions with community partners for supplemental learning/ professional development and interaction with clients to obtain real world perspectives. Third, the focus is to facilitate the empowerment of residents to create positive relationships with Social Workers, to participate in empowerment experiences, and to have holistic and multicultural sensitive opportunities for their personal and career development.

The authors continue to be strongly committed to the ecological systems approach and the necessity of all of partners owning their rights and roles in participating in what Warren and Warren (1984) reference as a well-functioning community. Examples of student task groups accomplishments, since publication include:

On the first tier level we engage Introduction to Social Work Students (1st semester sophomore year) in an orientation to low income housing communities by partnering with the NRHA Social Workers and community team members to provide a treatment group "At the Kitchen Table: Color Me Stress Free." Students provide an Art Experience for 33 residents and an educational lecture, by community experts, on how color impacts mood and how to use color in our homes and dress to reflect wellness. They were provided with art supplies to develop home décor resources.

The second tier involves students enrolled in Human Behavior in the Social Environment Class: Marriage and the Family (1st semester junior year) who facilitate a socialization and educational group, "Senior Citizen TEA: Give Thanks for Seniors" for 27 residents who provide care for their grandchildren. The faculty partnered with 4 community organizations to provide a formal TEA the week before Thanksgiving to introduce the residents of public housing to free resources for grandparents. It has been observed by the faculty and community partners that at many of the community events, there is an absence of participation of seniors who live in our public housing communities. We would like to follow up with research to determine the obstacles/barriers to participation.

The third tier involves a prevention focus with the faculty using a State of Virginia Certificate training, "Champion for Children: Darkness to Light Sexual Assault Prevention". Utilizing state certified trainers to train social work students in Human Behavior Class II (1st or 2nd semester sophomore year) on sexual assault prevention methods, students follow up in Generalist Practice: Groups, Communities, and Organizations (1st semester senior/field year) to develop a treatment group for residents of public housing. In addition, the educational/ mutual aid group has been offered to two groups of 15 residents. Prior to the offering of the Training to residents, the faculty facilitated the Training for all Norfolk Redevelopment and housing Authority (NRHA) Resident Specialist/Social Workers. An invitation has been extended to follow up with training for the NRHA Security Team. A third Training for residents is scheduled for April 2018 for Child Abuse Prevention Month and will engage BSW students in the assessment, coordination, and implementation.

We continue to focus on empowerment and fostering creative approaches to teaching and the delivery of services, without being limited by zero based budgets, limited resources, and historical experiences. We are committed to fostering positive growth and societal changes to enhance a population of citizens who share in developing healthy well-functioning families despite disparities.

Through these continued interactive experiences the authors hope students and all of our community team partners will continue to fully embrace the words:

"Never doubt that a small group of thoughtful committed citizens can change the world, indeed, it is the only thing that ever has." (attributed to Margaret Mead)

Brenda Exum and Mary Yanisko

Brenda Exum, MSW, ACSW recently retired and continues with community organization, leadership of race relations groups, training for healthy living/food insecurity programs, and leadership of educational groups for cancer support professionals and volunteers.

Mary M Yanisko has retired from the School of Social Work at Norfolk State University and has continued to conduct groups (in person and virtual) in the areas of hospice, bereavement and families of dementia patients as well as providing ongoing training for cancer support volunteers.

Reference

Warren, R.B. & Warren, D.E. (1984). How to diagnose a neighborhood. In F. Cox, J.L. Erlich, J. Rothman & J.E. Tropman (Eds), *Tactics and techniques of community practice* (2nd ed., pp 27-40). Itasca, IL: Peacock.

The model, a continuum of connecting the classroom and community: Utilizing group work

Brenda Exum and Mary Yanisko

This paper describes a sequential model for educating social work undergraduate students on group process, emphasizing the importance of task groups, integrating group work practice and cultural competence across three semesters. The model will demonstrate an empowerment partnership between the School of Social Work and the community to facilitate the strengthening of these partnerships to benefit students, communities and the populations at risk.

Introduction

After many years of clinical practice experience, their involvement in professional activities such as organizational boards and community task forces and from implementing classroom instruction, the authors realized that optimal learning occurred when students were able to experience in multiple modalities the content that is taught in the classroom. 'The model, a continuum of connecting the classroom and community: Utilizing group work' was created to address this need and also in response to the emergence of such arenas as evidenced based social work practice.

The model developers were also conscious that task groups are one of the most widely used forms of group work in social work practice. Yet, it continues to be an overlooked consideration in human service agencies (Toseland & Rivas, 2005). The authors realized early in their careers the significance of students being participants in task groups to create the change process in the community. Franklin and Hobson (2007) assert:

...the time has come for universities to take a greater responsibility for resolving the issues of implementation of evidenced based practice by making community agencies a part of the educational research enterprise (p.397).

There is a rich tradition in the field of social work that knowledge, skills and values focused experiences for multi level service delivery, be provided for students who are in CSWE accredited programs. In response to the challenge of strengthening the learning experience, this model is a continuum of instruction in the area of group work practice on the BSW undergraduate level. It links goals for students, community partners, and community clients in a three component educational approach. The model also incorporates the thread of cultural competence throughout.

This article will describe the model, outline the goals of each tier/ semester, demonstrate how each is operationalized and provide examples of the results of the task group experiences in impacting the community.

Group work as the modality of choice

Group work is the modality of choice for these model developers who are concerned about preparing students for the delivery of interventions for clients with consideration of the complexities related to funding and staffing organization. The purpose of using group work for this model is to provide students with experiential opportunities in and outside of the classroom. This modality fosters the opportunity to use Bandura's (1986) Modeling and Coaching techniques for students to replicate in the community practice arena. In addition, Soliman (1999), suggests that working in small groups can increase student motivation. The size of the groups changes each semester with the students experiencing smaller task groups as they develop increased competencies in leadership and membership participation. The learning experience is structured throughout the tiers for each student to have responsibility to increase their competencies. This prepares them for effective group leadership post graduation.

Model

To initiate the model, the approach included the development of the structure of the relationships between the faculty and the community partners. The goal is to provide formal reciprocal volunteer consultation services with the community professionals. This facilitates input into student learning activities that would result in a positive impact for the partners' client communities. Community partners are contacted at the beginning of each semester to explain the students' learning assignments, to give the names of the student group members, to establish a meeting with the groups and to develop a feedback mode for the agency partners, students and faculty members.

The model develops students' competencies over three tiers/ semesters that begin in the junior year and conclude in the capstone course, which is offered concurrently in the first semester of the field experience. The overarching goal is to increase student capacity building in understanding the dynamics of multi cultural task group work, the nature of community intervention, and the functions of organizations in the community (Warren & Warren, 1984). This model increases social workers' abilities to commit to the poor and underserved in a multi cultural context (Mulroy, 2010). Generalist practice learning objectives focus on, prior to the field experience, the integration of classroom study content, opportunities for observation of best practices and the special challenges in the community of clients. The reciprocal experience is critical for schools of social work because the training of students and practitioners is closely related and results in mutual gain for all participants (Franklin & Hobson, 2007).

The goals of the model are:

1. To formally introduce differential approaches of group work by exposing students to the benefits of task groups;
2. To decrease student anxiety related to participation and leadership in groups;
3. To involve students in experiential learning in the community in order to observe social work models;
4. To develop networking skills to encourage a vision for the student to see themselves as the future task group leaders and members of community organization task groups;
5. To facilitate the integration of community partnerships as a

resource in the classroom;

6. To challenge students to value community partnerships in providing community services, and

7. To increase cultural competencies through authentic interactions with diverse populations.

Tier one/first semester

The goal of this tier is to introduce students to a formal task group experience beginning in the introductory practice course. This is operationalized through the incorporation of a university required service learning component. Students are assigned to teams of 5-8 students, based on their interest, for a one semester exposure experience in addressing a community need. The faculty and community partner introduces the learning activity as an unmet need that requires the intervention of restoring, enhancing or creating a resource. The students meet in their first formal classroom task group to brainstorm to create a project that will impact resource for the community. They meet with the partner to develop a timeline and to observe the partner as a change agent. The project is completed by the last month of the semester and students participate in a poster presentation display at the university service learning showcase for a university wide audience.

Example of learning experience

The community agency referred to in this example is a long term care facility that borders the university campus. The students' task group provided a one time event that enhanced the well being of the residents. The literature warns of the danger of service learning in higher education becoming 'charity work' (Ward & Wolf-Wendal, 2000). Social work students are challenged to operationalize the core value of respecting the dignity and worth of persons served. The community partner, as a mentor, facilitated the learning objectives and ensured inclusion of the clients' perspectives.

Working under the creative supervision of the community partner, the students in this example provided an event called the 'Wall of Fame'. This event provided residents an opportunity to celebrate and honor their significant life events. The students created the Wall of Fame by exhibiting posters of residents with their pictures and stories in the facility and at the university.

Tier two/semester two

The goal of this tier is to have students develop skills in participating in a task group, while studying human behavior and families, and to understand treatment group approaches that impact diverse family groups in communities. The faculty and community partners meet to discuss the resources of the community organization. The goal is to facilitate student exposure to the family multicultural context and to learn about culturally sensitive social work practice. The community partners commit to accommodating observational experiences in the community and to support the classroom learning with presentations about the experiences of the population in their environment. A strong focus is on the ecological systems perspective to help students develop knowledge and values related to how families impact the environment and how the environment is impacted by families (Iatridis,1995).

The students are assigned to task groups of 4-6 persons that meet formally each week. In the first week of the course, the groups are given guidelines to use in the development of a formal presentation, for the class. The research findings and the learning outcomes from community partner coaching are shared in the final presentation. The partners assist the classroom learning by providing opportunities for students to learn/observe about ongoing treatment groups, social action and social reform initiatives and empowerment activities in their communities. In addition, students research diverse protective factors for various ethnic groups and share how they strengthen family units. The semester provides students with opportunities to experience shared traditions, rituals, customs, and celebrations that help to sustain families of different ethnic groups in the global society. The emphasis for the task groups in this tier is to recognize the responsibilities we all share in fulfilling the commitment to ensure social and economic justice thrives for all families.

Example of learning experience

The second tier semester involved 5 different task groups, in one class, with each group focusing on a different ethnic group. Throughout the semester each group researched ethnic strengths, patterns of family organization, core values, and coping philosophies. The learning included a study of contemporary issues related to immigration as it relates to ethnic family and community wellbeing. The task groups deliberated on the content to share with the total class to prepare them for a closing event. The teams collaborated to coordinate a 'Celebrating Families Forum', a closing class event, which was open to the university campus. The combined task groups provided a panel of individuals from different ethnic/cultural groups to speak on their challenges and strengths in an effort to preserve their ethnic heritage and wellbeing. It included a major showcase exhibit of memorabilia, religious objects, art, clothing, and food. A sweet potato pie throw down contest for the African American community was to demonstrate how families use preparation of food to facilitate family solidarity.

Tier three/semester three

The goal of this tier, which takes place in the capstone course, social work with groups, communities and organization, is to use task groups to implement a program for an unmet need in the community. Students work in formal task groups of 3-5 members (approximately 4 groups per class), based on their passion for addressing a gap in services in the local community for populations at risk. The focus of purposeful task group work is highlighted in the major assignment that requires each student task group to develop a new grassroots organization that will partner with an existing community service provider to address a barrier that creates an obstacle for clients in meeting their basic needs (Maslow, 1970).

The students work in partnership with the community partners and the network of key informants that they develop through attending staff meetings and/or focus groups for clients, etc. The partners assist the faculty with concrete, real life, experiential learning in the areas of membership in task groups, developing professional networking relationships, team building, fundraising, conducting needs assessments, and exposure to the current use of task and treatment groups in agencies.

The classroom learning involves instruction on how to do program development. In addition, budgeting, resource development, fundraising and marketing techniques and program evaluation are covered. Students use this knowledge and skill base to develop a new resource to implement for the partner's clients, prior to the end of the semester. The evaluation of the semester experience is done by the students in assessing if the goals stated by each student grassroots organization were met. The final presentations are conducted as mock proposal review panels to determine which task group project is worthy of funding for future replication. The community partners also give feedback to the groups.

Example of learning experience

One grassroots task group project was a Women's Wellness Forum for public housing residents. Students partnered with the local housing and redevelopment authority and case managers and collaborated with major health organizations who provided speakers, health screenings, and displays. Students developed directories to link residents to local services. The task groups with additional coaching from the community partners learned techniques to solicit in kind donations to provide a healthy dinner and gifts for the 100 residents who attended. In addition, a children's group was conducted concurrently by students and volunteer professional social workers for the participants' children.

The evaluation of this program, by the resident participants and the administrative teams from the housing authority and the health organizations, was so favorable that this has developed into an ongoing event each semester.

Each tier provided increasing levels of competency in group work practice. This increases the students' skill level and knowledge of group work modalities as an effective planned change process.

Outcomes

The outcomes for the students in this three tier model of connecting the classroom and the community were that each student successfully completing this model is able to actively participate as a member of a task group, assume leadership for a task group, develop a needs assessment with a community partner, and broker resources to support interventions using developmental group models. In addition they can apply macro skills such as collaboration, negotiation, team building, budgeting, marketing, and conduct evaluation of their interventions.

The outcomes for the community partners were the opportunity to assist the faculty with classroom learning based on the current/ contemporary needs of their clients, to have the resource of formal volunteer consultation by the faculty to plan intervention for their clients, to utilize the faculty member as a trainer for staff and community leaders, to utilize the energies and creativity of students in facilitating change in their communities.

Finally, the outcomes for the client community were access to new resources created by the students, access to empowerment opportunities, opportunities to serve as resources and consultants to students and faculty, and opportunities to be valued as major participants, in sharing their perspectives, in the education of future social workers. An unexpected benefit for the clients was the exposure and opportunity to explore their future personal, educational and career goals. Students served as models for clients and their children.

Discussion

This model has evolved over a five year period and the developers have had opportunities to receive formal and informal feedback from students in the three courses, other faculty, community partners and community clients. It was intentional to have the task group sizes decrease with each tier to increase the level of responsibility for each task group member. The task groups organized as committees and evolved in the third tier to using a board or taskforce format. The size was also tied to the number of community partners depending on the variance in class sizes. It was fortunate that the developers were able to sustain the commitment of a core group of community partners to facilitate the mutual advantage for continuity in the classroom and the community. Throughout the years the developers continued with high visibility in the partners' organizations.

This model has been evaluated from four perspectives. They include the formal university evaluation instrument that is implemented at the end of each semester/tier with students evaluating the course and the professor. The rating system includes a rating scale of very effective, effective, moderately effective, somewhat effective and ineffective. In 2009, for the category of faculty student interaction, students reported a 100% rating in the very effective to effective range in tier one and two and a 96% rating in that range for tier three. In the category of helpfulness of assignment in understanding course material, there was a 94% rating in the range of very effective to effective and 6% in the moderately effective for tier one and two and a 93% rating in the very effective and effective range and 7% in the somewhat effective category for tier three. Faculty, in each class, also have students complete an evaluation of the experience at the conclusion of their presentations in class (written analysis, verbal analysis and video tapings) in which 100% of the students in all three tiers rated their experience with the community partners in the very effective to effective range.

A second method of evaluation is to have students incorporate the learning from their research classes in the development of an instrument used to assess client satisfaction with the programs implemented in the community. This is required for tier two and three. In 2009, students developed a satisfaction survey, distributed it to clients who received services in the programs and 91% of the clients assessed the programs as very effective.

A third method is students, in the third tier, complete peer evaluations of the effective use of mezzo and macro skills in their grass roots organization.

A fourth method is the formal meetings between faculty and community partners throughout the semester and at the conclusion of the semester to evaluate the students and the outcomes of the learning activities in order to modify on going activities and to plan for future classes. These sessions have provided very positive feedback about the students and their contributions as well as thoughtful insights into additional activities that could be utilized in the future. Of the community agencies, 100% have continued their commitment to be community partners. Focus groups are also conducted to obtain the voice of client leadership groups and employees of the agencies served. Feedback from both of these populations was very positive and the client leadership expressed the hope that the students would provide even more educational groups for them in the future.

Future plans include the development of evaluative tools to measure benchmarks and final outcomes of the model, to develop procedures and instruments to assess changes in the service environment in order to provide competent practitioners to respond to community needs.

The developers would like to follow up with future research in the development of a model on sustaining the relationship with community partners in social work education.

Overall, there were many advantages to utilizing this model. It provided a win-win situation, as it contributed to the development of students to be effective generalist social work practitioners and group workers, it strengthened university relationships with community agencies and social work professionals, and increased community residents' involvement in providing positive interaction with social work professionals.

References

Bandura, A. (1986). *Social foundation of thought and action: A social cognitive theory.* Englewood Cliffs, NJ: Prentice-Hall.

Bloom, B.S. (1956). *Taxonomy of educational objectives. Handbook 1: The cognitive domain.* New York: David McKay Co., Inc.

Butin, D.W. (2006). Special Issue: Introduction. Future directions for service learning in higher education. *International Journal of Teaching and Learning in Higher Education, 18*(1), 1-4.

Franklin, C. & Hopson, L.M. (2007). Facilitating the issue of evidence-based practice in community organizations. *Journal of Social Work Education 43*(3), 377-404.

Iatridis, D.S.(1995). Policy practice. In R.L. Edwards (Ed.-in-chief), *Encyclopedia of social work* (19th edn., vol 3, pp.1855-1866). Washington, D.C.: NASW Press.

Krumer-Nevo, M. & Lev-Wiesel (2005). Attitudes of social work students toward clients with basic needs. *Journal of Social Work Education 41*(3), 545-556.

Maslow, A.H. (1970). *Motivation and personality.* New York: Harper & Row.

Mulroy, E.A. (2005). Group work in context: Organizational and community factors. In G.L. Greif & P.H. Ephross (Eds.), *Group work with populations at risk* (2nd edn., pp.446-456). New York: Oxford University Press.

Rothman, J. (2008). *Cultural competence in process and practice.* Boston, MA: Pearson Education, Inc.

Soliman, I. (1999). *Teaching small groups.* Biddeford, ME: University of New England.

Toseland, R.W. & Rivas, R.F. (2005). *An introduction to group work practice.* Boston: Pearson Education, Inc.

Troparon, J.E., Enlich, J.L. & Rothman, J. (2001). *Tactics and techniques of community intervention.* Itasca, IL: Peacock Publishers.

Ward, K. & Wolf-Wendel, L. (2000). Community centered service learning: Moving from doing for to doing with. *American Behavioural Scientist* 43(5), 767-780.

Warren, R.B. & Warren, D.E. (1984) How to diagnose a neighbourhood. In F. Cox, J.P.L. Erlich, J. Rothman & J.E. Tropman (Eds.), *Tactics and techniques of community practice* (2nd edn., pp.27-40). Itasca, IL: Peacock.

History

Based on a presentation at the XXXII AASWG Symposium, Montréal. Québec, 2010. First published in the Proceedings series in: Roy, V., Berteau, G. and Genest-Dufault, S. (Eds.) (2014) *Strengthening Social Solidarity through Group Work: Research and creative practice.* London:Whiting & Birch (pp.35-45)

Notes on authors (at time of first publication)

Brenda L. Exum, MSW, ACSW is a Social Work Professor at Norfolk State University. For over 30 years she has been committed to empowerment and encouraging civic engagement with a focus on diversity. She has been active in leadership in NASW-VA, an International Trainer in the Art of Dialogue and is the founder of Hampton Roads Trust Building Taskforce. Her advanced training has included Public Peace Process Training at Kettering Foundation and Community Building Fellowships at Initiatives of Change.

Mary Yanisko, MSW recently retired as an Assistant Professor in the School of Social Work at Norfolk State University. She continues to be active in the Hampton Roads community through volunteer activities, training, advocacy and hospice work.

Community social service projects: Working in task groups to create change

Preface to the 2021 reprint

The Community Social Service Project (CSSP) task group course has been taught for over 20 years. Originally designed as a sophomore level face-to-face course, task groups met in-class to talk about group dynamics, social issues they might address, and steps to complete their project. The last few years there has been an increasing use of on-line platforms for web conferencing such as Adobe Connect. Google docs and classroom management software have made it easier for students to share content and comment on each other's work.

Over the years, group techniques have become more refined. Several groups begin meetings with a one or two word check-in such as a weather report (e.g. sunny, rainy, partly cloudy) to quickly assess how group members are feeling. Some groups use a quick checkout at the end of a meeting. This has worked well for both virtual and in-person meetings.

To help with decision-making, several groups use rounds or a talking stick to assure that each member has an opportunity to participate if they choose. A couple groups use a "Pause," a moment for individual reflection when an important decision needs to be made or when the group atmosphere has become tense. This often leads to a new idea, a different way to address an issue, or a "group sigh" as tension is released.

Here is an example of a CSSP group that took the time to acknowledge and integrate the ideas, backgrounds and experiences of all its members:

The university serves a predominately white rural community. Recently immigrant and refugee families from Sudan and Somalia moved into the area. A CSSP group decided to raise awareness and funds for a battered women's shelter. A few task group members were from local communities, one grew up in Somalia, and another was from Sudan.

In addition to fundraising, the CSSP group found a short film about wife battering internationally and invited local Somali and Sudanese women to view and discuss the film. The Somali and Sudanese students served as translators, and the other group members assisted. I later learned that the student from Sudan had recently divorced her abusive husband -- something she could not have done in her home country. Student reflections illustrated the richness of this group experience.

To encourage meaningful dialogue and a collaborative brainstorming process, I would add an improvisational theater technique called *"Yes, and..."* In improvisation, each speaker acknowledges, and then expands upon what the previous person said. I participated in the use of this strength-based technique at a community meeting. By focusing on 'Yes, and..." our group was able to move beyond an initial "No, that won't work," response, integrate the ideas of various group members, and develop a creative group solution.

In an era of budget cuts and increasing expectations, it is unlikely a social work program could adopt an entire CSSP course. At the same time, in these complicated and changing times, we need to enhance our skills for working together. Social work and continuing education programs could provide more experiential opportunities for social workers and students to develop, enhance, and reflect upon the value of group work skills. For me, group work has always been at the heart of social work.

Today, the availability and increasing use of the Internet, laptops, tablets and smart phones provides opportunities as well as challenges. On-line sources for research abound and students need training to better assess the reliability of sources. Texting and checking social media during meetings presents challenges that become part of the learning process.

New technology has created additional opportunities for communication and collaboration. The Internet can make it easier to draw attention to an issue, organize an activity and fundraise. In this digital age students, faculty and community groups can interact, share content, and meet virtually. As we move together beyond walls, time zones, and international boundaries we need to continue to enhance our skills and understanding of the potential of group work.

Marilyn D. Frank

After 40 years as a social worker and social work educator, Dr. Frank continues to work with community groups, especially around issues of sustainability, aging, and health

Community social service projects: Working in task groups to create change

Marilyn D. Frank

This chapter presents a model for an introductory social work course that is learner-directed and experientially based and reports on students' perspectives of what they have learned. This 15-week course provides sophomore-level students with opportunities to learn about social work while they contribute to their communities and enhance their skills for working in task groups. Students learn and apply a four-step community social service model that has been adapted from a community intervention model initiated by Peterson (1973) and further developed by Peterson and Sandee (1990). Under the current model (Frank, 2005), undergraduate students work in task groups to identify a need arising from a social problem or issue, assess this need through library and web research, develop and implement a detailed project plan to address some aspect of this need, and formally present the results of their community social service project to their colleagues. Group work concepts are introduced throughout the course, and students are given ample individual and group opportunities to experience and reflect upon what they are learning about task group dynamics. Examples of projects and students' reflections from fall 2004 and spring 2005 task groups are presented.

Course overview

This introductory social work course provides students with an opportunity to work in task groups to address a social need in the community. Each task group chooses a social problem, a need arising from this problem, and a target group they hope to help. The task group develops at least two activities to help the selected target group with the identified need. Activities are generally focused on educating about the social need, creating opportunities for interaction between groups, or developing additional resources for a targeted group through fund-raising activities. Social problems addressed have included homelessness, chemical use and abuse, woman battering and suicide. Since each task group determines the social problem, need, and target group for their community service project, each project is unique and provides opportunities for creative problem solving within the group and community. Similar to what is described by Gumpert, Burrus, and Duffy (2003), this kind of experiential model helps students learn about themselves and others, interact directly with people in the community, and bring the experience back to the classroom.

This course comes early in the undergraduate social work curriculum and provides the student with opportunities to develop micro, mezzo and macro skills. Each student makes at least one contact with an agency, community group, or someone from a population at risk (micro); works in a task group throughout the semester discussing plans and writing reports (mezzo); and helps to implement and evaluate a social service project in the community (macro). For many students this is their first contact with a social service agency. Working in a task group students learn about establishing relationships with each other and people in the community, making agreements, and organizing others to help in accomplishing tasks (Kirlin, 2002).

Each year four sections of this introductory social work course are taught with an average of 25-30 students in each class. A manual developed by university faculty provides guidelines and protocols to help task groups move through the development and implementation of a community social service project. The manual provides information about group work and assignments to help students focus on group process as well as task completion.

The first day of the course the students, along with the instructor, determine how the task groups of 4-6 students will be formed. Generally students count off into the appropriate number of groups. This tends to lead to the random placement of students into groups. Occasionally groups form based on interest areas or to accommodate work schedules. Students meet in their task groups throughout the semester. Groups meet at least one time a week in the classroom and choose when and where they will meet outside of class time.

Through classroom discussion and meetings with individual task groups, the instructor serves as a consultant and mentor. In consultation with the instructor, each task group determines the social issue, need, target group, action system and activities to include in their community social service project. The instructor meets regularly with task groups to review task group goals and progress, to make suggestions about possible activities and potential contacts, and to discuss group dynamics.

Through lecture, discussion, and observation, task group members learn about principles of group dynamics such as communication (Fatout & Rose, 1995; Kirst-Ashman & Hull, 2006; Zastrow, 2001), group decision-making (Fatout & Rose, 1995), leadership (Zastrow, 2001), conflict (Toseland & Rivas, 2005; Zastrow, 2001) styles of conflict management (Cretilli, 1998), group atmosphere (Peterson & Sandee, 1990), task and maintenance behaviors and roles (Benne & Sheats, 1948), and stages in task group development (Catalyst Consulting Team, n.d.; Tuckman, 1965). The group serves as a laboratory to provide students with opportunities to observe and reflect upon group dynamics throughout the course. Reflective exercises focused on individual and task group experiences help students review and integrate what they have learned in the classroom, in their work within the task group, and in the community with people in need.

The community social service project model utilized in this course consists of four steps: 1) Issue and need identification, 2) Assessment of need, 3) Project plan and implementation, and 4) Analysis and presentation of results (Frank, 2005). Each of the four steps takes three to four weeks to accomplish and culminates with a task group report. Students have various opportunities to learn about and reflect upon group dynamics during each step.

Step 1: Issue and need identification

In this step, task groups choose two social problems or issues of interest, determine the needs that arise from this issue, then identify potential target groups, action systems, and activities that could help begin to address the identified needs. Classroom discussion focuses on building interpersonal communication skills and effective decision-making strategies (Fatout & Rose, 1995; Kirst-Ashman & Hull, 2006; Zastrow 2001). During this step, students write individual reflections that address their involvement in task group activities and their comfort level in the group. They also reflect on what learning from their work in the task group will be useful in the future, personally or professionally.

Step 2: Assessment of need

Each task group writes a literature review to learn more about the scope of the social problem they have chosen and the needs that arise from it, the populations that are affected, and the programs or services that are currently available to help address the social needs. At this point in the semester, stages of group development and issues surrounding conflict and conflict management strategies are discussed (Catalyst Consulting Team, n.d.; Cretilli, 1998; Toseland & Rivas, 2005; Tuckman, 1965; Zastrow, 2001). In the Step 2 report, task group members are expected to write about styles of conflict management which they have observed among themselves, the potential value of suppressing conflict or unpleasant feelings for short-term task achievement, and how suppression of unpleasant feelings might slow down their groups' goal accomplishment and potential to bring about change.

Step 3: Project plan and implementation

During this step, task groups write a mission statement, a detailed project plan, including an evaluation plan, and then implement the community social service project. The instructor discusses realistic goals and ways to evaluate project results with task groups. Students reflect upon the group atmosphere and how it has or has not changed throughout the semester and upon the impact of various task and maintenance roles on the group (Benne & Sheats, 1948; Peterson & Sandee, 1990).

Step 4: Analysis and presentation of results

This step provides each task group an opportunity to analyze the results of their community social service project and to formally present these results to their colleagues. A discussion of group dynamics is included in each task group presentation. Experiences with getting started, group decision-making strategies, leadership styles, and stages in task group development are shared. In addition, each task group member presents a personal reflection about what she or he learned about working in task groups. To illustrate the needs addressed using this community social service model two examples will be presented.

Social issues and community social service projects

Task groups are responsible for deciding what issue and needs to address in the community project. While the projects developed each semester are unique, two social issues that student groups frequently choose to address are teen pregnancy and sexually transmitted diseases, and domestic violence.

Teen pregnancy and sexually transmitted diseases

As graduates of local high schools, traditional-aged students feel that there is a lack of useful information presented in health classes about sex, teen pregnancy, and sexually transmitted diseases. Task groups have reached out to schools and local communities to speak to parents and teens about these issues and have designed and made presentations to health classes. Other groups have raised money for teen parents or provided teen parents with information about resources for returning to school and/or finding meaningful employment. These experiences have often been as meaningful for the task group members as they have been for the target group. For example, when a group member who had been a teen mom spoke to a high school class, the task group members gained a new appreciation for what their colleague had accomplished. Other times students expressed surprise at the attitudes and experiences of the adolescents with whom they have come in contact. These experiences have been important 'beyond the classroom' learning opportunities.

Domestic violence

While agencies are careful about confidentiality, task groups have received permission to implement projects ranging from collecting needed household goods and personal care supplies to hosting parties for children in a battered women's shelter. One task group that included a Somalian refugee and a Sudanese refugee arranged for the local women's shelter to present an international film about domestic violence to women from Sudan and Somalia. The students from Somalia and Sudan served as translators and helped to present information about available community services.

Task group members are often able to use their computer and technology skills to implement their community service project. A task group that held a Halloween party for children at the local women's shelter brought a digital camera and a photograph printer to take pictures which were given to the families. After the photographs were given to the families, they were erased from the camera.

This course provides social work students an opportunity to interact with people in need and helps them better understand issues related to social justice. For many students this is the first time they have worked on a project for an extended period of time or taken action to help people in need. By the end of the course, task group members have often illustrated increased sensitivity to the challenges faced by people and have developed confidence in being able to take steps to make a difference. A few students decided not to pursue a social work career after they saw the challenges faced by people in need and realized the time and energy it takes to effectively bring about change. Students' reflections demonstrate their learning process.

Student reflections

For many students, previous classroom group experiences have meant short-term group projects where, 'you do your part, I will do my part, and then we will staple our parts together and submit them.' In this course student groups are responsible for their own community projects and the task group serves as a laboratory for students to learn about group dynamics as well as working together to make a difference in the community. Reflection, which helps students integrate what they have learned and make meaning out of the experience, is a key element (Bringle & Hatcher, 1999). Students have opportunities to reflect upon task group dynamics and the development of their own personal and professional skills at each step of the model. Their perspectives in each of these domains illustrate the progression of their learning.

Task group dynamics

Several students commented on how things do not always go as planned – an important lesson to learn early in a social work career. Examples of student reflections on decision-making, communication, group atmosphere, and conflict demonstrate some of these lessons.

Decision-making

Many decisions need to be made throughout the semester. Major decisions include choosing a social need, target group interested in participating and a site to implement a community social service project. Other decisions include when and where a task group will meet and decisions around group process issues such as what to do if one of the group members does not follow through on an assigned task.

A range of decision-making styles is exhibited throughout each semester. Sometimes all group members want to share in the decisions and feel this leads to the strongest outcomes. A student from a highly motivated group reflected:

> *Because group members strive to reach a consensus on decisions, group sessions are time consuming; however they are also rewarding. This has led all members to take ownership in the project and in the problems that arise.*

Some students prefer quick decisions or rely on other group members to make decisions for them. Students, who rely on other group members to make decisions for them, tend to be less committed to the task group and are less involved with the community service project than other task group members.

Communication

Communication between two people can be difficult. Working in a time limited task group with three to five other colleagues can be especially challenging.

Task group members are active listeners and are encouraged to provide honest feedback as necessary. The manner in which they provide feedback is generally sensitive, leading group members to dare to take risks in expressing opinions and differences.

Nonverbally, the group members use facial expressions and head nodding to show their approval or disapproval of an idea or comment that another member has made... it makes idea swapping a lot easier because of that sort of instantaneous non-verbal feedback.

Again, the group was extremely busy, but I was also and I still got a lot of the work done. A lot more team communication is needed to succeed at this. It is not always easy working in groups.

Effective communication about group process and actions to take to successfully complete the community social service project is often mentioned as the key to a group's success.

Group atmosphere

The comfort level of students with the group and the ability of the task group to work together generally increases throughout the semester. While some groups have a challenging time working together at the beginning of the semester, by the middle of the semester typical student reflections include:

It is very safe to share what we want to share; and

We are building more trust as a team and therefore learning how to work better together.

End of the semester reflections on group atmosphere indicate greater acceptance of other task group members and greater comfort in working together.

A group is like a well-oiled machine; when one group member is stressed, the group as a whole will feel the stress and needs to focus in on alleviating the stress.

We have a couple of different working styles. Some of us are more relaxed and some like to finish their task immediately. We collaborate on all of our work though, and try to bend to fit each other's work styles. Those of us who are more used to putting things off try harder to accomplish projects earlier and those who are used to getting things done right away try to be a little bit more lenient about our own personal deadlines.

Occasionally student task groups or individual students have put in minimal effort to work together or complete a project. These students generally report discomfort with working in their group and/or with the community project that was chosen.

Conflict

Students do not like conflict or even having disagreements. They will often try to avoid conflict as long as possible. Task group members have used various strategies such as denial, suppression or compromise to deal with problems that arise. By the middle of the semester, one member of a task group commented:

One conflict that is occurring presently is that we have been lacking the presence of one of our group members at our meetings. This makes it difficult for our group to function as a whole. No one has wanted to address this issue because we have been hoping that it would change or self-correct. But, it is causing the remaining group members much distress and if it is left unaddressed, it could potentially bring our group and our service project down.

After discussions with the instructor and further attempts to contact the task group member, it became clear the task group could not count on this member. They decided to divide the work between the four of them. The fifth member joined the group when they went to speak at a school, but did not complete the course.

Professional and personal development

Students have an opportunity to reflect on their personal and professional growth throughout the semester. Students' written reflections at the end of the semester indicated a greater awareness of behaviors and roles in the group, increased skills, learning beyond the classroom, and influences on their careers.

Each student submitted written reflections regarding personal and professional growth after completing Step 1: Issue and need identification and Step 3: Project plan and implementation. At the end of the semester, each student reflects orally and in writing about working in a task group. Examples of student reflections on behavior and roles, group skills, impact beyond the classroom, and career direction follow.

Behavior and roles

Student reflections indicated a growth in understanding of the impact of their behavior in the task group.

The most important thing I learned about myself was how hard it is for me to compromise. I had to work at accepting other members' ideas. During this step there were some things that got overlooked because of miscommunication. I helped by encouraging an atmosphere where it's okay to ask questions.

An important thing I learned on a professional level would be that other people were counting on me to get my stuff done. That made me work harder and quicker on the tasks assigned to me so I wouldn't let my group down.

Skills

Students reflected upon task group skills that were acquired or enhanced and helped the group to function more effectively.

I learned different methods of diffusing tensions within the group. I think that every group needs to have one member who can crack jokes and help resolve tension

Two group members did not seem to understand each other when they gave ideas for talking to students about teen pregnancy. I was able to restate what each member said. This helped to clarify the different points of view. It also led to more ideas for activities related to teen pregnancy. I have learned the importance of speaking up when I don't feel things are being run fairly. Group work is not only being able to talk about your feelings and ideas for the project, but also about how the group is run.

Beyond the classroom.

A few students explained how the impact of working in the task group went beyond the classroom experience.

I'm not as scared of group work as I used to be and that's a HUGE step.

I am more willing to voice my opinions, even in other classes, from getting used to talking in my task group.

After completing a community service project, students reported a better understanding of challenges faced by people in the community, ability to access community resources, and greater confidence in creating and implementing projects to address the needs of people in the community.

I realized that there are more social issues to be addressed than I previously thought.

I learned how to make contacts in the community. I never dreamed people would be as willing to cooperate as they were.

I learned a lot about the problem of homelessness and how much impact a small group of people can really have.

Career direction

Completing a community social service project clarified career directions for some students.

I learned that social work is not the career for me because I became too personally involved and would rather do something else.

I started to feel like all of the papers and documentation were useless. After the final day of our project I realized how important all that work really is. I've regained my passion for this major and field of work.

Student reflections illustrate the impact working in task groups and completing a community project has had on personal and professional development whether a student chooses a career in social work or not.

Conclusion

By the end of this sophomore level course, students are better prepared to work in task groups and help people in need (Gumpert, Burrus, & Duffy, 2003). Their experience and increased understanding of task group dynamics form an important foundation for working in future task groups (Kirlin, 2002). This course, which comes early in the social work program, presents many students their first opportunity to work in a task group for an extended period of time and to personally interact with a social service agency, a community organization, and people in need. Through working with their colleagues, students are exposed to a variety of social issues, group dynamics, and learning styles. They have learned how task groups develop, have met challenges related to group dynamics, and have made a contribution to their community.

Both students and the communities have benefited. Each year approximately 100 students working in 16 different task groups complete a community social service project which impacts the work of numerous social service agencies, schools, church groups, homeless shelters, battered women's shelters, and community centers. On occasion, agencies have adopted materials such as resource manuals developed by students. Through this course undergraduate students have gained knowledge, skills and confidence in their abilities to work in a task group and have a positive impact on their communities. This experience has helped many students reaffirm their commitment to pursue a social work career.

References

Benne, K., & Sheats, P. (1948). Functional roles of group members. *Journal of Social Issues, 4,* 41-49.

Bringle, R. G., & Hatcher, J. A. (1999). Reflection in service-learning: Making meaning out of the experience. In *Introduction to service-learning toolkit: Readings and resources for faculty* (2nd ed.)(pp. 83-89). Providence, RI: Campus Compact.

Catalyst Consulting Team. (n.d.). Accelerating team development: The Tuckman Model. Retrieved August 15, 2003, from http://www.

catalystonline.com.

Cretilli, P. (1998, October). *Styles of conflict management.* Minnesota State University, Mankato, Department of Nursing.

Fatout, M., & Rose, S. R. (1995). *Task groups in the social services.* Thousand Oaks, CA: Sage.

Frank, M. D. (2005). Making change: A guide to developing community social service projects. Unpublished manuscript.

Gumpert, J., Burrus, S., & Duffy, J. M. (2003). Pushing the boundary and coming full circle: A contemporary role for social group work in service education. In J. Lindsay, D. Turcotte, & E. Hopmeyer (Eds.), *Crossing Boundaries and developing alliances through group work* (pp. 99-114). Binghampton, NY: Haworth Press.

Kirlin, M. (2002). Civic skill building: The missing component in service programs? In *Introduction to service-learning toolkit: Readings and resources for faculty* (2nd ed.)(pp. 163-169). Providence, RI: Campus Compact.

Kirst-Ashman, K. K., & Hull, G. H. (2006). *Generalist practice with organizations and communities* (3rd ed.). Belmont, CA: Thomson Higher Education.

Peterson, C. L. (1973). *A manual for social work intervention group projects.* Unpublished manuscript.

Peterson, C. L., & Sandee, W. R. (1990). *Beyond the classroom: A manual for social work intervention group projects.* Unpublished manuscript.

Toseland, R. W., & Rivas, R. F. (2005). *An introduction to group work practice* (4th ed.). Boston: Allyn and Bacon.

Tuckman, B. W. (1965). Developmental sequence in small groups. *Psychological Bulletin, 63*(6), 384-399.

Zastrow, C. (2001). *Social work with groups* (3rd ed.). Chicago: Nelson-Hall.

History

Based on a presentation at the XXVII AASWG Symposium, Minnesota, MN., 2005. First published in the Proceedings series in: Kuechler, C.F. (Ed.0 (2011) *Group Work: Building bridges of hope.* London:Whiting & Birch (pp.67-80).

Notes on author (at time of first publication)

Marilyn D. Frank, MSW, PhD, LISW, Associate Professor, Social Work Department, Minnesota State University, Mankato, Minnesota.

Constructing a bridge between research and practice:

A reflection on cooperative group learning

Preface to the 2021 reprint

Annette Gerten, MSW & PhD, was an Associate Professor at Augsburg College in Minnesota, US at the time of her death in 2014. Her loss was keenly felt by her family, colleagues, students and the communities she touched, who recalled her courage, humility, innovative spirit and strong relationships.

It is striking that in the first lines of her paper stress the centrality of educational practices that "honor the social work student." Her use of a bridge metaphor for student learning groups has enduring power. It elevates peer learning as not only a bridge, but also as the vehicle to share with others on the way to competent professional practice.

This paper reinforces the imperative to assess and capitalize on members' strengths (students in this case) to achieve their group's purposes. As Gerten points out, without honoring these inputs and desires, mutual aid and empowerment are challenged. Today, as we often pathologize members' identities and needs, her affirmative message and evidence of this successful learning strategy serves as an important counterpoint and strong rationale for effective social group work approaches.

Throughout, Gerten reflects on her own parallel process of learning. She reports how the implementation of a rigorous evaluation approach opened the possibility to understand learning through the eyes of students. Her investment and excitement for reciprocal learning among group workers and members illustrates how groups lead to growth, change and advancement for all participants, recalling the work of Hans Falk (1988) and Judith Lee (2004). Annette Gerten's formulations of worker role in this chapter are essential in understanding the development of the dual identities of social group worker and educator.

As her colleagues and former students reflected on her legacy, they spoke of her enthusiasm, and that she "dedicated her whole heart to her students and to her colleagues" (Augsburg College, 2014). These qualities were brought into service in developing strategies to teach research more effectively, in ways that inexorably link the demands for thoughtful evaluation and empirical evidence in professional practice.

This preface was written by the Editors, Carol S. Cohen and Mark J. Macgowan, due to the death of Annette Gerten in 2014.

References

Augsburg College (2014). *Augsburg College Mourns the Passing of Dr. Annette Gerten*, Associate Professor of Social Work http://www.augsburg.edu/alumni/2014/01/03/augsburg-college-mourns-the-passing-of-dr-annette-gerten-associate-professor-of-social-work/ Retrieved 10/15/18.

Falck, H.S. (1988). *Social Work: The Membership Perspective.* (Volume 14 of Springer series on social work. New York: Springer Publishing Co.

Lee, J.A. B. (2004). *The Empowerment Approach to Social Work Practice, 2nd Edition.* New York: Columbia University Press.

Constructing a bridge between research and practice:

A reflection on cooperative group learning

Annette Gerten

Introduction

It is evident in social work literature that social work educators want to build a bridge between research and practice in a way that honors the social work student. Quite likely the research professor is on one side of the bridge, students on the other, and the professor is coaxing, encouraging, or even forcing students to cross the bridge in order to gain knowledge of research methods for social work practice. Evidence of the desire to teach research methods in a way that students will understand can be seen by the multiplicity of approaches that have been tried, such as: using drama to teach research methods (Whiteman & Nielsen, 1990), teaching practice skills in research courses (Rubin, Franklin, & Selber, 1992), teaching research in practice courses (Berger, 2002), creating research projects in the field practicum (Cox & Burdick, 2001), and using cooperative learning groups (Swanberg, Platt, & Karolich, 2003). Furthermore, the following title suggests the position social work educators take with students: 'Pedagogy of the perturbed: Teaching research to the reluctants,' (Epstein, 1987). This title indicates the two positions that research educators and students find themselves in; generally they begin research courses facing each other across the river with no bridge to cross.

Specific methods of instruction can be the tools that educators use to build a bridge that reaches across this divide. The method of instruction which relies on cooperative group learning is a possible 'best practice' approach. Specific to the instruction of research methods in social work education, Garrett (1998) uses the work of Johnson, Johnson, and Smith (1991) as well as others to describe the benefits and implementation of the cooperative education model of instruction. Swanberg et al. (2003)

also present evidence of cooperative learning as an alternative approach to teaching research methods.

In this reflection, I share the excitement and enthusiasm that I experienced teaching research methods using cooperative learning groups. It has been three years now that I have been teaching the course using guidelines as formulated by Garrett (1998) and the cooperative group learning method as outlined by Johnson et al. (1991). Extremely positive feedback from students led to the present study of this method of instruction. The research design was formulated in order to build on previous research and included baseline data and a comparison group. Specifically, the design was a pretest posttest design with nonrandomized groups. Participants consisted of two sections of the course with 15 MSW students each. One section (which I taught) participated in cooperative learning groups and the other (taught by a colleague) experienced a multi-method approach. The results were surprising; the most significant findings will be highlighted in this reflection.

Building a bridge to student learning

The importance of baseline data

Collecting baseline data is an important step in allowing instructors to perceive students' knowledge and skills accurately. Lazar (1991) suggests that instructors may perceive students to be more negative towards research methods than the students perceive themselves. The importance of gathering baseline data in order to clarify where students begin the course was underscored by this study. I found that my assumptions regarding students were not true. Data indicated that the majority of students had some research knowledge and/or experience at the start of the course. Passage of time was a factor in reducing student confidence and retention of research content. A sample comment illustrates how one student felt at the start of the course:

[I have a] general understanding of research process and methodology, however, my current level of research knowledge is insufficient in conducting my own research.

It was illuminating to learn that students started the course with moderate levels of anxiety and nervousness; not the high levels that I had expected. On a five point scale ranging from 1 (*low*) to 5 (*high*), students in both groups had mean scores of approximately 3.1 for anxiety and 3.1 for nervousness. Students in both groups had low scores for confidence, calm, anger, and sadness. It is possible that MSW students returning to school after working in the field may approach many of their classes with a certain level of anxiety and nervousness. Perhaps Lazar (1991) is correct in his finding that changing faculty attitudes is as important as changing student attitudes. Using the bridge metaphor, the research instructor needs to perceive students as coming to the course with tools in their toolbox that can be used to construct a bridge. Albeit, the tools may be rusty and the students may not be confident in using them, nevertheless they are coming to the course with some knowledge with which to work. Additionally, it is important to acknowledge the emotions that students bring to the course without exaggerating or inflating their significance.

The importance of a comparison group

Prior research would suggest that the classroom that implemented the use of cooperative learning groups would be a better teaching method. However, results from this study suggest that outcomes from each classroom were similar. For both groups of students, feelings of anxiety and nervousness were reduced and confidence was increased from pretest to posttest. Furthermore, students reported favorably about the instruction in each classroom finding the instructor to be the primary source of knowledge regarding course material. In the collaborative learning section my course evaluations were slightly higher and student comments slightly more enthusiastic, but not enough to suggest that one method was superior to the other.

These findings suggest that a bridge between students and research knowledge can be facilitated by a highly skilled instructor. Epstein (1987) suggests that there are pedagogical principles of 'good' research instruction. He states that the research instructor should use humor, start where the student is, let students set the pace, and respect students and their desire to learn (Epstein, 1987, p.81). Evidence indicates that both instructors used all of these principles. It is very possible that in only looking at the comparison between student emotions this study was not measuring a critical variable, such as student learning, that might have detected a difference between the two sections. The focus of my study was on using cooperative learning groups to reduce negative feelings and increase confidence. In future studies it will be valuable to track how cooperative learning groups contributed to learning the content. Nevertheless further exploration of the qualitative data in the current study leads to a greater understanding of how *students* experience the process of being involved in cooperative group learning.

Hearing student voices

The data strongly support that the processes of empowerment and mutual aid were key to understanding the bridging function of cooperative learning groups. Qualitative comments indicate that the experience of cooperative group learning involved the following: humor, support, universality, and learning. Sample comments are as follows:

> *Small group learning was helpful. It gave me time to regroup during each class session. Our group's use of humor lifted the feeling of being so overwhelmed.*

> *I think it was a great experience because we knew that we could call on our group members anytime. We were able to share support, frustrations, when appropriate.*

> *Being in small groups helped me break down some things in class without feeling like a complete moron. It was nice to have a few people to always reflect with and talk about continued projects, etc. I felt supported and normal as opposed to thinking this class was only difficult for me.*

> *Small group learning in research was helpful when trying to understand material. Reading assignments on research literature and sharing of ideas helped build reassurance in our understanding. Group members worked well together so a positive experience was had (this includes both base group and other small group activities).*

These comments illustrate how peer support through small groups helps reduce negative feelings as a barrier to learning. Comments reveal why students are so enthusiastic about the course. Not only do they learn 'how' to do research but they end up feeling empowered. Cooperative learning groups as implemented in this study use a new paradigm of learning. Johnson et al. (1991) state that 'in the new paradigm, students actively construct their own knowledge. Learning is conceived of as something a learner does, not something that is done to a learner' (p.16). Additionally, cooperative learning groups enable the instructor to implement principles of good teaching which include encouraging cooperation among students and an emphasis on active learning (Chickering & Gamson, 1987).

Conclusion

At the end of the course students were asked to use a metaphor to describe what they learned. One cooperative learning group used a pair of handcuffs as a prop. They placed handcuffs on me and a student. I was asked to hold up a sign that said 'research' and the student held up a sign that said 'practice.' Students explained that what they had learned from the course was that research and practice were linked together: research informs practice and practice informs research. Whether using the metaphor of the bridge or handcuffs, this example illustrates that students understood the connection between the two. Finally, I remain convinced that the instructor who teaches research need not approach the course with trepidation. Both instructors and students alike can have a positive experience. Future research is necessary in order to further identify best practices in research pedagogy. For now it seems that cooperative learning groups have much to offer in terms of building a bridge not only between research and practice but between instructors and students. Colleagues ask me 'Given this data will you continue to use cooperative group learning to teach research?' My answer is yes. The importance of hearing the voices of social work students and incorporating those into ongoing course development needs to be emphasized. The process of gathering data enabled me to see course learning through their eyes and thus establish a bridge between teaching and learning.

References

Berger, R. (2002). Teaching research in practice courses. *Social Work Education, 21*(3), 347– 358.

Chickering, A., & Gamson, Z. (1987). Seven principles for good practice. *AAHE Bulletin, 39*(7), 3-7.

Cox, L., & Burdick, D. (2001). Integrating research projects into field work experiences: Enhanced training for undergraduate geriatric social work students. *Educational Gerontology, 27,* 597-608.

Epstein, I. (1987). Pedagogy of the perturbed: Teaching research to the reluctants. *Journal of Teaching in Social Work, 1*(1), 71-89.

Garrett, K. (1998). Cooperative learning in social work research courses: Helping students help one another. *Journal of Social Work Education, 34*(2), 237-246.

Johnson, D., Johnson, R., & Smith, K. (1991). *Active learning: Cooperation in the college classroom.* Edina, MN: Interaction Book Company.

Lazar, A. (1991). Faculty, practitioner, and student attitudes toward research. *Journal of Social Work Education, 27*(1), 34-41.

Rubin, A., Franklin, C., & Selber, K.(1992). Integrating research and practice into an interviewing skills project: An evaluation. *Journal of Social Work Education, 28* (2), 141-153.

Swanberg, J., Platt, P., & Karolich, R. (2003). Cooperative learning in social work education: An alternative approach to teaching research methods. *Arete, 27*(2), 36-49.

Whiteman, V., & Nielsen, M. (1990). Drama in teaching survey research methods: An experimental evaluation. *Journal of Teaching in Social Work, 4*(2), 67-81.

History

Based on a presentation at the XXVII AASWG Symposium, Minnesota, MN., 2005. First published in the Proceedings series in: Kuechler, C.F. (Ed.) (2011) *Group Work: Building bridges of hope.* London:Whiting & Birch (pp.81-86).

Notes on author (at time of first publication)

Annette Gerten, PhD, LICSW, Associate Professor, Augsburg College Department of Social Work, Minneapolis, Minnesota

Teaching social work from a group-as-a-whole perspective: A classroom case study

Preface to the 2021 reprint

I wrote the following article ten years ago during my twenty-fifth year as a clinical social worker and my tenth year as a professor in social work education. I wrote the article following a challenge by students in the classroom to my grasp of racial bias in my course material. The event and the changes that followed helped me to grow as a group leader and teacher. The challenge occurred during an event that I describe in detail in the article. The experience of the event itself, and later, reflecting and writing about it have revealed the unpredictable and astonishing capacity of small groups to transform themselves and their members (including the leader) from a state of ordinary, agreeable being-together, to a state of radical, positive, and unbalancing developmental movement.

Re-reading the article, today, still surprises - still inspires me to teach from a stance of group leader, to probe with my students the processes of our learning and to point to the *group as a whole* as an ever-present context of our work together. A re-reading also causes me to value more than before the group of author/theorists of the British School of object-relations, Melanie Klein (1946/1952); Wilfred Bion (1961, 1970), Donald Winnicott (1987, 1988), and Michael Eigen (2001), whose work and ideas I examine in the article. I did not mentioned John Bowlby (1969, 1988) in the article, but should have. My omission is due to Bowlby's strong influence on me. He is an internalized good father, an ever-present guiding figure in my object world.

My re-reading has made me ask: How does one learn to teach? Perhaps, like many who will read this, and like my first teachers in social work, I learned to teach largely through leading groups and by supervising and being supervised. One learns to attend closely to student's external experiences and, at the same time, to their and to one's own subjectivity. Taking an "intentional stance" (Fonagy, Gergely, Jurist & Target, 2002; Dennett, 1987) one attunes to the other and shares the exploration of the object of study. My style of intentional stance allows room for the concepts of the object-relational writers whom I mentioned above. I return often to their writings. They continue to deepen my understanding of our human separateness and togetherness.

Concepts such as *container/contained* of Wilfred Bion (1970), *holding* of Donald Winnicott 1987, 1988), and *projective-identification* of Melanie Klein (1946/1952) are unusual because they stimulate thought and imagination, resist closure, and, like rich garden beds, they continue to sprout new growth. They touch on what Plato called an ideal or eternal reality. Such concepts are open but are not vague. They do not constrict. Nor are they subject to wearing thin by overuse. An example comes from Kimberlyn Leary (2004), mentioned in the article, who assumes an object-relational, intentional stance in diplomatic conflict resolution. Leary elsewhere names *critical moments* in negotiations where "something has collapsed or newly emerged, leaving the participants tense or vulnerable or, on other occasions, expectant and hopeful" (Leary, 2004, p. 143). The concept has relevance for teaching and for group work and informs the case example in my article.

James J. Canning

James Canning is professor emeritus at Springfield College School of Social Work.

References

Bion, W. (1961). *Experience in groups.* London: Tavistock Publications.
Bion, W. (1970). *Attention and interpretation.* London: Tavistock Publications.
Bowlby, J. (1969). *Attachment, Vol. 1: Attachment and loss.* New York: Basic Books, Inc.
Bowlby, J. (1988). *A secure base: parent-child attachment and healthy human development.* New York: Basic Books.
Dennett, D. C. (1987). *The intentional stance.* Cambridge, MA: The MIT Press.
Eigen, M. (2001). *Damaged bonds.* London: H. Karnac.
Fonagy, P., Gergely, G., Jurist, E. L.& Target, M. (2002). *Affect regulation, mentalization, and the development of the self.* New York: Other Press.

Klein, M. (1946/1952). Notes on some schizoid mechanisms. In, Juliet Mitchell (Ed.), *The selected Melanie Klein*. New York: The Free Press.

Leary, K. (2004, April). Critical moments in negotiation. *Negotiation Journal*, 143-145

Winnicott, D. W. (1987). *Babies and their mothers*, C. Winnicott, R. Shepherd; & M. Davis (Eds.). Reading, MA: Addison-Wesley.

Winnicott, D. W. (1988). *Human nature*. New York: Schoken Books.

Teaching social work from a group-as-a-whole perspective: A classroom case study

James J. Canning

Introduction

Practice with groups has been a principal way of providing social work services since the early 20th century. Until recently, education for group work was included in most United States social work graduate programs. Unfortunately education for group work is now less available in these programs. Competence in group practice has become a secondary requirement in many graduate programs. Many MSW students graduate today without having taken a course in group work, even though they are likely to plan and to lead groups in practice settings (Kurland & Salmon, 2006; Birnbaum & Auerbach, 1992).

The lack of group work courses in social work schools diminishes social work practice with groups. It also indirectly diminishes classroom teaching of group work; in the past, social work practitioners and teachers applied their knowledge of group behavior and their skills as group leaders in their teaching, thereby directly and indirectly exposing students to group-conscious practice and maintaining the group tradition in social work.

A surprising synergy occurs when teachers share with students their group knowledge and skills by providing actual group experiences in the classroom. This chapter presents a case study of a social work classroom experience that illustrates a group approach to classroom teaching and demonstrates the impact that this has on the students' (as well as the teacher's) learning. It is fair to say that if group practice is not reestablished as an expected competency of professional social workers, the group work tradition that has distinguished social work education from education in related disciplines is at risk of disappearing by becoming a speck on the horizon of social work history.

Purpose and premises of this chapter

The purpose of this chapter is to advocate the preservation of an interest in group work education and practice among social work teachers, and to benefit group practitioners who teach group work. In addition, it is intended to interest social work teachers and practitioners in group-as-a-whole and related object-relations theories and concepts that deepen our awareness of the life of a small group.

A first premise of this chapter is that the teacher who is educated about practice in social work with groups is better able to grasp what is happening in a classroom. This chapter includes a case study, a description of a classroom incident experienced by this writer and his classroom students when they were challenged by the topic of racial bias. The example demonstrates the teacher's use of group leadership and group-as-a-whole theory to work through the teaching impasse.

A second premise of this chapter is that understanding and applying relevant object-relational concepts and theories to the classroom enhances the effectiveness of the social work classroom teacher, and increases the classroom learning for both the teacher and the student. Group work, and the teaching of social work, are intimate, inter-subjective processes and can be effectively examined through relevant object-relations concepts and theories. In other words, in order to teach well, one must grasp, as fully as possible, what one and one's students are experiencing in the here and now of teaching and learning. Teaching and learning are not separate processes. They occur mutually and within the same interaction. Good teaching requires the empathy and self-awareness of the teacher. Learning requires the learner to consider where the teacher is coming from. One assumes that an empathic and aware teacher imparts these qualities to students by modeling them, not by prescribing them or stating them explicitly.

Classroom case study:
Relevant theories and terms

Theories relevant to the classroom case study

Empathy and group awareness in teaching are enriched by object-relations theorists of the British School, namely Melanie Klein, Donald Winnicott, John Bowlby, Wilfred Bion and, more recently, Michael Eigen. Their theories require a finely tuned sense of 'the other'. Their subjectivity defies the current trend in social work practice and teaching toward only what is conscious and objectively observable. These authors place a value on not knowing, on what theories and empirically-based studies cannot explain adequately.

I shall examine an event that occurred in my social work practice classroom by using the concept of *projective- identification. Projective-identification*, first described by Melanie Klein (1946), then modified and elaborated by Bion and Winnicott, is representative of a real and very useful phenomenon that cannot be objectively observed. I will also utilize two other useful concepts, Bion's (1967, 1970) *nameless dread* and Winnicott's (1965) concept of *holding*. Finally, I will introduce ideas of a new theorist, psychoanalyst Kimberlyn Leary (2006), who has applied object-relational concepts in understanding race and racism.

I use theories parsimoniously in teaching practice, respecting both their ability to open areas for exploration and their limitations. I encourage students to use theorists and their theories to generate an inner discussion of the things they wish to understand. I encourage use of what might be called a 'mental messaging'. In my own 'mental messaging', I invite a broad range of 'correspondents'. I value the contributions of all. I allow old and new theorists to enter, and to leave. These are qualities that Bion (1961) says are ingredients of 'good group spirit'. Following Donald Winnicott (1971), I leave plenty of space for play and creativity.

Terms relevant to the classroom case study

Projective-identification

Melanie Klein (1946) used the term *projective-identification* to describe how babies may attain a sense of protection against 'annihilation', by putting into the mother negative sensations, emotions, and fantasies that they (the babies) are unable to tolerate. Wilfred Bion (1965, cited by Sandler, 2005), found that patients projectively identified with him at times when they experienced intense confusion. Bion (1965) describes a patient whose negative projections appeared motivated not by wanting to be rid of awful feelings and sensations intolerable to the patient, but, instead, by the patient's strong wish to be understood, to have his therapist, Bion, experience what the patient experienced and to understand specifically his identity confusion. Bion describes the identity confusion as his patient's inability to know his own mind, as separate from Bion's mind. In receiving the patient's projection, Bion describes himself as feeling helpless. He attributes this feeling as coming from the patient. He decides that it is this feeling of helplessness that he, as a therapist, must experience, reflect upon, and return to the patient in words that the patient can process mentally.

Beta element, alpha-function, nameless dread

Bion (1970) uses the term *beta element* for the patient's initial projected feeling, and the term *alpha-function* for the process that Daniel Goleman terms *mindfulness,* and Peter Fonagy and others (Fonagy, Gergely, Jurist & Target, 2002) term, *mentalization.* The *alpha-function* transforms *beta elements* into thinkable entities. Bion (1970) believes it works similarly to the digestive process. He further suggests that while projective-identification is sometimes a mechanism for getting rid of something that is unwanted by putting it into something or someone else, it can also be a normal means of (intimate) communication. Bion, following Klein, believed that *projective-identification* began in the infant-mother relationship. In cases where the infant's *projective-identification* failed, where the mother could not accommodate it, the infant experienced what Bion (1963/1993) describes as the *nameless dread* of annihilation.

Container/contained, mock containment

Bion's (1970) concept, *container/contained*, describes the conflicting human wishes to be protectively contained by something greater than oneself, and at the same time to be the container, oneself, to contain or control the other, or a whole group of others. The concept addresses the disparity between these wishes and the reality that mental life, even an individual mental life, is too complex to contain or be contained, either by a skilled leader, a religion, a group, or a theory. Bion suggests that human needs for containment (for safety), and to be containers (to understand), are based in the helplessness of infancy. Containing and containment of mental life are sought in adulthood but are possible only in fantasy, since mental life is complex, changing, and ongoing. According to Bion, theorists or theologians who believe a theory or religion can contain a person's mental life or behavior are engaging in delusion (Bion, 1970). Eigen (2001) describes the *mock containment* that can result from one's denial of the dread of living fully. Mock containment constricts impulses needed to live creatively and in contact with others.

Holding, dropped, falling

Winnicott (1965), like Bion, a disciple of Melanie Klein, theorizes *holding* as a provision of the good enough mother. The good enough mother tolerates her infant's distress sufficiently but not perfectly, contains it, and then reflects the infant's experience back in such a way that the infant feels regulated and understood. Winnicott (1971) dismissed *projective-identification* as a confounding concept since it assumes that infants are miserable. Winnicott thought that infants did not normally experience intolerable emotions or misery but became miserable when they were not adequately held. He emphasized that an absence of holding by the mother resulted in the infant feeling *dropped* or *falling*. He assumed adults in therapy also require a *holding* environment, in order to organize, to reflect, and to create. Klein's, Bion's, and Winnicott's notions of inter-subjective relationships, however different and theoretically distinctive from each other, share a core truth about how we teach and learn from each other, in individual therapy, in group work, and in the classroom.

Relational opportunities

Kimberlyn Leary (2007) goes beyond Klein, Bion, and Winnicott by describing a process similar, but more interesting, than what Bion calls the individual's *alpha-function*. Leary describes a more complex, multiple, or group inter-subjective exchange, as may occur in a diplomatic negotiation where raw elements such as dread are gradually expressed, refined, and mutually understood. What Bion terms *beta elements*, raw thoughts, sensations, and impulses that issue unannounced from an individual mind, Leary views as *relational opportunities*. A raw element projected from the mind of one subject is reflected upon by the mind of others and is returned by participants to the sender in an ongoing process of mutual influence. Leary (2007) has successfully applied her theory as a participant in Indonesian government negotiations with a rebel group. Leary would say that the diplomat, teacher, therapist, or group leader that seeks to influence others will need also to be influenced.

Additional comments on theories and terms relevant to the classroom case study

The four theorists cited above, Winnicott, Bion, Klein, and Leary are dedicated to understanding the ways by which individuals mutually influence each other. They do not pretend to know the answers. Bion says it well. A theory cannot 'contain' the mental domain because it is not a 'container' but a 'probe' (1970, p.73).

Klein discovered an inter-subjective process that led Bion to probe group processes. Bion wrote only one book directly related to group work (1961). However, it has been observed that his interest in group work, which began as a combat field officer in World War I, seems to have led him to probe the ways individuals influence one other in the army, in therapy, in families, and in organizations. His later writing continues to inform the complexities of human interaction in all these contexts (Sutherland, 1992). Similarly, Winnicott's studies inform family work, group work, and teaching. Leary (2007), who is a contemporary feminist theorist, has adapted object-relational concepts to social problems, the oppression of women, racism, and international terrorism.

I see these theorists as offering much to social work teachers. They do not provide formulae. They, instead, refresh our observational skills and our thinking. Reading them is like viewing drawings of the old masters. Their works are useful to us in the ways that fine art is useful to us. We cannot do what they did. But they inspire us. They revel in the inner worlds of individuals and their relationships. They present awesome mental landscapes. They reveal the dignity of mental life and make us hopeful.

Classroom case study:
A social work class experience

I have chosen a recent event in a social work course I taught to illustrate my two premises of this chapter:

1. that one is a more effective social work classroom teacher if one has been educated about practice in social work groups, and that the teaching of social work benefits if the teacher is an effective group facilitator;
2. that relevant object relations concepts and theories can be applied to teaching and learning.

I will tell the story of this classroom event in three parts: a surprise in the classroom, a 'class-as-a-whole' debate regarding its meanings, and the consequences.

A surprise in the classroom

All members of the class were in their second year of a three-year social work graduate weekend program. The course was the foundation year practice course, and addressed practice with groups, organizations, and communities. There were 22 women and three men. In regard to race and ethnicity, I am a Caucasian, middle-aged male, of Irish descent. Among the students, five were African American women, two were Latina. The remaining class members were Caucasian. All class members were employed in social work positions in various fields: child protection, juvenile justice, home-based family support; or youth, medical, geriatric, disability, or services for people who are homeless.

The 'class-as-a-whole' was friendly, talkative, and serious about their work and their education. Since weekend classes took place on Saturdays and Sundays, from 9:00 a.m. to 4:00 p.m., all acknowledged being *tired* from going to school and managing work and family life. Most class members drove an hour or two to get to class.

A few students were experienced in working with groups but most were inexperienced. About a quarter of the class members expressed strong interest in practice with groups. Others expressed moderate interest, with one or two expressing mild interest. Faculty colleagues had warned that some members of this particular class talked excessively and on occasion made negative or irrelevant contributions to classes. I was told that I 'might have to set limits' on these individuals, since they might try to 'highjack the class', meaning that they could move the class focus in a direction that the teacher might not want to go, resulting in a from the stated and sacred 'course content'.

As the first class began, I noted that the five African American women in the class sat together in the back row of the classroom. Two of the women talked more than the other three members, and seemed to speak for the group of five. In keeping with my group-as-a-whole approach I noted this sub-group, and wondered how this would play out in the 'class-as-a-whole'.

In my class sessions I always include exercises, role-plays or discussions of practice vignettes related to groups. In this first class, I randomly divided the students into three 'experiential groups', and had them meet unsupervised for fifty minutes. These groups would continue to meet for fifty minutes during each of our remaining six classes. The groups were not to be therapy groups but could be support or task groups. Each group was charged with deciding the purpose of their group during the first meeting. For example, one group named their group SWAT (students working against tension). We would discuss the phases, processes, and progress of the three groups as a class following each of their group meetings. I named this part, 'class-as-supervisor', since it offered students an opportunity to reflect on group process as both outsiders and insiders. Group process was to be described generally by the elected leaders of each group. Names of individuals were not to be stated. Confidentiality would be preserved at the group and classroom levels.

The first day of class went according to plan. Toward the end of the day I showed a film entitled *Circle of recovery: healing the wounds of drugs and alcohol*, a '60 Minutes' production narrated by Bill Moyers. The film presents a support group created by several black men who are recovering from drug addiction. In the film, Moyers interviews the group leader who tells a moving story of his neglect as a child, his traumatic isolation and loss of self-esteem as an adolescent, his combat experiences in Vietnam, his PTSD diagnosis and ineffective PTSD treatments, and his deepening substance addiction. The film describes his eventual recovery with the help of a mentor and a support group which provided him with emotional support and inspiration. It lets the camera record the process of several group meetings. Each support group member speaks, close-up, sharing experiences intimately and movingly with the group. I had shown this film many times because it is one of very few available that demonstrates actual group process. The stories of the men are moving, genuine, tragic, sad, and hopeful. There are accounts of prison stays, broken family ties, and extraordinary suffering. There is also joy, humor, caring, and spirituality.

When the recording of the film ended, there was a long silence in the class. In past showings, this silence was evidence of the positive, emotional impact on students of the men in the film openly sharing their feelings. Students have said things like, 'I never thought men could talk like that'. Comments like this often led to students' increased awareness of group interactions, and increased their interest in practice with groups.

On this day, the first student to speak was one of the African American women. 'I am so *upset* with this tape. Why is it that in a graduate program that is supposed to focus on people's strengths, they keep showing us things like this, black folks in trouble, black folks who are lonely and depressed, black folks who commit crimes, are addicted, and who have done all sorts of bad things?' Her voice trembled. She said tearfully, 'there are so many *good things* that my people do! Why don't you ever show us these things?' The class was silent.

I was unprepared for her comments. My first thoughts were defensive.

I liked this tape. I had shown it for three or four years. Others had liked it. I liked these men. I had even grown fond of Bill Moyers. Maybe my class was being hijacked! Maybe I needed to set limits. Had I gone with my first impulse, I might have acknowledged the student's opinion and then asked if the video had not allowed us to see significant strengths in these men and in their group and group leader. I imagined using my influence as a teacher to re-frame and turn her comments around. However, I remained silent. Speechless might be a better choice of words. Then, I experienced sadness. I felt strangely unbalanced, perhaps dropped, or maybe I had dropped the woman speaking, or had 'let the class down'. Without hesitating I said, 'I think you might be right. Let's hear what others think about this.' Several students said that they thought the tape was okay and provided a rationale for showing educational tapes that present persons who are oppressed and at risk. The two Latina women commented that they agreed with the student who had spoken. I told the class that I thought the student who had spoken had revealed something important, that it had taken courage for her to do so. I said that we would take up the issue of negative imagery in the next class.

A 'class-as-a-whole' debate regarding its meanings

During the two-week class break that followed, I reflected on the student's criticism of the tape, and my feelings about the incident. I decided that she had exposed a serious problem in our visual materials, in textbooks, in other educational media, and perhaps in me. I decided that the class might benefit by exploring together the hidden, pejorative meanings in our educational visual media, specifically negative visual representations of persons of color. I decided to create a 'task group' within the class for this purpose. Since it was February, American Black History Month, I would name the project the 'The American Black History Month Project'. Besides validating the student's criticism and acknowledging the issue at hand, it would contribute to learning about task groups. We could begin to create a new sort of visual imagery in our courses and in the school. I received an e-mail from the woman who had spoken, thanking me for supporting her comments. She attached a video clip from a television news broadcast that showed black children of age four to five choosing white rather than black dolls to play with.

At the beginning of our next class, I was disappointed that the woman who had spoken was not in class. I announced my plan to form task groups to meet for thirty minutes for the next four weeks to examine course and school materials and come up with recommendations for creating positive images of people of color. Following my announcement one of the black women said, 'This is not going to work'. Others chimed in. Some shook their heads. Some hung their heads. Some grumbled. I asked that we proceed with the class and talk again about the project after the lunch break. They agreed.

As we met following lunch, the woman who had spoken the week before was present. I said that I thought that the subject of color and race and negative representations of persons of color were difficult subjects for the class to talk about. Nevertheless, thanks to the student, we had what seemed to be a promising start. I suggested that we not abandon the project. A Caucasian woman said, 'I think we are definitely off the track with this. It just makes everybody feel uncomfortable and guilty'. I acknowledged her with a neutral nod. Another Caucasian woman who had initially supported the criticism of the film said, 'I think we are making a mountain out of a molehill. We paid to learn about groups. So why are we wasting time on this stuff'? I thanked her and asked the class for a show of hands of those who thought we were addressing a 'molehill'. A white woman, who had earlier described herself as an experienced group leader, raised her hand. I then asked for a show of hands of those who thought we were dealing with a 'mountain'. About two-thirds of the students raised a hand. There was silence. I suggested that since it seemed the subject was mountainous we might begin a climb and see if we could get a view. The experienced group leader who had seen a 'molehill' said, 'I think that the class is getting out of control'. After my mountain climb comment I did indeed feel mildly out of control. I thanked her, acknowledging her experience, and said that I was sure that if we all participated as a class-as-a whole we would work this out.

The discussion that followed addressed color. The women in the back row related painful experiences of racism. One described arriving in NYC from the Dominican Republic at age nine, and being puzzled and then angry that grown-ups identified individuals by skin color. She had never heard experienced adults giving skin color any attention. Some awkward and even outlandish thoughts and feelings were expressed. I listened thoughtfully to all, remaining relaxed and emotionally interested and neutral. As time ran out a man said, 'Four times is just too much. We already have a lot of work to do'. Someone else said that they wanted to continue the conversation but not for four more classes. Before class ended, we agreed that on the last day of class we would spend one hour developing a set of recommendations for introducing positive images of individuals, families and groups of people of color in the fall.

Following the class described above, I received a number of positive emails from students. More than one said that they had never before spoken about race, color, and racism in a class or in a group. Between the second and final class, students brought in biased news stories, pictures and examples of negative images from the press and elsewhere. I viewed each of these and discussed them with the student(s) who brought them to me. A notable color photo from the front page of the *New York Times* showed the members of the Rutgers women's basketball team looking downcast and victimized after Don Imus had ridiculed them on the radio. I was asked if the team would have made the front page looking proud and joyful as champions? And, did I know that some of the women on the team were white and were not included in the photo?

The consequences

During our final class, scores of suggestions came forth. A student volunteered to collect them on the board. A Student Diversity Committee would be formed for weekend students. Students would make video-recordings of ordinary social and family events in their Black and Latino communities. These could depict local life as it is lived, including actual social gatherings, work, festivities, holidays, and cultural rites of passage, as opposed to how life is presented in commercial and educational productions. Such videos could be provided to teachers as alternative course material. A festival of Black and Latino films was suggested. The women of color and others formed an *ad hoc* committee to approach the dean with their ideas in the fall.

As the course progressed there was less lateness coming to class, more energy, more discussion, and less fatigue at the end of the day than there had been in the beginning. Class members were less dependent on their instructor in discussions, and more interested and responsive to each other. There was a positive bond within the separate experiential groups and in the class-as-a-whole. In Bion's terms, the class was dependably a work group. Good group spirit was evident in the creativity expressed in the final class.

Discussion of the 'classroom case study'

In terms of object-relations, I believe that the woman who spoke out can be seen as projecting into the class a reality that had been denied, the reality that the lives of people of color were hidden from view in the classroom and in the graduate program. It is likely that she had received similar projections from others, before and during her months as a student, had reflected on them, had exercised her alpha function, and put something understandable and usable into the class-as-a-whole. Most of us identified strongly with her. I allowed myself to be influenced because of what might be termed the rightness and courage of her statements. I now believe that the *alpha-function* serves to express what one knows to be true. Perhaps the *alpha-function* constitutes a central individual strength. While projections are usually thought about in terms of distortions of reality, projections can be of what is true, of what has been reflected upon, and of what we need to hear. The student projected what was true and what needed to be understood if we were to remain a class-as-a-whole or to come together in what Bion (1961) refers to as *good group spirit*. Finally, the video became for the class a symbol of a form of stereotyping that is disguised as caring and concern.

My views of teaching, of group work, of influence, and of ways that individuals are represented visually, have been expanded. I shall remember this event as allowing me to teach and to be taught in the same moment. I have become a sharper observer of images, of who creates them, of their motivations for doing so, and of the effects they have upon me and others. My fondness for Bill Moyers is less. In viewing the tape again he seemed a little dry and condescending. Was this a dawning of awareness of my own dryness and privilege? I wonder what has become of the men in the tape, if they benefited from making the tape, and if others have benefited from it. I cannot know. In regard to the object-relations theorists and concepts with which I started, I have found them useful as always. However, they have new meanings for me. The class-as-a-whole has transformed them and enriched them.

When the class member warned that the class was 'getting out of control', she was both right and wrong. I had removed external controls. I had not set firm limits. However, the class members, given control, were able to listen, just as I was doing, and to make sense of things. Had I set rules and limits to regulate the class, they might have provided what Michael Eigen (2001) has called a mock containment that restricts but does not protect. I provided holding, and held fast, but not rigidly, to a plan of action. Students took courage from the first student to express thoughts and feelings that were less than fully 'digested'. Blunders were made and were accepted as valid contributions, with the awareness that they were meant in the spirit of working together on the same goal.

Both classroom teaching and leading groups might be described as imparting and supporting the *alpha-function*, in ourselves and in others. In doing so, and in keeping with Bion, one assumes that the raw thoughts and feelings of persons are presented for a purpose; that they are raw forms of subjectivity that can be transformed by inter-subjectivity, provided that there is safety to do so. In giving permission to speak out and by suppressing judgment, I helped to create a holding environment. This allowed individuals to feel included, to not fear being dropped, to think, to influence, and to be influenced.

Was this event a 'mountain' or a 'molehill'? On the molehill side, you might say that our class-as-a-whole, including its teacher, accomplished less than other groups and other classes that have discussed race, racism, and color. I have become aware of the 'mole' in myself, who tends to excavate snug tunnels within which to avoid what is dreadful. Perhaps other groups and classes in social work have accomplished more to address racism and biased media representations than we did. On the mountain side of things, I think that the woman who dared to speak against negative imagery saw a mountain that I, and other teachers like me, had not seen. Her words contained mountains. The class-as-a-whole held her and supported her courage.

One could say that our class-as-a-whole was a holding environment. It allowed its members to express and receive raw thoughts and emotions, to transform them, and to transform dread into creative action. Dread seems like an appropriate name for the fear of speaking in a group about race, color, and oppression. Students managed to replace dread with empathy and understanding. Leary (2007) urges us to be influenced as we attempt to influence, to be moved by those whom we are attempting to move. I suggest that this enriches the concept of *projective-identification*, and leads to hope that we do not have to dread our differences. Leary (2007) states:

> If Winnicott was correct in suggesting that there is no such thing as a baby, then perhaps there is no such thing as black or white (without the other). Whenever patients talk about the Other, they are inevitably talking about Themselves. And so are we (p.87).

Conclusion

The above discussion supports the concept that group work and teaching go hand-in-hand. Group work, done in the classroom, clinic, schools and elsewhere, provides more opportunities for individual change and interpersonal learning than any other practice method if the group leader or teacher understands how groups work, especially at the level of inter-subjective experience. The authors of the British school of object-relations are a rich resource of knowledge in this regard. It is noteworthy that besides their wealth of knowledge regarding mental functioning, they have grasped human development and have used it to ground their understanding of subjectivity and their capacities for empathy. Together they bring, more than other theorists, a sense of justice that can guide workers, therapists, group leaders, or teachers in areas of love, fairness, reason and reparation. It will be a great loss if such theorists become lost to social work education and practice. If politics is about understanding groups and how people understand each other, it may make a significant difference in our futures in social work.

References

Bion, W. (1970). *Attention and interpretation.* London: Tavistock Publications Ltd.

Bion, W. (1963/1993). *Second thoughts: selected papers on psycho-analysis.* Northvale, NJ: Jason Aronson Inc.

Bion, W. (1965/1984). *Transformations.* London: H. Karnac (Books) Ltd.

Bion, W. (1961). *Experience in groups.* London: Tavistock Publications Ltd.

Birnbaum, M. & Auerbach, C. (1992). *Group work in graduate social work education: The price of neglect.* Presented at the CSWE Annual Program Meeting in Kansas City, Kansas and cited in R. Kurland & R. Salmon (eds.) (2006).

Eigen, M. (2001). *Damaged bonds.* London: H. Karnac (Books) Ltd.

Fonagy, P., Gergely, P., Jurist, E. & Target, M. (2002). *Affect regulation, mentalization, and the development of the self.* New York: Other Press.

Klein, M. (1946/1986). Notes on some schizoid mechanisms, in Juliet Mitchell (ed.), *The selected Melanie Klein*. New York: The Free Press.

Kurland, R. & Salmon, R. (2006). Making joyful noise: Presenting, promoting, and portraying group work to and for the profession. *Social Work in Groups, 29* (2/3), 1-15.

Leary, K. (2007). *On being influential*. Paper presented as Lydia Rapoport Lecture at Smith College School for Social Work, Northampton, MA.

Leary, K. (2006). The John Bowlby Memorial Lecture: How race is lived in the consulting room, in K.W. White (ed.), *Unmasking race, culture, and attachment in the psychoanalytic space*. London: H. Karnac.

Sandler, P.C. (2005). *The language of Bion: a dictionary of concepts*. London: H. Karnac.

Sutherland, J.D. (1992). Bion revisited: group dynamics and group psychotherapy, in M. Pines (ed.) *Bion and group psychotherapy*. London: Jessica Kingsley Publishers.

Winnicott, D.W. (1971). *Playing and reality*. London: Tavistock.

Winnicott, D.W. (1965). *The maturational processes and the facilitating environment*. London: Tavistock.

Videotape (see page 141)

Circle of recovery: healing the wounds of drugs and alcohol (1997). Princeton, NJ: The Bill Moyers Collection, Films for the Humanities & Sciences.

History
Based on a presentation at the XXIX AASWG Symposium in Jersey City, NJ., 2007. First published in the Proceedings series in: Tully, G.J., Sweeney, K., and Palombo,S.E. (Eds.) (2012) *Group Work: Gateways to growth London: Whiting & Birch (pp.39-54)*

Notes on authors (at time of first publication)
James J. Canning, MSW, PhD, Associate Professor, Springfield College, Massachusetts.

A magical mystery tour:
Education and social work with groups across borders

Preface to the 2021 reprint

The Canada-Russia Disability Program (CRDP) was a four-year project (2003-2007) to foster the development of civil society and good governance in Russia. Now, thirteen years later, reflections on some outcomes of the CRDP program, the current state of social work education and social work in Russia, gleaned from recent publications, and a consultation with Dr. Don Fuchs (2017), provide some small insights into current realities and the value of social group work as primary teaching methodology.

The CRDP Program was conceived and implemented within a socioeconomic and political environment in Russia that was in the midst of change (Canadian Centre on Disability Studies, 2007). In the ensuing years the social work stream of the CRDP program assumed: equal partnership among the disability community, governments and universities; a Social Model of Disability and promotion of human rights; consumers' participation in the development and implementation of the project; a Social Work Curriculum with a shift from medical to social content; and curriculum based on human rights and anti-oppression, person-in-environment frameworks (Fuchs, 2011).

The Social Development outcomes included:

- Approval and implementation of two specializations in the three focal regions of the project, one in social work and disability and the other social work and mental health.
- Approval of three teaching learning centres for providing practical education and service innovation.
- Increased instructional capacity to provide classroom and field education for social work students.
- Implementation of a model of field education in all three regions.
- Movement of social work education standards more in line with

those approved by IASSW Standards and scope of practice (Fuchs, 2011).

Iarskaia-Smirnova and Rasell (2014), in their analysis of the disconnection between social work education in Russian universities and the field of social work, note that while

... social work education in Russia is affected by the weak status of the profession in addition to vagaries in the higher education system, requiring changes in both the welfare and university sectors to promote professionalization, there are some creative developments within universities and social service agencies to build partnerships to train staff (p. 230).

Iarskaia-Smirnova and Rasell go on to note that

Overall awareness of social work's goals, methods and values is stronger now among Russian academics than in the last two decades, especially in terms of fighting discrimination and marginalization. (p. 231)

In 2013, occupational standards for professions, including social work, were developed with support from the federal Ministry of Labour and Social Protection. These standards have the potential to increase the professional orientation of future educational curricula. "Ultimately, social work education could enhance the status, influence and voice of social work in Russia by giving graduates a distinctive value base, professional orientation and shared identity" (p. 231).

In 2016, a summit in Vladivostok marked the 25th anniversary of social work in Russia, organized by the Government of Vladivostok, The Union of Social Workers and Professional Pedagogues (USWSP), an International Federation of Social Workers' (IFSW) Member, Council of Europe, and the Ministry of Labour and Social Protection in Russia. Participants included representatives from nearly 30 regions of Russia, social workers from China, Korea, Singapore, Thailand, Vietnam and academics from Japan, the United Kingdom, France, Hong Kong, Australia and the Czech Republic, and the first visit to Russia by representatives from the International Association of Schools of Social Work (IASSW). The summit focused on education and training of social workers, workplace safety of social workers, social responsibilities and social control. IFSW Secretary-General, Rory Truell (2017) noted:

The success of the summit and wide range of participants is a testament to the effective work of the USWSP. It takes significant leadership to promote, legitimize and make relevant a profession that is new to a country ... (Retrieved 11/22/2017 from http://ifsw.org/news/celebrating-25-years-of-social-work-in-Russia).

Ellen Sue Mesbur

Ellen Sue Mesbur, MSW, Ed.D, is a group work consultant. She served as Director and Professor at School of Social Work, Ryerson University and the School of Social Work, Renison University College, University of Waterloo

References

Canadian Centre on Disability Studies (2007). Canada Russia Disability Program 2003-2007: Final Report. Winnipeg Manitoba: Monograph.

Fuchs, D. (December 2017). Personal Communication.

Fuchs, D. (2011). Promoting Human Rights and Full Citizenship of Persons with Disabilities in Russia: The Role Social Work Education in a Global Context. Presentation at the ENSACT Conference, *Social action in Europe: Social sustainable development and economical challenges*, Brussels April 11-14.

Iarskaia-Smirnova, E. & Rassell, M. (2014). Integrating practice into Russian social work education: Institutional logics and curriculum regulation. *International Social Work* 2014, Vol. 57(3) 222–234.

Truell, R. (2017). Retrieved 11/22/2017 from http://ifsw.org/news/celebrating-25-years-of-social-work-in-Russia

A magical mystery tour:
Education and social work with groups across borders
Ellen Sue Mesbur

Introduction

This paper describes my experience of the use of social group work in teaching in Russia across language, culture, history and tradition. I was invited to participate in the development and delivery of a Field Education Training Program in Russia as part of an international project, the Canada–Russia Disability Program (CRDP). The multi-year, multi-million dollar project, funded by the Canadian International Development Agency, included Canadian representatives of social work education, government, non-government and disability communities. The project was undertaken using a tripartite model of engagement including the voluntary, government and education sectors in both Canada and Russia. Activities were focused within four components: education, demonstration models, policy promotion, and network and information dissemination in three Russian cities: Moscow, Stavropol, and Omsk. The project encompassed three streams: Social Work, Mental Health, and Disability Studies.

I will begin by laying out the social and historical context and the state of social work practice and education in Russia. Further, the tensions around cross-national teaching in social work in the context of international development assistance will be discussed. The following brief section of the paper will describe the teaching context and the characteristics of the participants. I will continue by outlining the conceptual framework for the social group work approach utilized for the training and illustrate the use of this method with examples from the training. Next, the qualitative analysis of major themes generated by the participants through classroom discussions will be presented. I will conclude with my reflections on this unique learning experience.

Leviathan: Social change and the rise of social work in Russia

For more than two decades after the collapse of the Soviet Union, Russia has been going through a 'transition,' a complex social transformation that includes the replacement of the communist state and planned economy with a capitalist free-market and democratic institutions. Such rapid political, social, and economic change has rendered Russia akin to a third world country – experiencing widespread and endemic social problems such as unemployment, poverty, and homelessness without the necessary social infrastructure and supports to address or ameliorate them (Freed, 1995; Templeman, 2001). The resultant social, economic, and political conditions have revealed acute social welfare needs requiring the development and expansion of a social service infrastructure and a workforce of professionally educated and trained social workers (George, 1999; Gray & Simpson, 1998; Tunney, 2001; Whitmore & Wilson, 1997).

As a result, in the early 1990's, the first formal social work training programs were introduced in Russia, alongside a fledgling targeted social welfare system, replacing the Soviet-type universal social assistance and protection (Kolkov, Shapiro & Solovyov, 2000; Rutgers University Center, 2008; Templeman, 2001). The decade following perestroika saw the emergence of three professional social work associations, specialized periodicals, and over 150 schools of social work in Russia (Iarskaia-Smirnova, Romanov & Lovtsova, 2004; Penn, 2007; Templeman, 2001). Despite these promising initial steps, social work as a profession in Russia remains in its early phase of formation and faces many challenges as well as pedagogical obstacles (Iarskaia-Smirnova & Romanov, 2008; Iarskaia-Smirnova, Romanov & Lovtsova, 2004; Penn, 2007).

For example, the majority of those working in the social services industry in Russia have no formal training or education (Iarskaia-Smirnova & Romanov, 2002; Templeman, 2001). Yet, in spite of this it is commonplace for those working in social services to self identify as social workers and to be recognized as such (Templeman, 2001). Additionally, social work credentials have yet to be established, and informal professional standards and a code of ethics are known by only a small group of Russian educators and graduates (Iarskaia-Smirnova & Romanov, 2002). Moreover, social workers are typically viewed as welfare workers or, as they are commonly referred to, 'visitors,' and are charged with such commonplace tasks as aiding clients with their house chores and purchasing groceries rather than providing professional interventions (Kolkov, Shapiro & Solovyov, 2000; Iarskaia-Smirnova & Romanov, 2002; Templeman, 2001). The profession's lack of legitimacy is reinforced by the limited funding of social services and low salaries of social workers, who are predominantly women (Iarskaia-Smirnova & Romanov, 2008).

Similarly to professional practice, social work education in Russia faces major challenges. First, with such a brief history, social work theory relevant to the post-Soviet context is underdeveloped, while social work theories and approaches traditionally grounding social work in Western countries face cultural barriers in Russia (Penn, 2007). Second, an understanding of the scope of practice is limited. Few guidelines exist for social workers, and many workers are untrained, having entered the profession as a result of governmental, economic, and social changes (Templeman, 2001). Likewise, most social work instructors do not have social work education (Penn, 2007). Next, social work training in Russia has been criticized for the weak integration between theoretical education and practice (Penn, 2007; Rutgers University Center, 2008). Furthermore, field education suffers from the lack of regulation of the relationship between universities and social work agencies and from the lack of supervision of students' fieldwork (Penn, 2007). Overall, social work training is geared toward general education, and programs of study in specialized areas of practice and/or with specific populations are insufficient (Rutgers University Center, 2008). Unsurprisingly, the attrition of social work students is high (Penn, 2007); moreover, less than 30% of social work graduates become employed in the profession (Iarskaia-Smirnova & Romanov, 2002).

International technical assistance: Can social work knowledge be transferred across borders?

Since social work started to emerge and grow in post-Soviet countries, the need for technical assistance to strengthen professional practice and education was recognized both by foreign aid agencies and local counterparts (Rutgers University Center, 2008; Trygged & Eriksson, 2009). A number of internationally-funded projects and programs to support various areas of social work in Russia have been reported in the literature (Rutgers University Center, 2008). Also, Western universities have been involved in building the capacity of social work educators in Russia and in a variety of activities, including providing access to information, sharing educational materials, expert assistance with curriculum development, scholar exchange, and faculty training (Penn, 2007; Rutgers University Center, 2008).

While there has been genuine and mutual desire to share knowledge on the part of Western social workers and to adopt knowledge on the part of Russian counterparts, the outcomes of these activities have been mixed in introducing and sustaining new approaches to practice and training. For instance, Trygged and Erikkson (2009) describe the difference in the outcomes of two similar projects aimed at transferring Swedish social work models to Russia. Likewise, Penn (2007) reports obstacles to international collaboration in social work from the perspective of Russian partners, who often found that foreign models are not suitable for the Russian context and need to be adjusted, felt that 'Western visitors' cannot understand the experiences of local partners and believed that local actors had limited contribution to the project decision making.

The conventional asymmetry-based approach to capacity building has been heavily criticized for being colonial in spirit and was held responsible for foreign aid that brought limited benefit to receiving countries (Torres, 2001). According to Torres (2001), the asymmetry-based aid has an inherent assumption that universal and high-quality knowledge can (only) be produced by an aid-giving party for an aid-receiving party; consequently, capacity building has been predominantly expert-driven, while the local expertise of those who work in the field is often devaluated and ignored. As a result, projects utilizing asymmetrical, top-down, one-way knowledge transfer approaches have lead to the introduction of models irrelevant to the local context and are therefore unsustainable (Torres, 2001). Knowledge in the international assistance context is not to be transferred; it has to be generated by participating and interacting organizations, social groups, and individuals. In this context, a knowledge-transfer model should be replaced by an interactive model of knowledge utilization, which holds that in order to be relevant and useful, knowledge has to be co-produced and validated by knowledge users (Denis, Lehoux,

& Champagne, 2004). Moreover, learning in this context can be conceptualized as 'mutual trade,' an interactive, engaging experience that has an impact on all parties involved, including both local and Western participants (Doel & Penn, 2007).

The debate around asymmetry-based international technical assistance resonates with the social work profession's existential struggle to balance the contextual, specific, local and the universal, common, global (Gray & Fook, 2004). Social workers involved in international projects face a number of essential questions, such as: Is social work knowledge transferable from one social, historical, cultural context to another? Which elements of social work are universal and which ones are context-specific? Will social work theory and methods developed and tested in a Western country be relevant in a developing country? How social work approaches rooted in liberal societies' values will be accepted in a post-communist society? Finally, is cross-national technical assistance compatible with social work ethics which is sensitive to the relationships of power and inequality? While there is no definitive answer to any of these questions, social workers have to embrace the complex nature of this work that may simultaneously comprise the elements of technical assistance, neocolonialism, and mutual trade (Doel & Penn, 2007).

The teaching context

My teaching of the Field Education Training Program occurred in two cities: at the Russia State Social University (RSSU) in Moscow and at the Omsk State Technical University (OSTU) in Omsk. I taught for five days, six hours a day, in each city. The Field Education Training Program and Manual was developed to provide Russian schools of social work with the information necessary to offer comprehensive and globally recognized field instructor training to their agency-based field instructors. The content was designed to mix the broadest standards in social work education, such as the International Association of Schools of Social Work (IASSW) and the International Federation of Social Workers (IFSW) Global Standards for Social Work Education, the latest research findings from Canada and the United States, with more detailed Russian-specific information for field instructors and case-study examples to use as discussion points. The curriculum was designed to incorporate discussion activities and practical applications to maximize learning through the interaction of course content with the experience and knowledge of participants.

The two trainings brought together a range of representatives across sectors, reflecting the general diversity of the workforce in Russia. At the RSSU, between 25–40 individuals (with a gender breakdown of approximately 95% females and 5% males) participated in training, including a few students, professors of social pedagogy, social work and medical rehabilitation departments, social service providers, representatives of government, and disability organizations. At the OSTU, between 80–85 individuals participated in training (with a gender breakdown of approximately 85% females and 15% males) including students, professors, social service providers for children, youth, families and the aged, the disability community, and government. Most participants had little formal socialization to the profession of social work and no formal training in social work. In addition to local participants, representatives of the CRDP's Working Groups and participants from Stavropol region attended and participated in the training course offered in Omsk region.

Since language can be a major obstacle to effective communication in cross-national projects, the quality of translation is a crucial component of the training process. The Field Education Training Manual that I wrote had been translated into Russian, and copies were made available to the participants. Local bilingual interpreters assisted me in the course of training. In Moscow the two young translators, who were students in the Department of Languages, worked diligently beginning with a 'crash course' on social work terminology to acquaint them with the culture of the professional language. In Omsk, I initially worked with an experienced translator who was a professor in the Department of Languages, and for the last three days one of the CRDP Russian-speaking staff filled in until another experienced translator was located.

Social group work and teaching

In my teaching of the Field Education Training Program, I applied a social group work approach, drawing upon ample evidence in the literature that social group work skills can contribute to effective teaching (Birnbaum, 1984; Kurland & Salmon, 1998; Schwartz, 1960, 1980; Shulman, 1970; Somers, 1971). Schwartz (1960), who viewed teaching as a special case of the helping process in a group, identified five essential tasks of the teacher in the education experience.These tasks are as follows: searching out the common ground between the learner's perceptions of his own needs and the subject matter; detecting and challenging the obstacles which obscure the common ground; contributing data – ideas, facts, values, concepts, which are not available to the learner; 'lending a vision' to the learner in which the instructor is revealed as one whose hopes and aspirations are strongly invested in the interaction between the learner and the subject area; and defining the requirements and the limits of the learning situation.

Schwartz (1980) noted that the substance of communication and the circumstances under which it takes place must be understood as an integrated whole, encompassing both process and content. He viewed content and process as a 'seamless whole,' characterizing *how* we work and *what* we are working on as possessing the same focus and impetus. In describing the interactive nature of the teaching-learning transaction, Schwartz (1960) suggested that communication from the teacher/group worker will only be effective to the extent that '...the members are alive to the possibilities of the learning situation, feel a personal stake in its effects, and learn to use it in their own behalf. It thus remains for the worker to utilize what he knows and feels in such a way that it may become that valuable to others' (pp. 33-34).

This conceptualization framed my teaching in the Russian social work project, particularly in addressing the participants' current realities and balancing my own valuing of group process in learning with participants' experiences with a different approach to education. One cannot overestimate the challenges of teaching with translators; interacting with individuals who have different histories, cultures, languages, and frames of reference for practice; and engaging participants who have experienced mainly a didactic authoritarian tradition of education. To overcome these challenges, I adapted Schwartz's idea (1960, 1980) of teaching as a special case of the helping process in a group and drew upon personal experience in social work education to engage the participants in a 'Magical Mystery Tour' (The Beatles, 1967) of education to a social group work beat. The use of social group work in the classroom to engage the participants as group members in a collaborative journey of discovery was the key to building trust and connections and promoting cross-national professional dialogue.

The following three examples illustrate the use of social group work in cross-national teaching. The first example shows how social work was defined through the training. Social work is a contextual profession, described as a socially constructed phenomenon, an activity which is to a large extent defined by the economic, social and cultural conditions in which it takes place (Payne, 1991). Therefore, instead of being exposed to lecturing about what social work is in Canada or the US, the participants were asked to reflect on the current state of social work practice and education in Russia. In the process of developing their definitions of social work, the participants generated the following themes: (a) Practical work (social work as providing help to those people in the community in need); (b) Paradigm approach (social work as helping people in difficult life situations versus social work as an integration of a human being in society to create optimum conditions for self-realization); (c) Competencies (social work as professional knowledge and skills such as paperwork skills, communication skills, applying theoretical knowledge in practice, knowledge of the legislation to facilitate clients' access to benefits, quality of task performance, knowledge of client populations); (d) Social workers' roles.

The second example is the use of social group work to help the participants to identify what information from the field regarding societal trends, conditions, and social work needs are important for universities and their communities to know. The groups generated the following themes: (a) raising the legitimacy of the field and of social workers in the society through public awareness campaigns and higher social workers' salaries; (b) clarifying social workers' and clients' responsibilities; (c) the need for advocacy and legal protection of social workers. These findings indicate a major concern about the field's lack of recognition and social workers' being de-valued in the society.

The third example demonstrates the participants' exploration of the core values of the profession. Despite not having formal social work education and a lack of established professional codes of ethics, the participants showed strong commitment to what appeared to be the underlying values of social work. They spoke of the 'ideal' and the 'real,' with many striving for the ideal in challenging environments. The key themes emerged in the Omsk group discussion about social work values were as follows:

(a) humanism (human beings are the top priority of any society);
(b) social justice (people who need help should get help);
(c) ethics, norms, rules (specialists base their work on the national code);
(d) respect of human rights and freedom;
(e) individual approach (personal approach connected to humanism);
(f) social partnerships (effective social work efficient requires partnership between systems at government levels and different agencies and organization);
(g) a client-centered approach;
(h) personal qualities of social workers: humanity, empathy, altruism, tolerance, responsiveness, good communication skills, creativity, positive attitude, honesty, kindness, self-development; and
(i) professionalism (an integration of knowledge and experience).

As expected, social group work revealed that each participant as well as each group as a whole represented a specific historical, cultural, regional, and social context. However, I was struck by what appeared to be intuitive understandings of social work as a profession, even though the participants generally lacked the knowledge of theoretical foundations of social work. The core values and understanding of helping, the notions of professional practice and competencies, the need for knowledge, and their understandings of the limitations of their own social/political/economic context were evident in the participants' discussions.

The data generated by the participants reflect what Taylor (1999) describes as some basic, acceptable universals: firstly, that of social work's altruistic mission of helping others and preventing harm, a mission that is bolstered by a belief that society and its institutions, must be responsive to human needs and interests; secondly, social work's pursuit of social justice. One can claim that the fundamental humanitarian values of social work are transferable, whereas the social, cultural, economic and political conditions of individual countries define how these primary values are to be achieved.

In evaluating the course, the participants acknowledged an interactive, participatory social group work approach, which allowed for positive exchange among the participants and between the participants and the facilitator, as well as contributed to the friendly and open learning atmosphere in the classroom. The participants noted and greatly valued an opportunity for networking and for shared learning of knowledge, experiences and perspectives from their colleagues. Moreover, I found that a social group work approach to training was useful not only for generating knowledge through participant engagement but also for conveying certain tools while adapting them to local contexts. The participants appreciated the tools used and provided to them, in the form of small-group exercises, handouts and the course reference manual itself. Specifically identified as highly relevant and of value were modules covering 'how-to' of effective field supervision, understanding learning styles, addressing special challenges in field instruction, and operational principles of field education.

With respect to the content of the course, the majority of the participants reported a significantly better understanding of field education principles and practices as a result of their involvement in the course. The key topic areas identified as areas of learning included ethics, stress, and addressing student challenges. Specific reference was made relating to knowledge gained with respect to the Canadian context and its application to the current status of field education in Russia. Finally, the participants found that the course complemented already existing knowledge by developing links – most specifically, by providing a framework for understanding the importance of integration of theory-based knowledge with practical components of skill development in social work.

Conclusions and reflections

Teaching social work cross nationally is a formidable task that involves the challenges of teaching with translators; connecting with individuals who have different histories, cultures, languages, and frames of reference for practice; and engaging participants who have experienced mainly a didactic authoritarian tradition of education. The use of a social group work approach for teaching field education in the Russian project allowed me to engage the participants into an interactive, participatory mutual-learning process through which knowledge was generated, shared, reinvented, and interpreted by transforming participants' experiences rather than transferred as a ready-to-use product. Adapting Schwartz's idea (1960, 1980) of teaching as a special case of the helping process in a group and drawing upon personal experience in social work education, I engaged the participants in a 'Magical Mystery Tour' (The Beatles, 1967) of education to a social group work beat. Through social group work, the key to building trust and connections and promoting cross-national professional dialogue, the participants as group members - and I as a facilitator - embarked on a collaborative journey of discovery.

The discussion of cross-national teaching in social work contributes to a larger debate of the issues of Westernization-indigenization in social work and universal, international versus local, context-specific social work (Gray & Fook, 2004). Certainly, social workers participating in cross-national social work projects have to critically appraise their own assumptions of universality and transferability of their understandings of social work core values as well as approaches to practice and education. Moreover, social workers have to be open to exploring cultural, historical, social, geographical contexts different from their own backgrounds, which shape their social work practice and education. However, as Doel and Penn (2007) note, recognizing difference while ignoring what is common can be yet another form of discriminating and constructing 'the Other.' They argue that mutual learning in cross-national interaction 'can only happen when we break through the experience of difference and allow ourselves to understand the *commonalities*, too' (p.378).

There are numerous cultural challenges inherent in the role of a social work educator teaching abroad, including understanding the local needs and issues and promoting social work's professional identity (Tunney, 2002). Western social work education models cannot be simply transplanted to other countries. I was conscious of and guided by the cultural relativity of my North American view of field education programs. For instance, organizational change, social justice, and advocacy are accepted field practice goals in North America; in Russia, where the tradition of social change necessary for activism has been lost, creation of an organization around a profession has yet to be achieved. Notions of 'advocacy' for vulnerable persons, for example, are difficult to promote when general cultural attitudes in Russia view persons with disabilities and physical and mental illnesses as 'defective' (Tunney, 2002). This view was reinforced when participants in my classes discussed programs of 'correctology.' Yet, throughout both courses, participants noted the need for advocacy, promotion of human rights, and structural changes in society.

A qualitative analysis of data generated by the participants of the training through small-group tasks and discussions demonstrates the universal themes of social work practice and education in two Russian cities. While the social, cultural, and historical differences between North American social work and social work emerging in post-communist Russia are hard to overestimate, Russian social workers grapple with issues familiar to their colleagues across borders: issues of social work ethics, client-worker relationships, professional competencies, integration of social work theory and practice, and the place of the field in the society. My experience with the participants in Russia taught me that we have much to learn from each other. Through that journey—a 'Magical Mystery Tour'—in two Russian cities, the commonalities of a commitment to humanity and the fundamental principles of social work and social work field education were articulated and shared once again.

References

Birnbaum, M. (1984). The integration of didactic and experiential learning in the teaching of group work. *Journal of Education for Social Work*, 20(1), 50-58.

Denis, J-L., Lehoux, P., & Champagne, F. (2004). A knowledge utilization perspective in fine-tuning dissemination and contextualizing knowledge. In L. Lemieux-Charles & F. Champagne (Eds.). *Using Knowledge and Evidence in Health Care: Multidisciplinary Perspectives* (pp. 18-40). Toronto: University of Toronto Press.

Doel, M. & Penn, J. (2007). Technical assistance, neo-colonialism or mutual trade? The experience of an Anglo/Ukrainian/Russian social work practice learning projects. *European Journal of Social Work*, 10 (3), 367-381.

Freed, A.O. (1995). Bulgarian social services and social work education. *International Social Work*, 38, 39-51.

George, J. (1999). Conceptual muddle, practical dilemma: Human rights, social development and social work education. *International Social Work*, 42, 15-26.

Gray, M. & Fook, J. (2004). The quest for a universal social work: Some issues and implications. *Social Work Education*, 23(5), 625–644.

Gray, M. & Simpson, B. (1998). Developmental social work education: A field example. *International Social Work*, 41, 227-237.

Hrycak, A. (2002). From mothers' rights to equal rights. In N.A. Naples & M. Desai (Eds.) *Women's Activism and Globalization*, (pp. 64-82). New York: Routledge.

Iarskaia-Smirnova, E. & Romanov, P. (2002). A salary is not important here: The professionalization of social work in contemporary Russia. *Social Policy & Administration*, 36(2), 123-141.

Iarskaia-Smirnova, E., Romanov, P. & Lovtsova, N. (2004). Professional development of social work in Russia. *Social Work & Society*, 2(1), 132-138.

Iarskaia-Smirnova, E. & Romanov, P. (2008). Gendering social work in Russia: towards anti-discriminatory practices. *Equal Opportunities International*, 27(1), 64-76.

Kolb, D. (1984). *Experiential Learning: Experience as the Source of Learning and Development*. Englewood Cliffs, N.J: Prentice-Hall.

Kolkov, V., Shapiro, B., & Solovyov, A. (2000). Managing the development of social work in Russia. In E. Harlow & J. Lawler (Eds.) *Management, Social Work and Change* (pp. 133-166). Aldershot, UK: Ashgate.

Kurland, R. & Salmon, R. (1998). *Teaching a Methods Course in Social ?Work with Groups*. Alexandria, VA: CSWE.

Mesbur, E.S. and Glassman, U. (1991). From commitment to curriculum: The humanistic foundations of field instruction. In D. Schneck, B. Grossman, & U. Glassman (Eds.). *Field Education in Social Work: Contemporary Issues and Trends* (pp. 47-58). Dubuque, Iowa: Kendall/Hunt.

Penn, J. (2007). The development of social work education in Russia since 1995. *European Journal of Social Work*, 10(4), 513-527.

Payne, M. (1991). *Modern Social Work Theory: A Critical Introduction*. London: Macmillan Press.

Rutgers University Center for International Social Work. (2008). *Social Work Education and the Practice Environment in Europe and Eurasia*. Report produced for the Social Transition Team, Office of Democracy, Governance and Social Transition of the United States Agency for International Development. Retrieved on 20 August 2010 from www.usaid.gov/ locations/ europe_eurasia/dem_gov/docs/ best_practice_in_social_work_final_121008.pdf.

Schwartz, W. (1960). *Content and Process in the Educative Experience*. Unpublished dissertation, Columbia University.

Schwartz, W. (1980). Education in the classroom. *Journal of Higher Education*, 51(3), 235-254.

Shulman, L. (1970). The hidden group in the classroom. *Learning and Development*, 2, 1-6.

Somers, M.L. (1971). Dimensions and dynamics of engaging the learner. *Journal of Education for Social Work*, 5(2), 61-73.

Taylor, Z. (1999). Values, theories and methods in social work education: A culturally transferable core? *International Social Work*, 42(3), 309-318.

Templeman, S.B. (2001). Social work in the new Russia at the start of the millennium. *International Social Work* 47(1), 95-107.

Torres, R.-M. (2001). Knowledge-based international aid. Do we want it, do we need it?' In W. Gmelin, K. King, & S. McGrath (Eds), *Development Knowledge, National Research and International Cooperation* (pp. 103-124). University of Edinburgh. CAS-DSE-NORRAG, Edinburgh, Bonn, Geneva.

Tunney, K. (2002). Learning to teach abroad: Reflections on the role of the visiting social work educator. *International Social Work*, 45(4), 435-446.

Trygged, S. & Eriksson, B. (2009). Implementing Swedish models of social work in a Russian context. *Social Work & Society*, 7(2), 273-284.

Whitmore, E. & M. Wilson (1997). Accompanying the process: Social work and international development practice. *International Social Work, 40*, 57-74.

History
Based on a presentation at the XXVIII AASWG Symposium, San Diego, CA., 2006. First published in the Proceedings series in: Moyse Steinberg, D. (Ed.) (2010) *Orchestrating the Power of Groups: Beginnings, middles, and endings (overture, movements, and finales)*. London: Whiting & Birch (pp.40-53).

Notes on authors (at time of first publication)
Ellen Sue Mesbur, MSW, EdD is Director and Professor at the School of Social Work, Renison University College, University of Waterloo, where she teaches social work with groups and field education. She has published in the areas of: the history of social group work in Canada; teaching and learning within the context of a small group; on-line teaching; and field education.

Walking the talk: Utilizing groupwork in gatekeeping social work education

Preface to the 2021 reprint

Three changes in legislation, policy and practice have occurred since this paper was written. One of the most significant for social work education programmes was enacted by the 2011 social work byelaw (*Code of Professional Conduct and Ethics for Social Workers* (CORU), 2011). Registration is now mandatory for all practising social workers in Ireland. This effectively transferred responsibility for the professional registration and recognition of the degree and title of social worker from the University to CORU (2011), a new statutory entity for the regulation of health and social care professionals. The name CORU is derived from the Irish word, *coir*, meaning fair, just and proper.

Allied to registration, since 2015, CORU has responsibility for Fitness to Practise. As each professional register is statutorily rather than voluntarily regulated, CORU has the power to take legal proceedings against a practitioner they deem to be in breach of their professional code of conduct and ethics. One social worker has been struck off the social workers' register for embezzlement of Health Service Executive funds. There is also an alert system in place through the EU professional recognition scheme where each EU member is informed if a professional is struck off in that country.

The introduction of the Social Work Bylaw 2011 placed responsibility on individual practitioners for ethical and professional conduct as outlined by CORU. The implications for social work course providers is to ensure that students are aware of and compliant with expected standards of professional conduct. The University's Fitness to Practice Code has been established in line with CORU guidelines. Its focus ensures that students are aware of and compliant with the standards expected of registered social workers. This has relieved some of the pressure on social work educators who now have a network of peers and professionals to support ethical and professional decision making when reviewing students' suitability for progression. In addition, it places responsibility on students to 'own' their health-issues by the Disclosure Requirement in matters affecting their Fitness to Practise.

CORU has also introduced the requirement for Continuing Professional Development (CPD). The audit began in May 2017. When it is completed in 2018 it will be reviewed for effectiveness and required changes to the code of ethics and professional conduct required by CORU. The implementation of CPD rests with the individual professional. The implications of these changes for social work education are being responded to with initiatives from Universities in Cork and Galway who now offer postgraduate training for practitioners to undertake field instruction to social work students in training. The IASW, which is the professional association for social workers in Ireland, has also implemented a CPD programme. Both protocols have yet to be fully evaluated and research is underway to consider their effectiveness in combining support for *good-best practice* with protection of the public from *bad practice*. Reflecting the proclivity for litigation, the IASW has also introduced legal cover insurance for social workers whose practice may come under scrutiny.

These legislative changes have placed greater responsibility on individual social workers to comply with professional standards while enabling social work educators to enlist the support of the wider University and professional community to provide selection and ongoing screening that is open, transparent and accountable. This shift in focus to service user protection aligns more coherently with the changes suggested in this paper.

Mary Wilson

Dr Mary Wilson was attached to the Bachelor of Social Work (BSW) programme at the National University of Ireland, Cork. She currently delivers an online programme, *The Mask Paradox* exploring the issues for fieldwork instructors delivering an assessment of student competence while masked.

Reference

Code of Professional Conduct and Ethics for Social Workers Byelaw 2011: Statutory Instrument No 143: in accordance with powers conferred by Section 31 of the Health and Social Care Professionals Act 2005. Available at Coru.ie.

Walking the talk: Utilizing groupwork in gatekeeping social work education

Mary Wilson

Introduction

This chapter explores using groupwork as a gatekeeping mechanism. It will consider the challenges that arise in maintaining professional standards while actualising principles of access and social inclusion in social work education and training for non-traditional students. Professional behaviour formation is at the core of programmes which seek to educate the professional. This task may be enhanced or impeded by many issues including the students' previous life and work experiences, professional accreditation criteria, field work agency values, and institutional norms and parameters regarding access and participation. Gatekeeping is a core process in the delivery of professional social work education.

The chapter will explore gatekeeping as social inclusion, a core value in programmes seeking to construct the professional identity of a non-traditional student. Then, a review of screening out or inclusion that is required when students are found to be unsuitable for professional practice will be undertaken. The use of the groupwork modality to support tutors, practitioners and service users in student selection and progression will be considered for its relevance in achieving successful outcomes in both spheres. The BASS (Bachelor of Applied Social Studies), an exit route programme devised for students who are deemed unsuitable for professional training at University College Cork Ireland, will be used to provide an example of resolving the gatekeeping debate in practice.

Background

Principles of human rights and social justice are fundamental to social work. These values are central to defining who we are as a profession, why we do what we do and how we do it! "Human rights and social justice serve as the motivation and justification for social work action. In solidarity with those who are disadvantaged, the profession strives to alleviate poverty and to liberate vulnerable and oppressed people in order to promote social inclusion" (NSWQB 2003). Education is a major strategy for fostering social inclusion. Thus, issues of access and widening participation are fundamental to the ethos of professional training programmes for the non-traditional student cohort. This approach emphasises commitment and willingness to walk the tight rope between oppressed/marginalised people and the social and political structures that have contributed to their exclusion (Friere, 1973; Lee, 1994; Lordan & Wilson, 2002; Parker, 2007). In practice, social inclusion involves actualising the values of equality, recognition and participation. As a social work educator, I believe that groupwork is the modality best suited to managing the tension inherent in that polarity and for modelling reflective functioning for best practice.

Gatekeeping is central to the process of professional formation. The term *gatekeeping* evokes different responses among those who are responsible for the evaluation, selection and retention of students. One view encompasses a process where students are nurtured through the educational enterprise to ensure that they successfully complete the course and are competent to practise when they graduate. Another is to see it as a way of selectively shutting the gate at some point in the student's journey when s/he is found to be unsuitable for practice in the field of social work. Gatekeeping issues can be present when the student applies to the programme or manifest at a later stage. Unsuitability for practice can occur for any number of reasons, such as difficulty with integrating theory into practice, the wounded-impaired helper phenomenon, extreme egotism or inappropriate behaviour (Gibbs & Macy, 2000; Lafrance, Gray, & Herbert 2004). Regardless, the script for the gatekeeping process cannot be written specifically, as one size does not always fit all. Differences in programme content, institutional contexts and the student cohort will be influential in determining the kinds of responses that will 'fit'. In the following pages the issues that have arisen at the University College Cork Ireland will be reviewed, and some specific gatekeeping responses explored.

Gatekeeping at the entry level stage

Consideration of licensing and application processes within global and local contexts

The introduction of the Byelaw in May 2011, the first statutory instrument of its kind under the Health and Social Care Professionals Act, 2005, completes the process by which the profession of social work in Ireland will be regulated in the 21st century. The right to apply for registration which had previously been issued by the University on completion of either a BSW or MSW degree will now be issued via application for registration to CORU (Health and Social Care Professionals Council, Dublin, Ireland), the new regulatory authority. CORU is also responsible for the licensing of continuing professional development initiatives, course accreditation and fitness to practice. These changes bring Ireland into line with the USA, UK and some jurisdictions in the EU, where the licensing power rests outside of the remit of the university.

At the local level, University College Cork offers two professional social work education programmes, an MSW and a BSW. Both courses integrate university based and agency based learning to provide the requisite academic and professional knowledge, skills and values for professional practice. Graduates from both courses gain the same license to practice in the profession on completion of their programme. The BSW course is unique in its focus on the mature/non-traditional student cohort and its mission to combat social exclusion.

Students wishing to come on the BSW course make application through the Central Admissions Office (CAO). This is a twofold process involving an aptitude test as a pre-selection mechanism and an interview. The course team, practitioners and service users make up the panel of interviewers who make the final selection of the 25 students who will gain entry to Year one. The average age of students who apply is mid to late thirties. While a gender imbalance exists, with more women than men represented in the student cohort, there is also greater evidence of multiculturalism from increasing participation by students from Africa and Eastern Europe. In the main, the students are typically those who are returning to full time education for a 'second chance' or those who seek retraining from another career. They are assertive, highly articulate and most are cognisant of the privilege of being at university. The exit route programme, the Bachelor of Applied

Social Studies (BASS) was inaugurated in 2008, and runs concurrently with the BSW in years three and four. Currently three students have been offered and/or are completing the BASS.

Consideration of previous life and work experience

For activate inclusion in the educational sphere we must create an environment within which people can develop to their fullest potential. Students come to the social work course with a wealth of prior knowledge and life experience. This previous life and work experience serves as a rich resource for learners and teachers alike. Within contemporary social work education there has been much discussion on the use and relevance of principles of adult education (Foley, 2004; Sankaran, 2001; Bamber, 1995). One of main issues facing us as educators is to create an educational environment in which the previous life and work experiences of students can be validated and used in the teaching process as well as examined for its applicability and transfer to the arena of professional practice. In this context, the support for the learning endeavour becomes central. We employ a number of group based educational methods which are designed to support the formation of the professional in training.

Gatekeeping during the educational process

Initially when a group of students embark on a course there will be different needs, styles of learning, levels of motivation and/or resistance to the learning endeavour. In terms of professional formation, balancing participants' needs with the requirements of the university will pose a challenge to the creativity of any programme team. Non-traditional students generally have high support needs for the different stages of the learning process. Many students begin by identifying and articulating the discontinuities between previous work contexts where the emphasis is on task, productivity and an external locus of control with the university's emphasis on theory, applied knowledge and professionalism. The idea of professional formation is one that needs to be acknowledged and integrated in the new learning context, and must be constructed collaboratively with students.

A triad of approaches using groupwork principles

Small tutorial groups are formed at the outset of programme and facilitated by course tutors to build the learning community. Three models/approaches using groupwork principles are central to the success of this collaboration:

1. Models of adult education, which foster equality and participation by students in the learning process, are used. The knowledge building process is one that students struggle with continually and sometimes resist. There are a number of stages in this process. Initially many students come as consumers of the service of education and articulate themselves as service users. The next stage concerns the engagement and use of self in the learning process; and later the students come to understand their responsibility towards the other: the service user, who is the invisible presence in all our relationships as tutors and practice teachers, and is the *end user* of this process of education and training. Collaborative small group and active learning approaches are particularly useful in addressing the learning needs of the non-traditional student group while developing and enhancing their sense of professional identity (Smith, 2009). Participation in small learning groups focuses on developing the reflective functioning skills upon which practitioner frames of reference are constructed. Tutors model professional engagement and facilitate its articulation and application to other spheres of work. For example, the social work service user may be reframed as an adult learner using this paradigm, indicating its transferability and applicability to the practice context where it can be used to facilitate service users who are also 'experts by experience' (Preston-Shoot, 2007), to collaborate in the construction of meaning associated with their experiences and to take action based upon it.
2. Enquiry based learning (EBL) utilises and builds on students' prior ways of doing and knowing. EBL is a particularly useful tool for addressing the theory practice dissonance that non-traditional students struggle with and frequently articulate. EBL describes an environment in which the learning is driven by a process of enquiry owned by the student (Kolb, 1984). Using small groups, the

teaching focus emphasises student centered learning, experiential learning, and collaborative work which can help to actualise the value of social inclusion in the teaching and learning context. Small groupwork, facilitated by tutors, enables students to identify their own issues and questions, which actualises the purpose of the group. Knowledge gained through this process is more readily retained because it has been acquired by experience and in relation to a real issue/problem.

3. Creative means of working, which support alternative discourses in teaching and learning, are utilized. The discourse of social inclusion has become marginal to the world view that social work is promulgating. It would appear that engaging in the provision of 'packages' of care in the field, and profitable 'packages' of education, are indicators of what is now increasingly valued and affirmed. A Canadian study (Lafrance et al, 2004) suggests that social workers have become overly aligned with the work system that employs them, creating an over-identification with bureaucratic systems instead of the profession or clients served. Social workers' responses to meeting needs with ever declining resources risk neglecting and ignoring the reality of peoples' existence and their struggles. Managerialism has become the dominant discourse in agencies to the exclusion of dialogue and bridge building between social workers and service users. As educators, we need to contest this world view by offering more creative and intuitive forms of engagement that seek to work in partnership with students and service users in challenging the oppression or injustice of expert systems. Conceptually, social exchange theory and groupwork theory cohere in the strengths perspectives (Saleeby, 2002), thus enabling robust and creative responses to the brief/problem/solving/outcomes driven models currently dominating professional practice. As an educator I believe in parity of esteem for educational initiatives that value cognitive, affective and intuitive processes. My own experiences as an educator have led me to groupwork and maskmaking, (Lordan, Wilson & Quirke, 2007; 2009). These tools support creativity and reflexivity in addressing the post-modern dilemmas of uncertainty, chaos and crisis that are everyday events in the lives of social workers and service users. Social workers in training also learn to acknowledge the equality of cognitive and intuitive processes and endeavour to integrate them in an inclusive pedagogy which supports a diversity of approaches in education and training and produces critically reflective professionals (Wilson & Quirke, 2009).

Groupwork gatekeeping strategies: Group panels and group forums

The role of service users as contributors to the gatekeeping evaluation process

Service users have a vast practice wisdom, which has not as yet been recognised as contributing to the dominant discourse. Its meaningful inclusion in the educational domain requires greater attention in institutional responses to professional education and training. The BSW programme has inaugurated a group panel of service users to assist in the student selection process. The composition includes those who have engaged with child protection and welfare; adoption; disability and the mental health services. For selection in 2012 new members include young people formerly in residential care now living independently. The Selection Co-ordinator conducts a single session training group with the Panel to clarify roles, offer support and ensure that materials are relevant. The service user Panel has been providing this service for four years. Each year it is evident that the group has grown in personal confidence and capacity which is a welcome but secondary outcome of their involvement. Their principal contribution lies in the richness of the wisdom that they bring to the interviewing process. A caveat exists currently, service users do not receive direct payment for their time or expertise. Travel expenses, book vouchers and lunch are offered. Perhaps the next challenge for the activation of social inclusion will be to payment of 'real' money to service users for their services. This is an issue that the course teams are reviewing urgently and creatively as resource allocation becomes more contested.

Service user involvement is a continuous resource for student learning. Current BSW students on fieldwork placement are expected to engage with users in evaluating the quality (or otherwise!) of the service they have delivered. This conversation with service users (Elliott et al 2005) seeks to establish an alternative discourse based on service user need rather than service delivery, and recognition of the service user as a co-equal end user of the professional formation experience. Providing increased opportunities for more meaningful engagement by service users in course delivery and assessment continues to be an evolving objective.

Support for staff serving as gatekeepers

Responding to high support needs of mature students however has its own 'hidden curriculum', which is the need to 'model' good practice in the educational arena. Specifically, for those who are delivering professional education and training it can mean the erosion of self and the lack of institutional recognition of the impact made by the welfare/support component in the teaching, tutoring and academic progression spheres. To contextualise, to date the BSW programme has necessitated attendance at pre-death rites and funerals of three students, attended the 'afters' of a couple of weddings, arranged maternity leave for others, encountered those who have experienced incidents of sexual abuse, domestic violence, mental illness, child and parental hospitalisation, dealt with police clearances that were not clear and interviewed/confronted students who tried intimidation inside and outside of class because of failure to progress. In addition there is a support role to colleagues and other students who have been affected by these experiences. Responding to these challenges, lead to the establishment of a group Tutor's Forum. This remit of this small group was to support team members, clarify and find solutions to the complex issues that professional formation raises for students. The facilitator of the Forum was a practitioner whose long experience in fieldwork supervision has been extremely useful in addressing and resolving the issues that have emerged. As a group, the Forum brought 'the outside in' and takes 'the inside out'. As groupworkers we well know the importance of challenging the isolation that can accompany course delivery with non-traditional students.

Practice Advisory Panels as contributors to the gatekeeping evaluation process

The Tutor's Forum has evolved from the BSW to encompass the wider arena of professional programmes within the School. This segue has been formalised into group Practice Advisory Panels whose membership consists of 6 or so experienced practitioners from a wide variety of contexts. The Practice Advisory Panel meets twice yearly to review the written work undertaken by students from fieldwork as quality control and professional oversight mechanisms. Members of the Panel also offer professional support to Fieldwork personnel and are available to act as mediators in the event of disputes arising from failed practice assessments.

Considerations when screening out unsuitable students

Duty of care

Unsuitability for practice can occur for any number of reasons, including difficulty with incorporating theory into practice, the wounded helper phenomenon, extreme narcissism, or behaviours related to the inability to function within the parameters of professional expectation (Gibbs & Macy, 2003; Lafrance et al., 2004). As social work educators we have a duty of care to service users who are the end users of all our interventions. We and our colleagues in practice are all gate keepers of professional standards. In light of these issues, there is increasing agreement that screening out social work students whose difficulties are non-academic is a major challenge for educators and consequently for the profession as a whole. Yet given the reality that not all students will meet the necessary professional standards, and in order to protect service users, it is crucial that social work programmes 'do not avoid the difficult issue of failing inadequate students' (Cowburn et al, 2000). Some of the issues that have emerged in actualising the principle of duty of care include:

Promoting diversity

A key principle of social work education concerns the elimination of institutional barriers that impact negatively on dis-advantaged and oppressed groups. Reconciling the need to eliminate discriminatory practices against minorities with the commitment to gatekeeping in professional social work education is an ongoing challenge that frequently leaves staff uncertain and often afraid. In relation to ethnic minorities, does affirmative action mean lowering standards to ensure entry and automatic progression to professional qualification?

Does this become discriminatory of non minorities who fail to meet and maintain programme standards? Posing this question serves to highlight how gatekeeping is a particularly sensitive area for teachers and students alike. In my experience, the ability to write clearly and comprehensively in the language of the society within which license to practice will be granted must be a requirement. Indeed report writing and record keeping are core proficiencies in professional social work education, not least for their impact on the lives of service users. In keeping with principles of access and inclusion, support mechanisms are provided and literacy support is offered for dealing with writing and literacy issues. However in a minority of cases this is insufficient to meet the need and leads to inevitable failure on fieldwork placement. Colleagues in the field are understandably perplexed that students seem to pass academic assignments in the first two years of the course while failing report writing while on fieldwork placement in years three and four. Agreed standards of literacy are developed in partnership with accreditation bodies, educators and practitioners requiring on-going dialogue and clarification. From 2012 passing grades on the BSW have been increased from 40% to 50% . This provision will need on-going review and re-evaluation for its effectiveness in raising and maintaining standards of professional training.

Student rights

Ensuring that students' rights are honoured is an ever present challenge in the gatekeeping process. Student's rights are a valued principle that underpins all our work, but are sometimes misinterpreted or misused as with disability legislation. In this context, access to a degree is often seen as an entitlement rather than an opportunity. However carte blanche entitlement to a degree that gives a professional license to practice in the social professions is fraught with dangers that frequently go unrecognised and/or are minimised. In the absence of universal policies and practices that support the screening out of unsuitable or impaired students, we strive to balance the competing needs and rights of both students and service users in the hope that we get the balance right!

Impaired helpers, wounded healers

Impairment in professionals resulting from addiction to substances or behaviours that legitimate abuse; mental illness or emotional (dis)stress is becoming a more visible issue in students applying for professional programmes. Social work students report a greater incidence of psychosocial trauma and dysfunctional families than students in other faculties (Black, Jeffreys, & Hartley, 1993). While further study may be needed to assess the correlation between difficult early life experiences and the choice of social work as a career, it cannot be ignored as an important factor in the selection and preparation of candidates for professional training (Lafrance et al, 2004). When a professionally questionable behaviour emerges it is often first experienced in the small group tutorial. The tutor uses the opportunities to explore the professional practice implications of the behaviour. In the skills lab in particular, students also have an opportunity to view themselves on film and are facilitated to make the connections to good practice. If this fails the tutor will meet the student individually. This conversation often begins the process of self realisation leading to a decision to take time out or to transfer to the BASS. When rigorous attendance and behavioural requirements have been made explicit and contextualised to professional behaviours, there has been a marked improvement in attendance, assignment submissions and codes of behaviour.

Legal issues

Legal issues are the most commonly cited institutional obstacle to effective gatekeeping (Gibbs & Macy, 2000). Today's litigious society couples a conservative political climate with endangerment of resource allocation to dramatically compromise the commitment to gatekeeping. Foremost is the fear of legal action. Pressures from institutional administrators and their legal advisors were barriers identified to the development of sound policies and practices that support programmes to 'screen out' students who are not suitable for a career in social work. Institutions of higher education must accept that the implications of offering access to non-traditional students begin rather than end at the point of entry.

Providing an exit route

For the mature student the stakes for failing to complete the course successfully are very high. Prior to 2008, it was possible for a BSW student to reach year three or even the final year when a failed fieldwork placement resulted in no degree being awarded. This position appeared iniquitous in the extreme and suggested a degree of institutional oppression that rested uneasily with mission statements on access and social inclusion. There was a need to provide, as a matter of urgency, an alternative academic route for those deemed unsuitable for professional progression. The discourse of social inclusion seems relevant for addressing the contested issues of rights and responsibilities that arise. An inclusive response to the gatekeeping issues that arose on the BSW was to provide an exit route for those deemed unsuitable for professional training or who failed fieldwork practice placements. Consequently the Bachelor of Applied Social Studies (BASS) was inaugurated in 2008. This is purely an academic qualification and has no professional implications or obligations. The BASS route acknowledges students strengths and offers an alternative path to university qualification. The duty of care to all stakeholders is addressed by this initiative, which acknowledges issues of access and inclusion while protecting vulnerable service users. The issues that laid the foundation for the BASS exit route are among those commonly encountered when a tension exists in balancing professional standards with open access. These issues can militate against the development of clear procedures and actions to support the 'duty of care' aspect of professional formation. As a social work educator it is my responsibility to ensure that students whose impairments will interfere with their professional judgement and performance should be diverted towards the exit route. It is not enough to pass the buck in the hope that agency or professional licensing will stop those who are dangerous or harmful. In Ireland we know all too well, as recent enquiries and reports into clerical and institutional abuse attest, where that particular route has led. The current reality is that few social work programmes have well defined policies for non-admission or termination of students for reasons other than academic failure. A compelling argument can be made it seems that in professional programmes, appropriate professional behaviour should be viewed as an academic requirement rather than as a misconduct issue (Cobb & Jordan, 1989; Moore & Urwin, 1990). Research suggests that successful outcomes in this domain begin at the point of entry. Students are made aware that certain behaviours are expected and that others will not be tolerated. Additionally, the need for standardised assessment frameworks, that include professional behavioural requirements need to be included in Marks and Standards to support all colleagues, particularly those who are delivering courses from disciplines external to the professional context concerned. However, to sail safely between the Charybdis of professional formation and the Scylla of social inclusion, these Fitness to Practise Guidelines/Protocols need to be in place pre-course commencement in order to minimise the exclusionary effects of this provision.

Further reflections on using groupwork to gatekeep

At an institutional level there is a growing awareness that fitness to practise is an on-going issue for all professional and clinical programmes. The university has established a Fitness to Practise Group to develop guidelines and codes of conduct to ensure that professional standards are maintained though assessment and sanction in order to meet the challenges arising in professional and clinical education. This initiative is evidence of a shift in wider university policies recalibrating social inclusion and professional formation. The guidelines are likely to be protocol by late 2013.

The pathfinding role of groupwork in delivering multi-dimensional interventions that value other voices and alternative world views can be acknowledged from the UCC experience. It is the central element holding diverse interventions coherently together. It is the means by which contested issues can be raised and resolved. By valuing the practice wisdom of colleagues, practitioners, service users and students knowledge for best practice is built. This is an outcome that is not only desirable but possible for constructing humanistic responses to the issues that arise in the professional formation of the non-traditional student cohort. Gatekeeping is an on-going process of evolving ideas about what constitutes the common good. Groupwork for gatekeeping enables the collective exercise and exploration of the professional challenges that arise in delivering to that ideal.

Conclusion

The possibilities, challenges and outcomes that arise in maintaining professional standards in the delivery of professional social work education and training to non-traditional students have been explored in this paper. Thoughts evidencing the use of groupwork in gatekeeping, and in building collaborative relationships and inclusive structures that foster corporate responsibility with users, professionals and institutions, were reviewed as central to programme integrity. Future issues concerning access are likely to be contested as competing needs and rights are debated. The continued relevance and use of groupwork for this collective exploration must encourage us to be hopeful about the creative synergies that can be fostered by walking the talk!

References

Bamber, Anthony L. 1995. *Supporting adult learners,* London: Library Association.

Black, P.N., Jeffreys, D., & Hartley, E.K. (1993). Personal History of Psychosocial trauma in the early life of social work and business students in *Journal of Social Work Education 29:* 171-180.

Cobb,N., & Jordan,C. (1989). Students with questionable values or threatening behaviour: precedent and policy from discipline to dismissal, in *Journal of Social Work Education, 25 (2):87-97.*

Cowburn, M., Nelson, P., & Williams, J. (2000). Assessment of Social Work Students: standpoint and strong objectivity. In *Social Work Education,* 19 (6):627-637.

Elliott, T., Frazer, T., Garrard, D., Hickinbotham, J., Horton, V.,Mann, J.,Soper, S., Turner, J., Turner, M., & Whiteford, A. (2005). Practice learning and assessment on Social Work Service User Conversations. In *Social Work Education,* Vol 24, No 4, June 2005, 451-466.

Foley,G (2004). *Dimensions of Adult Learning,* UK: Open University Press.

Friere, P. (1973). *The Pedagogy of the Oppressed.* New York: Herder and Herder.

Gibbs, P., & Macy, H., (2000). The arena of gatekeeping. In *Gatekeeping in BSW Programs.* Patty Gibbs & Eleanor H. Blakely (eds) 2000. New York: Columbia University Press, 3-21.

Kolb, D. (1984). *Experiential Learning.* USA Englewood Cliffs: Prentice Hall.

Lafrance, J., Gray , E.,& Herbert, M. (2004) Gate-keeping for Professional Social

Work Practice. *Social Work Education, 23(3): 325-340.*

Lee, J.A.B. (1994). *The Empowerment Approach to Social Work Practice.* New York: Columbia University Press.

Lordan, N., Wilson, M., and Quirke, D. (2009). Mask Making and Social Groupwork. In: *Strength and Diversity in Social Work with Groups.* Carol S. Cohen, Michael H Phillips and Meredith Hanson (eds). New York: Routledge.

Lordan, N., Wilson, M., & Quirke, D. (2007). Masks in Social Work. In: *Visual Practices across the University,* Jim Elkins, (ed). Munchen: Wilhelm Fink.

Lordan, N. & Wilson, M. (2002). Groupwork in Europe: Tools to Combat Social Exclusion in a Multicultural Environmet. In: *Social Work with Groups: Mining the Gold.* Sue Henry, Jean East and Catheryne Schmitz (eds). New York: The Haworth Press.

Moore, L. & Urwin, C. (1990). Quality control in social work: the gatekeeping role in social work education. In: *Journal of Teaching in Social Work, 4 (1):113-128.*

National Social Work Qualifications Board (NSWQB) Handbook 2003. Dublin: NSWQB.

Parker, J. (2007). Disadvantage, stigma and anti-oppressive practice. In: *Social Work and Disadvantage* Burke, P. and Parker, J. (eds). London: Jessica Kingsley.

Preston-Shoot, M. (2007). *Effective Groupwork.* Basingstoke: Palgrave.

Saleeby, D. (2002). *The Strengths Perspective in Social Work Practice.* New York: Longman.

Sankaran, S. (2001). *Effective Change Management: Using Action Learning and Action Research,* Lismore NSW: Southern Cross University Press.

Smith, Mark. (2009). Developing critical conversations about practice. In: *Groupwork Research.* Oded Manor (ed). London: Whiting and Birch.

Wilson, M. & Quirke, D. (2009). Promoting Partnership and Empowerment through Groupwork: The way forward for social work education. In: *Social Professional Activity: The search for a minimum common denominator in difference.* Claire Dorrity and Peter Herrmann (eds). New York: Nova Science Publishers, Inc.

History

Based on a presentation at the XXXIV IASWG Symposium, Long Island, NY., 2012. First published in the Proceedings series in: Tully, G.J., Bacon, J., Dolan-Reilly, G., and Lo Re, A. (Eds.) (2013) *Group Work: An international conversation highlighting diversity in practice.* London: Whiting & Birch (pp.74-89).

Notes on authors (at time of first publication)

Mary Wilson, PhD, is Senior Lecturer at the School of Applied Studies, University College Cork, Ireland.

Academic mentoring of social work faculty: A group experience with a feminist influence

Preface to the 2021 reprint

The original paper on group mentoring of social work faculty by Atchinson et al. was published in 2011. It is still relevant or perhaps even more timely today, as increasing numbers of social work faculty are retiring due to the plethora of faculty from the baby boomer generation (Hayslip, Patrick & Panek, 2011). This phenomenon means there will be a stream of tenure track positions available for new faculty members who enter the evermore challenging tenure track world where they will be expected to publish quality research studies, seek and secure grant funding, teach effectively, and perform relevant university and community/professional service. Mentoring these new faculty members will be even more critical in supporting their career growth and the effective navigation of academic expectations, which ultimately affects students' education and social work practice.

The value of mentoring is documented across professions (Block & Florczak, 2017; Eby, Allen, Evans, Ng, and DuBois, 2008; Washington, 2006). However, there continues to be minimal research on individual or group mentoring of social work faculty. A recent article on individual mentoring of BSW faculty found that many newer faculty members did not have mentors (Ellison, Moore, & Johnson, 2014). There were mixed results regarding formal mentoring programs, including minimal institutional support for mentors with little oversight of formal mentoring programs (Ellison et al., 2014). There was more positive feedback regarding informal mentoring, but a disconnect was discovered between what mentees believed they needed, primarily more help with scholarship, versus what mentors provided (Blue & Kominkiewica,

2013; Ellison et al, 2014). A study of field director mentorship (Ellison & Raskin, 2014) also found that new field directors wanted assistance with conducting research, but this was rarely part of the mentorship. No recent articles regarding group mentoring of social work faculty were found. However, group mentoring may be even more advantageous than individual mentoring (Pelech, Basso, Lee, & Gandarilla, 2016; Toseland and Rivas, 2017). The multiple perspectives and supports within a group experience - mutual aid, universality (feelings of being in the same boat in academic pursuits), the sharing of information and experiences among peers, the provision of hope for academic success through peer examples, and the opportunity for safe, open dialogue can all contribute to the impact of the experience.

One of this article's strengths is its foundation in feminist theory, which highlights some of the stresses and discrimination that many female faculty members experience when balancing work with family and personal responsibilities. An additional strength of the study is the structure and format of the group in that it was conducted once a month through telephone mediated technology, thereby allowing for participation from faculty members from geographically diverse universities with minimal time expectations.

Building trust and safety in many groups is a challenge. This was true in the academic mentoring group. Given the hierarchical nature of the tenure track system, the relatively small social work academic community, members' past devaluing academic experiences, and the lack of face-to-face connections among group members, the development of intimacy and cohesion was slower to develop. Trust was eventually obtained, but the recommendations of the study – to use video conferencing so that body language can be observed, and restrict group membership to faculty members from different universities – are particularly relevant.

This qualitative study found that one of the instrumental tasks of the group was met - the untenured faculty and one of the tenured faculty advanced their careers by the end of the two-year group. In light of current theory, it would be good to discuss the diversity of the members' backgrounds early on in a group to build trust and reduce later conflicts (Pelech et al., 2016). For example, two of the members had young children, and there were many other forms of diversity among the members that could have been sensitively explored in the foundation sessions. This recommendation applies to many groups. It is hoped that the re-publication of this chapter will inspire additional mentoring groups for social work faculty members as well as the pursuit of additional research on this important topic.

Cheryl D. Lee and Shirley R. Simon

Cheryl D. Lee, Ph.D., MSW is Professor Emeritus, California State University, School of Social Work

Shirley R. Simon is Associate Professor, Loyola University of Chicago, School of Social Work

References

Block, M. & Florczak, K.L. (2017). Mentoring: An evolving relationship. *Nursing Science Quarterly, 30*(2) 100–104.

Blue, E. T. & Kominkiewica, F. B. (2013). All faculty need mentors: Learning beyond the classroom. Paper presented at an annual conference of the Baccalaureate Program Directors, Myrtle Beach, South Carolina.

Eby, L.T. , Allen, T. D., Evans, S., Ng, T. and DuBois, D. (2008). Does mentoring matter? A multidisciplinary meta-analysis comparing mentored and non-mentored individuals. *J Vocat Behav., 72*(2), 254–267.

Ellison, M., Moore, W., & Johnson, A. (2014). Mentoring experiences of undergraduate social work faculty: Navigating the academic maze. *Journal of Sociology and Social Work, 2*(2), 191-218.

Ellison, M., & Raskin M. (2014).Mentoring field directors: A national exploratory study. *Journal of Social Work Education, 50,* 1-15.

Hayslip, B., Patrick, J.H. & Panek, P. (2011) *Adult development and aging, 5th edition.* Malabar FL: Krieger Publishing Co

Pelech, W., Basso, R., Lee, C. D., & Gandarilla, M. (2016). *Inclusive group work.* New York, NY: Oxford University Press.

Toseland, R., & Rivas, R. (2017). *An introduction to group work practice* (8th ed.). Boston, MA: Pearson/Allyn and Bacon.

Washington, D. (2006). *A hand to guide me: Legends and leaders celebrate the people who shaped their lives.* Des Moines, Iowa: Meredith Books.

Academic mentoring of social work faculty: A group experience with a feminist influence

Alana B. Atchinson, Lisa M. Murphy,
Maria A. Gurrola, Cheryl D. Lee,
and Shirley R. Simon

Introduction

The start of a new tenure-track faculty member's career can be a stressful time filled with job insecurities and questions about expectations. As the number of tenure-track faculty appointments has declined and new hires are held to increasingly higher standards of productivity, the sense of vulnerability on the part of new faculty has intensified (Finkelstein, 2003; Graubard, 2001). Mentoring can help new faculty succeed in academic life. The mentor-protégé relationship has been a subject of discussion and research in both the business and academic worlds for many years. Although the mentoring relationship may be an especially important tool for academic success for new social work faculty, discipline specific research exploring mentoring of junior faculty has been scant. This lack is evidenced not only in research journals but also in primary professional publications. For example, there was no entry for "mentor" in either the *Social Work Dictionary*, 3rd edition (1995), or the *Encyclopedia of Social Work*, 19th edition (1995). A more recent entry in the *Encyclopedia of Social Work with Groups* addresses mentoring but is not specifically about junior faculty in an academic environment (Lee & Montiel, 2009). Additionally, the few studies that specifically explore mentoring of *new* social work faculty focus exclusively on individual mentoring relationships (Wilson, Pereira, & Valentine, 2002).

Using theory and principles of group process, and influenced by feminist theory of co-mentoring (McGuire & Reger, 2003), a group of social work educators, four untenured and two tenured, met monthly, via telephone conference calls, to support the work of individual members and the group as a whole. This paper offers an analysis of this experience. Suggestions for improved mentoring of social work faculty are explored, and areas for further research are identified.

Review of literature

Women in academics

The field of academia has changed over recent decades as the number of women taking tenure track positions in universities grows; however, despite the increased presence of women on campuses, a disproportionate number of men continue to hold the majority of both high ranking administrative and full-time tenure track positions (Bakian & Sullivan, 2010). While men are more likely to hold full-time positions in research, women are commonly found as part-time faculty focused on teaching (Hart, 2011; Carr, 2001). This division is especially troublesome, as statistics show that in the last decade similar number of PhDs were awarded to men and women (Cantor, 2010). It is important to note that while the total number of PhDs awarded was split nearly evenly between men and women, when examining the individual numbers by field, gender division reflected a gross imbalance. Fields such as nursing and the humanities were dominated by women, while mathematics and sciences were heavily laden with males (Carr, 2001). Additionally, within this context, women experience advancement of research careers to a lesser degree than their male counterparts (Gardiner, Tiggemann, Kearns, & Marshall, 2007).

Mentoring

Research has shown that the mentoring process is essential for new professors to successfully navigate the world of academia (Gee &

Norton, 2009; Wasserstein, Quistberg & Shea, 2007). This is particularly true for women, and examining gender bifurcation within the mentoring dyad has shown that within academia, the total number of male mentors outnumber female mentors, but those female mentors often had many more female than male protégés (Perna, Lerner & Yura, 1995). After a woman is hired in a tenure track position, the experience can be isolating, as demonstrated in an auto-ethnographic study by Hellsten, Martin, McIntyre, and Kinzel (2011), and women frequently experience the tenure track very differently from their male counterparts. In addition to isolation, women in the academy have reported discrimination and a social network that they are unable to access as two marked difficulties faced when navigating the world of academia (Foster et al., 2000; Wolfinger, Mason, Goulden, 2008). In 1999, Australia adopted an action plan to target inequalities in Australian universities, through which formal mentoring was used, under the assumption that when mentoring is informal, women may often be excluded (Gardiner, Tiggemann, Kearns, & Marshall, 2007). It seems universal that mentoring plays a positive role in improving the status of women in academia, and is shown to be most effective when there is a complementary fit between the mentor and the protégé, especially when the mentor is formally recognized and/or rewarded for his or her efforts in the process (Gee & Norton, 2009). Gee and Norton (2009) also observed that women should be cautious of time commitments outside of specific field work, as committee work can be time consuming and ultimately less advantageous in career advancement. Of course, it is also imperative for a successful mentoring relationship that a hierarchal system of oppression is not in place; to avoid that, some institutions favor peer mentoring as a means to connect similarly aligned faculty to reduce insecurities, which ultimately leads to further isolation (Driscoll, Parkes, Tilley-Lubbs, Brill & Pitts Bannister, 2009).

Family and social obligations

Family seems to be another area where, in the context of success in academia, women face more difficulties than male colleagues. This is particularly true for women who have children under the age of six (Wolfinger, Manson & Goulden, 2008). In fact, even when programs and services have been created to assist women with families, they are often reluctant to use these services through fear of appearing to be taking advantage of their position or being viewed as doing less work than women with no children or their male counterparts, regardless of the males' parental status (Hellsten, Martin, McIntyre & Kinzel, 2011). Wolfinger, Manson and Goulden (2008) also found that having a family has a different effect based on gender. For men, having a family, including children, has a positive effect; yet for women, the opposite was found. The same study also found that for single Ph.D. graduates, gender was not strongly indicative of their future success in academia; in fact, single women fared slightly better than men (Wolfinger, Manson & Goulden, 2008). Additionally, women often finish Ph.D. degrees during what is often viewed as prime childbearing years. This often creates a predicament for women who may be forced to choose between a family and a career (Mavriplis et al., 2010).

Mentoring social work faculty

New social work educators have reported that mentoring was especially beneficial to their teaching and research (Wilson, Pereira & Valentine, 2002). This qualitative study also found that new female social work educators valued the mentoring they received, especially with regard to networking and research (2002). It is important to note that even in the field of social work, a profession where women are the majority, high end administrative positions are still largely filled by men (Bent-Goodley & Sarnoff, 2008; Sakamoto, Anastas, McPhail & Colarossi, 2008). Social work as a discipline and practice strives for social justice, and the lack of women in administrative positions is an ongoing issue that is currently being confronted in this profession (Bent-Goodley & Sarnoff, 2008). In conjunction with social justice themes, knowledge about mentoring in social work education within underrepresented minority groups is not readily available; however, Simon, Perry and Roff (2008) found that a group of African American women sought and received more mentoring regarding their doctoral studies and faculty expectations than regarding balancing their career and family issues. The limited research on mentoring across cultural, racial, and gender barriers often addresses new models of mentoring, including new conceptualizations of roles, implementing practices that promote mentoring within academia, and the relatively new concept of multiple mentoring (Sorcinelli & Yun, 2007). For multiple mentoring, the mentoring process is a group- or partner-based journey, typically non-hierarchical, collaborative, and designed to mentor specific subject areas (Sorcinelli & Yun, 2007). In a study of gender differentiation among social work faculty at both Canadian and United States universities, Sakamoto et al. (2008) found that similarities exist between the two countries in regard to gender disparities. While there are far too many variables to make concrete assertions, similar patterns of underrepresentation emerge in terms of tenure, administrative positions, and promotions of female faculty members in both countries (Sakamoto et al., 2008).

Trust and mentoring in academia

Trust is a very significant factor that emerges in the literature regarding mentoring, and it is especially vital in those mentoring relationships that bridge gender and culture. It is easy to establish and perceive trust when both mentor and protégé have commonalities; yet, when differences exist, discomfort may arise, which if not properly navigated may develop into distrust (Shollen, Bland, Taylor, Weber-Main & Mulcahy, 2008). Shollen et al. also observed that trust leads to mutual understanding and symbiosis, and provides a space for growth and learning within the mentoring dyad (2008). Trust within academia is often difficult to achieve due to the constant competition for resources and promotions (Hart, 2011). Due in part to these reasons, trust is often avoided in order to reduce the vulnerability of women within academia. Often, non-spoken rules dictate actions that create a hostile environment, even when there is no clear threat to these women (Cantor, 2010). Research is vital to upward mobility in academia, and trust and expertise can have a negative effect on the mentoring relationship if both the mentor and protégé have a vested interest in the same area of research. In a study of female social work faculty, a new educator shared an area of interest in research with her mentor, and found that the mentor assumed a patronizing role, rather than offering expertise and respect as a colleague to the new faculty member (Wilson, Pereira, & Valentine, 2002).

Methodology

Design, data collection and analysis

The mentoring group met by phone for one hour once a month for a two year period. After meeting for 18 months, the group participants anonymously answered 10 open-ended questions (Appendix A) after receiving University Institutional Review Board approval. The results for each question were compiled and analyzed for themes in the responses. Two members of the group (not the group organizer) independently analyzed the responses. Inter-rater reliability was at an 85% level.

Sample

In this group of six, all of the members were female and ranged in age from 32-62. Three of the group members were white, two were Mexican-American, and one group member was Native American/White. Group members varied in academic rank. Four group members were untenured assistant professors. Among this group of untenured assistant professors, one each had finished her second, third, fourth, and fifth year. A fifth group member was a tenured assistant professor. The sixth group member was a tenured full professor. One of the group members was at a research one institution, three group members were at research two institutions and two group members were at primarily teaching institutions.

Results

The main overarching theme that came up during several questions was "trust." This theme was interesting for several reasons. First, most of the group members had never met one another in person. It is often difficult to trust people one has never met in person. Trust can be particularly difficult when one cannot see and observe the body language of the other group members during meetings. Also, the field of academia, like many other professions, is very small, and one is not always aware of the external relationships group members may have and how those relationships might influence one's future. Third, the different academic ranks of some of the participants created issues of trust and feelings of vulnerability. Lastly, because of trust and vulnerability at their home institutions, several group members had problems trusting the group in the beginning. For example, one group participant stated, "When I started with the group, I was hesitant to share issues that I felt vulnerable about. Over time I have come to trust the other group members and tend to trust more and share more."

Most of the group participants had experienced some form of mentoring at various points in their career. Many had experienced dissertation mentoring. Some participants had experienced mentoring at their home institution, while others had not. One group member said, "I work with a group of colleagues where the senior researcher serves as a mentor. She is guiding the group to projects and gets us involved in different projects to increase our research, publications and be successful in the tenure process." This was one example of a supportive mentoring environment. However, there were many examples of non-supportive home institution environments. One participant said, "I have looked for mentoring in my home institution but have not been particularly successful." A few of the group participants who had not experienced mentoring at their home institution had sought mentoring through professional organizations. For example, one group member said, "Prior to this experience I had approached mentoring through the Division on Women and Crime. There are several feminist scholars who are part of the Division that have been great resources."

Participants were motivated to join the mentoring group for several different reasons. A few group members were having trust issues at their home institutions and were looking for support during the tenure and promotion process. One participant explained her situation and her decision to join the group:

> *I met the group organizer at the group camp/group conference in 2008. After several conversations about academic life and the importance of mentoring, she invited me to join the group. Having been unsuccessful finding a mentor in my home institution, I was excited to join this group. I am nervous about the tenure and promotion process at my institution and was looking for support and input from other faculty. After a very difficult first year at my home institution, I was very hesitant to talk with*

colleagues because I did not trust them to not use information I shared against me during the evaluation process. I particularly like being able to talk with faculty from other institutions because of the trust issues I have at home.

A second reason members were motivated to join the group was to get support and feedback from others. One group member said,

It seemed like a good opportunity to learn more about the experiences of others and get support/feedback on issues that emerge regarding teaching and publishing from the point of view of someone outside of one's institution.

The convenience of the group was another reason members chose to join. Since the group did not require a large time commitment on the part of the group members and the meetings were via telephone once a month, members believed it was something they could fit into their schedules. One member said,

I also decided to join because I knew it was going to be by phone, this is convenient because I do not have to go out of my house and I can do it while I am cooking dinner or getting ready to put my kids to bed. Time is very limited when you have young children, and there is no time to go out of the home to meet with others and talk about what is going on in our job. This also gave us the opportunity to talk to people in other universities.

Lastly, some group members thought by joining the group they might be able to help other group members. One group member explained

I joined the mentoring group to help some of my colleagues. I believe in mentoring and wanted to give something which I wish I would have had.

Group members were asked if they thought mentoring in the group was different from individual mentoring. A few participants stated they did not notice any differences between individual and group mentoring. However, several group members listed some of the advantages and disadvantages they thought were present with this style of group mentoring. One participant thought an advantage of group mentoring was that it involved a "more collaborative process with equality among peers." Another participant said, "Mentoring in a group is nice because

I like when other people bring up issues that I have been thinking about. It makes me feel like I am not alone in my experiences or how I am feeling." However, mentoring group participants did believe there were a couple of disadvantages. One participant believed there was "less time to focus on one's personal issues." Another participant stated, "At least in my case, I do not personally know all of the group members so this may play a role in how much I'm willing to share about specific issues." The disadvantages listed by participants were considerably fewer than the advantages listed. Overall, group members saw much benefit to the group mentoring process.

Participants were asked what they would change about the group. Group members suggested they wanted to work on building the trust in the group. One group member explained,

> *I am little more cautious about some of the issues I raise in the group setting. I have had some very bad experiences and don't always have confidence that people will keep things within a group. When I was going through some of the stuff with my former employer I didn't say everything that was going on. However, I did share some of it. This group was nice because they listened and kept stuff in the group. As I was seeking mentoring in my former department, I attempted individual mentoring and those people were not trustworthy so I guess it just depends on the group and the individual person and you always need to be aware of who you can trust and who you can't.*

Two of the group members work in the same department at the same institution, which also led to some hesitancy about which subjects might be discussed in the group, especially because one member had a higher rank than the other group member. There seemed to be a fear among group members that what was said in the group might not stay in the group.

The meeting time was another thing some members wanted to change. However, there was some discrepancy among group members about the time of day that worked the best. For example, one group member stated, "The time is difficult for me. I am the only member on the East Coast so the calls are late for me. However, I find the benefits of being a part of the group to outweigh this inconvenience." On the other hand, one group member suggested, "It would be nice to have conversations a little later in the evening so I can participate a little more." The mentoring phone calls usually took place around five o'clock in the evening Pacific Coast time. A few group members wanted to change the structure of the meetings. One suggestion was to initiate a better method of communication (i.e., video chat or other online processes)." The role of the group participants was another issue that was suggested as a way to improve closeness and trust in the group. One participant observed, "Our current project is this research. It's brought us closer together I think so maybe more projects. Not sure of that since we are all so incredibly busy." These were all minor suggestions to improve the group overall but they appear to pertain to building trust and better group cohesion in the future.

Last, group members were asked how they thought diversity was dealt with within the mentoring group. Some group members reported that diversity was not addressed in the group while others thought it was adequately addressed. For example, one group member considered diversity to be a difficult issue for people to address so it was not dealt with at all, even though group members were very diverse. She stated, "We are diverse in many ways and we talk about it yet I don't think we touch on every issue of diversity. I think even in this setting it is difficult to talk about some issues." Yet, another group member found that there was an acceptance of the roles of others. She said, "One of the biggest differences is the parents and non-parents. Group members seem to be accepting of these differences. I feel the group members are open- minded about differences in culture. We could discuss this more." There seems to be room to discuss diversity in all of its different forms that affect women in academia, including the issues of parenthood and the decision to have or not to have children as an academic.

Overall, there are advantages and disadvantages to mentoring over the telephone but members seemed to enjoy the process and have benefitted from the group. One member stated, "When I started with the group, I was hesitant to share issues that I felt vulnerable about. Over time I have come to trust the other group members and tend to trust more and share more." Another participant shared, "I see how the group members help when individuals are down and out. This gives me a very positive feeling like the group is worth it. I've received a lot of support." These results support a feminist model of group mentoring that seems to have benefitted several junior faculty members as they navigate the tenure and promotion process. One group member summed up the group mentoring experience in the following way:

Rather than seeking guidance with help related to the specific process at my home institution, I tend to turn to the group for three things:
1. As a place to discuss issues related to teaching

2. As a place to find support and encouragement for scholarship
3. For general camaraderie with other academics, ones I have grown to trust.

Limitations

The study had a small sample size and may not be generalizable to other female social work faculty. Members of the group analyzed the data, which may have biased the results. Qualitative data by its nature has a subjective element.

Summary and recommendations

It was apparent in this qualitative study that mentoring of newer social work female faculty is desirable to improve success in the academic arena, which is consistent with prior research (Bent-Goodley & Sarnoff, 2008; Sakamoto et al., 2008; Wilson et al., 2007). Like other studies of mentoring in academia, this study found that mentoring is essential for traversing the tenure track process (Gee & Norton, 2009; Wasserstein, Quistberg & Shea, 2007). Members of the mentoring group who consisted of social work faculty found the group to be a place to discuss teaching and scholarship issues and to find friends to prevent isolation (Hellsten et al., 2011). Further, members received tenure, retention and/or promotions during the two year period of the group. Group mentoring, as opposed to individual one-on-one mentoring, allowed the members to discover that their issues were experienced by others and to garner mutual aid (Gitterman & Shulman, 2005). The use of telephone technology made the group accessible, especially for female faculty who also had young families. The literature discusses discrimination toward women with young children in academia who are often viewed as not doing their fair share of the work (Wolfinger et al., 2008; Hellstein et al., 2011). In contrast, the women who were parents of young children in this study felt they received support from other group members, including those who did not have young children.

As in other mentoring studies, trust was a major theme and is essential for mentoring to progress (Shollen et al., 2008). There were several factors that inhibited trust from developing in this group: most members had not met each other in person and feared that information would not be kept confidential within the relatively small social work academic community. In addition, the academic work place, which is highly competitive for resources, is known as a barrier to trust among faculty in general (Cantor, 2011; Hart, 2011). The results indicated that over time, the group became a safe place where members felt they could be more open and receive support even though members expressed past experiences in academia where trust was not found in individual one-on-one mentoring relationships.

Several recommendations emanate from this study. The results indicate that although mentoring in a group has some drawbacks such as less time to attend to an individual problem and a greater possibility of a breach in confidentiality, the members overall were satisfied with the group experience, felt they learned more from peer input than would be possible in one-to-one mentoring, and liked the convenience of meeting monthly by telephone. The implementation of additional mentoring groups are recommended but will require additional research since very few group mentoring studies have been completed.

The establishment of a mentoring group of members from varied institutions should be considered due to the competitive nature in most home institutions. Meeting by telephone was considered a plus but did preclude the reading of body language. The use of video technology is recommended to improve communication. The group decided to evaluate their mentoring experience, and this project brought the group closer together as they planned the research, wrote a manuscript, analyzed the data, and created a proposal and presentation for the IASWG international symposium. The group participants highly recommend group projects for this type of group. The fact that this mentoring group could meet in person at the IASWG Long Beach Symposium was a special way to foster cohesion. A combination of technology mediated sessions with at least one face-to-face meeting at some point in person is highly recommendation.

References

Bakian, A. V., & Sullivan, K. A. (2010). The effectiveness of institutional intervention on minimizing the demographic inertia and improving the representation of women faculty in higher education. *International Journal of Gender, Science and Technology, 2*(2), 206-234.

Bent-Goodley, T.B., & Sarnoff, S.K. (2008). The role and status of women in social work education: Past and future considerations. *Journal of Social Work Education, 44*(1), 1-8.

Cantor, N. (2010). Women in the academy: Reflections on best practices for survival and success. *Office of the Chancellor.* Paper 2.

Carr, F. (2001). The gender gap in the academic labor crisis. *The Minnesota Review, Number 52-54 (New Series),* 271-279.

Driscoll, L. G., Parkes, K. A., Tilley-Lubbs, G. A., Brill, J. M., & Pitts Bannister, V. R. (2009). Navigating the lonely sea: Peer mentoring and collaboration among aspiring women scholars. *Mentoring & Tutoring: Partnership in Learning, 17*(1), 5-21.

Finkelstein, M. J. (2003). The morphing of the professoriate. *Liberal Education, 89*(4), 6–15.

Foster, S.W., McMurray, J.E., Linzer, M., Leavitt, J.W., Rosenberg, M., & Carnes, M. (2000). Results of a gender-climate and work-environment survey at a midwestern academic health center. *Academic Medicine, 75,* 653-660.

Gardiner, M., Tiggemann, M., Kearns, H., & Marshall, K. (2007). Show me the money! An empirical analysis of mentoring outcomes for women in academia. *Higher Education Research & Development, 26*(4), 425-442.

Gee, M. V., & Norton, S. M. (2009). Improving the status of women in the academy. *Thought & Action: The NEA Higher Education Journal,* 163-170.

Graubard, S. R. (2001). *The American academic profession.* New Brunswick, NJ: Transaction.

Gitterman, A. & Shulman, L. (Eds., 2005). *Mutual aid Groups, vulnerable and resilient populations, and the life cycle (Third Edition).* New York: Columbia University Press.

Hart, J. (2011). Non-tenure track women faculty: Opening the door. *Journal of the Professoriate, 4*(1), 96-124.

Hellsten, L. M., Martin, S. L., McIntyre, L. J., & Kinzel, A. L. (2011). Women on the academic tenure track: An auto-ethnographic inquiry. *International Journal for Cross-Disciplinary Subjects in Education, 2*(1), 271-275.

Lee, C. D. & Montiel, E. (2009). Mentoring. In A. Gitterman & R. Salmon, Eds., *Encyclopedia of social work with groups,* 306-308. New York, NY:

Routledge.

Mavriplis, C., Heller, R., Beil, C., Dam, K., Yassinskaya, N., Shaw, M., & Sorensen, C. (2010). Mind the gap: Women in stem career breaks. *Journal of Technology Management & Innovation, 5*(1).

McGuire, G. M., & Reger, J. (2003). Feminist co-mentoring: A model for academic professional development. *Feminist Formations, 15*(1), 54-72.

Perna, F. M., Lerner, B. M., & Yura, M. T. (1995). Mentoring and career development among university faculty. *Journal of Education, 177*(2), 31-45.

Sakamoto, I., Anastas, J. W., McPhail, B. A., & Colarossi, L. G. (2008). Status of women in social work education. *Journal of Social Work Education, 44*(1), 37-62.

Seritan, A. L., Bhangoo, R., Garma, S., DuBe', J., Park, J. H., & Hales, R. (2007). Society for women in academic psychiatry: A peer mentoring approach. *Academic Psychiatry, 31*(5), 363-366.

Shollen, S. L., Bland, C. J., Taylor, A. L., Weber-Main, A. M., & Mulcahy, P. A. (2008). Establishing effective mentoring relationships for faculty, especially across gender and ethnicity. *American Academic.4*, 131-158.

Simon, C.E., Perry, A.R., & Roff, L.L. (2008). Psychosocial and career mentoring: Female African American social work education administrators' experiences. *Journal of Social Work Education, 44*(1), 9-22.

Sorcinelli, M. D., & Yun, J. (2007). From mentor to mentoring networks: Mentoring in the new academy. *Change: the Magazine of Higher Learning*, 58-61.

Wasserstein, A. G., Quistberg, D. A., & Shea, J. A. (2007). Mentoring at the University of Pennsylvania: Results of a faculty study. *Society of General Internal Medicine, 22*, 210-214.

Wilson, P., Pereira, A., & Valentine, D. (2002). Perceptions of new social work faculty about mentoring experiences. *Journal of Social Work Education, 38*(2), 317-333.

Wolfinger, N. H., Mason, M. A., & Goulden, M. (2008). Problems in the pipeline: Gender, marriage, and fertility in the ivory tower. *Journal of Higher Education, 79*(4), 388-405.

Appendix A. Qualitative questionnaire

- What other ways have you approached faculty mentoring prior to this experience?
- Tell me about your decision/motivation to join the mentoring group?
- How is mentoring in a group different from individual mentoring for you?
- What are the differences between issues you raise in a group setting and those you raise in individual mentoring sessions?
- How has the group changed over time for you?
- What have you taken from the group mentoring experience?
- How can we improve the group mentoring experience?
- What are the advantages and disadvantages of mentoring over the telephone?
- What are other comments you have about the mentoring group?

History

Based on a presentation at the XXXIII AASWG Symposium, Long Beach, CA., 2011.First published in the Proceedings series in: Lee, C.D. (Ed.) (2014) *Social Group Work: We are all in the same boat.* London:Whiting & Birch (pp.31-45).

Notes on authors (at time of first publication)

Alana Atchinson, PhD, MSW, is a quintessential generalist social worker and has over 30 years of social work experience. She has worked in various fields including domestic violence, HIV/AIDS prevention and education research, child and adolescent mental health, rural poverty, and LGBT advocacy. In 2007 she joined the social work faculty at Bloomsburg University, Department of Social Work, in Bloomsburg, Pennsylvania, USA. She is an Associate Professor and teaches group work, introductory practice experience, and introduction to social work and social welfare.

Lisa M. Murphy, PhD, MA, is an assistant professor of Criminal Justice at La Sierra University. She also has a teaching credential in Special Education.

Maria A. Gurrola, PhD, MSW, MA, is Associate Professor, School of Social Work, New Mexico State University, Las Cruces, New Mexico, USA. She teaches Human Behavior in the Social Environment. Her research interest is in transnational families and their resiliency while adapting to two different environments emphasizing mental health and gender issues.

Cheryl D. Lee, PhD, MSW, is Professor, School of Social Work, California State University, Long Beach, California, USA.

Shirley R. Simon, ACSW, LCSW is Associate Professor, School of Social Work, Loyola University Chicago, Illinois, USA. She has been a social work educator for over thirty years, has published on group work education, practice and history, and has facilitated over one hundred student and alumni presentations at professional association conferences, particularly IASWG. Research and scholarship interests include group work education in MSW programs, hybrid-online group work instruction, curricular strategies for connecting students and professional associations, and social work dissertations on group work.

Orchestrating the power of a group of AASWG members in partnership for change with colleagues at a university social work program

Preface to the 2021 reprint

This paper describes the work of a Chapter of the Association for the Advancement of Social Work with Groups (AASWG) that developed an Ad Hoc task group to promote group work education at a local university. Enhancing group work and group work education is also in line with the primary focus of the International Association of Social Work with Groups (IASWG), formerly the AASWG.

Although the Ad Hoc task group as described in this paper ended, the impact of the actions of this group have continued to this day. Group work continues to be part of the curriculum of the social work program at the targeted university, and the endowed lectureship, focused on group work, continues to be offered. In addition, the group work components of the curriculum at another university were also enhanced.

In reflecting on the efforts of the Ad Hoc task group, it seems that one of the key components that aided the group's development, and was instrumental in the success of its efforts was the leadership of the group. This factor was very briefly addressed in the paper and deserves expansion. One of the co-leaders of the group was very devoted to group work and promoting group work education. Moreover, she was very mindful of the goal of the Ad Hoc group, but was also mindful of each group member's needs and expertise, and keeping each member of the group involved in the efforts of the group. This co-leader had a talent for connecting with each member of the group and making each one feel important and needed. Moreover, she was very skilled at helping the group arrive at consensus.

Another skill that she had was the ability to mediate the efforts and goals of the Ad Hoc group with the goals of the university social work program. Thus, the strong democratic leadership component was an important element that contributed to the success of the efforts to promote group work education.

One of the authors of this article, Anna Fritz, exemplified this type of strong democratic leadership. She was very dedicated to group work and promoting group work education. She had a gift for inclusion and for connecting to people in different fields of group work, and she was a strong advocate for AASWG. She was a powerful force in the promotion of group work and group work education; although she died in June 2009, her impact and legacy continue.

Thelma Silver

Thelma Silver, PhD LISW-S is retired as Professor in the Department of Social Work at Youngstown State University, where she taught group work

Anna S Fritz, MSSA was a former faculty member of the Mandel School of Applied Social Sciences at Case Western Reserve University where she taught group work

Orchestrating the power of a group of AASWG members in partnership for change with colleagues at a university social work program

Thelma Silver and Anna Fritz

Introduction

Change is needed in group work education as the movement towards a generalist curriculum model, which began in 1969, has resulted in the decline of group work education, a phenomenon noted by Birnbaum and Wayne (2000). Moreover, while group work educational opportunities decreased, social group work practice increased. As recently reported, there has been an increase in the wide use of treatment groups and task groups in social agencies in the United States (Goodman & Munoz, 2004; Sweifach & LaPorte, 2009). This discrepancy challenges social work academic institutions and social work practitioners to better educate social work students and social workers in social group work methods.

On a national level, the Association for the Advancement of Social Work with Groups (AASWG) is an organization with the mission of support and advocacy for education and training about social work with groups (www.AASWG.org). This organization collaborates with the Council on Social Work Education (CSWE), the accrediting body for social work educational institutions, to strengthen education for practice with groups (Birnbaum & Wayne, 2000). However, while national organizations can set broad policy guidelines and educational efforts, it needs to be local communities that will put change efforts into effect in academic programs.

Pre-group planning and development

The process for promoting group work in the curriculum of local universities in one Midwest region began about 15 years ago. Over the years it has involved a few different task and advocacy groups of one local chapter of the AASWG by using macro level task groups in an evolving group process effort.

In the spring of 1996 the local chapter of the AASWG was approached by the head of the social work school of one local university to be one of 14 stakeholder groups that were giving input to them as they were reevaluating their curriculum. An Assessment Task Force Stakeholder Group of the local chapter of the AASWG was convened as a one session group to address this request. This stakeholder group met together and provided the University with a list of skills and knowledge that should be required of social work graduates. However, the result of this process of curriculum restructuring with regard to content on group work was that it only produced an elective course on groups that few students accessed. This lack of prominence of group work in the curriculum was of great concern to the members of the local chapter of AASWG. Thus, the members of the chapter identified a need for enhanced education in group work at the University and looked for ways to address this need.

In the summer of 2003 a situation arose in which two members of the local chapter of AASWG were able to take leadership in advocating for more visibility of group work at the school, including greater content on group work in the curriculum. The two AASWG members had met the new administrator of the social work school, who invited their input for the vision of the school. This led to the two AASWG members' making a financial donation to the school to set up a lectureship program with the condition that it be used to promote group work. A second outcome was setting the agenda between the AASWG members and the social work administrator for continuing the discussion on increasing group work content in their curriculum. The two AASWG members then sought the involvement of an ad hoc sub-group of nine members of the AASWG Chapter Education Committee who were all alumni of the school.

As one reviews this pre-group planning phase, one sees some of the elements that should be considered in the formation of a group (Kurland,1978; Kurland & Salmon, 1998). These elements are need, purpose, composition, structure, content, pre-group contact, and social and agency context. There was a clarity of need and purpose of the Ad Hoc Group, namely, to engage in a cooperative effort with the educational institution to enhance group work education.

In regard to group composition (Kurland & Salmon, 1998), the members of the Ad Hoc Group were people who had similar beliefs and values about the importance of group work education; all were members of the AASWG Chapter Education Committee which had this as their agenda. The members of the Ad Hoc Group also had a similar educational background as Alumni of the university. They were also familiar with the history of the curriculum when the social work school had a richer content regarding group work.

The organizational and social context (Kurland & Salmon,1998) were also important in the formation of the Ad Hoc Group. The new administration of the school presented an opportunity for the group to impact the future direction of the school's curriculum. Moreover, the administrator was welcoming this input which created the conditions for collaboration.

Beginning phase

In the fall of 2003 the Ad Hoc Group of the Education Committee of the local chapter of the AASWG and the administration of the school of social work scheduled a meeting to pursue the agenda of enhancing social work education. The Director of the Alumni Office acted as a liaison between AASWG and the school. This also reflected the dual membership of the Ad Hoc Group as both members of the AASWG who wanted to promote group work and as Alumni who, out of concern for the school, wanted to strengthen the curriculum of the school in regards to group work. Thus, the Ad Hoc Group was part of the system that was targeted for change. This interconnection strengthened the cohesion of the group members and aided the change process. At this time it was also clear that the timing of the change was a positive factor. There was a new administration, and the institution was undergoing a curriculum review; thus, there was openness to change.

During the meeting the Ad Hoc Group and the administration acknowledged the need for increasing the visibility of group work in the curriculum. Both also agreed on how AASWG could continue to be involved in the promotion of group work at the school. The administration suggested that AASWG prepare a position statement that would outline what students need to know about groups and group work. Another objective was to promote group work at the school through an endowed lectureship on group work. Therefore, the Ad Hoc Group and the administration shared concerns and the commitment that AASWG would assist the school in their quest for change.

In the pre-group planning and beginning phases there was a clarity of tasks, namely, the promotion of group work in the school and group work content in the curriculum. This clarity of purpose and function and the establishment of goals are important in the beginning stage of a group (Kurland & Salmon, 1998; Toseland & Rivas, 2005) for a group to be effective. There was also leadership in the effort by the two Alumni who brought AASWG into the process, continued to push the agenda, and helped the Ad Hoc Group stay on task.

Moreover, the composition of the Ad Hoc Group of members who shared values about the importance of group work education and who also had a similar educational background was influential in keeping the group on task. Another important factor was that the social context and organizational context were creating the conditions of change to support the work of this group. All these factors are important in the beginning stage of groups (Kurland & Salmon, 1998) and helped create an effective advocacy group.

Middle phase

The work of the Ad Hoc Group centered on writing the position paper, which included four steps. The first step was to clearly research the historical development of group work and group work content at the school. The second step was to conduct a literature search on group work publications and document available group work literature in the school's library. The third and fourth steps were to specify the essential knowledge and essential skills of group work.

When the Ad Hoc Group met to work on these tasks, some conflict developed regarding the type of group work content that should be advocated for the curriculum. There was a disagreement about whether the content should be clinically focused, or whether it should be focused on basic foundation knowledge and skills in group work. A lively discussion occurred among the members of the Ad Hoc Group who were strongly committed to either the clinical focus or the foundation focus. After listing the possible content of each focus, members noted the common knowledge and skills of both a clinical focus and a foundation focus. This activity helped create a consensus in the group about the content. Thus, those who advocated for foundation knowledge dominated, although the position statement did state a specific need for clinical skills training in social group work practice.

By early December the Ad Hoc Group had developed a draft of the "Position Statement on Groups and Group Work". In their recommendation section, the committee presented guidelines for the knowledge and skills that they thought should be required of all social work students. They made recommendations for the expansion of content on group dynamics and small-group theory and for the expansion of content on group work in the foundation course. They also acknowledged the importance of developing clinical skills. The Ad Hoc Group presented the Position Statement to the University and the recommendations as outlined in the position statement were accepted by the school's Curriculum Committee.

The members of AASWG continued to advance the agenda of the promotion of a group work course by staying active in the process of engaging in partnering with the university. Consequently, the co-leader of the Ad Hoc Group sent a letter to the administration outlining the advocacy steps cited above that had been accomplished and asking for clarification about the status of the development of a required course in group work. The co-leader had received assurance that there were plans to develop this course for the next school year and that AASWG, Alumni, and community practitioners would be consulted during the process of course development.

During this phase there was a commonality of purpose established as the administration moved ahead with consideration of course development on a macro practice course with group content. In addition, a faculty member who was developing the course solicited the help of the Ad Hoc Group in reviewing the draft proposal of the course.

In the middle phase of the group process the Ad Hoc Group focused on some of the required activities of this work phase, namely, making decisions, solving problems, developing plans, and keeping the members informed and involved (Maier, 1963; Toseland & Rivas, 2005). Much of this work centered on the task of writing the position paper regarding group work in the curriculum.

Outcomes and ending

Through a partnership with AASWG and the school of social work, some of the major recommendations to enhance work at the school that were outlined by the Ad Hoc Group in the position statement were realized. The major goal of expansion of content in group work seemed to have been met through the development of a required course of macro methods with group work content and this course was expected to be part of the foundation curriculum. Moreover, during the development of this macro practice course the Ad Hoc Group of AASWG was consulted to review the course description and make recommendations.

In the evaluation stage of the task group, the tasks are evaluated to determine if the group's purposes have been realized (Toseland & Rivas, 2005). When the Ad Hoc Group discovered that the proposed macro practice course on macro methods had not been accepted for implementation, they needed to reevaluate the process and the ongoing tasks. It was also discovered that the new faculty members were now part of the process, and the AASWG chapter needed to decide whether or not to establish a new partnership with the new faculty in order to continue their goal to enhance group work content in the curriculum.

The decision was made to continue to advocate as the macro practice course with groups was being finalized. This meant that one of the leaders of the Ad Hoc Group continued to have contact with school faculty to inquire about the status of the course. Once this course was scheduled in the social work curriculum, the Education Committee of AASWG, several of whom were members of the Ad Hoc Group, reviewed the accomplishments of the Ad Hoc Group. It was determined that the latter group had met its goal of enhancing group work education at the school. As there was no longer a reason for the Ad Hoc Group to meet, it was disbanded.

This advocacy effort by AASWG to promote group work at the University accomplished some of the tasks established in the position paper. There was a clarity of focus outlined in the position paper that enabled the Ad Hoc Group to be clear about its direction as the members went through the advocacy process. Once the task was accomplished, the group ended.

Summary and conclusion

This paper outlines how one chapter of the AASWG utilized a task group, the Ad Hoc Group, to engage with a social work education program to expand group work education. The efforts of the Ad Hoc Group were presented as proceeding through the stages of group -- pre-group planning, beginning, middle and ending -- as outlined by Toseland and Rivas (2005).

The discussion also utilized the planning model presented by Kurland and Salmon (1998) to identify the factors that were important in the formation, cohesion and effectiveness of the Ad Hoc Group, especially need and purpose, content, group composition and social and organizational context.

As stated above, the Ad Hoc Group had a defined purpose (Kurland & Salmon, 1998) to enhance social group work education in a specific social work program and this clear task kept the group focused on its goal. Moreover, the composition of the Ad Hoc Group included people who had a strong commitment to the task of furthering group work education since, as members of the AASWG, they were committed to group work. Furthermore, as alumni of the University, they were also concerned about the lack of attention to group work at the school and wanted to change this.

As described above, the organizational context was ripe for change (Kurland & Salmon, 1998) because of the new administration and a curriculum review. The environmental context also included AASWG involvement and the financial resources of the alumni. In addition, the use of groups in agencies had increased, which possibly also put pressure on the institution to respond. All of these factors of group planning led to an effective beginning for the Ad Hoc Group as it had clarity of purpose and function. Moreover, there was leadership by the two alumni who initiated the advocacy effort by establishing the lectureship, and beginning the collaboration with the University.

In the work phase (Toseland & Rivas, 2005), the Ad Hoc Group was able to stay focused on the task of writing the position statement on group work. Conflict in this process arose about whether there should be a foundation focus or a clinical focus; the commonality of values and beliefs about the importance of group work and the shared educational background helped the group achieve a consensus.

The group also evaluated its progress in the achievement of its goals and continued to pursue its goals of creating a required group work course until this was finalized. Then, once the task was accomplished and the goal was achieved, the Ad Hoc Group was quickly ended.

In reviewing the stages (Toseland & Rivas, 2005) of the Ad Hoc Group, one can see the effective progression through the planning, beginning, and middle stages. However, the ending stage was abrupt without an evaluation of the group process that may have been useful. Instead of the focus on process at that stage, the focus was on the accomplishment of the task. Toseland and Rivas (2005) state that this balance of process and task is often a challenge in task groups.

Enhancing social work education needs to involve both practitioners and educators. Both types of social workers were involved in this advocacy effort, since the Ad Hoc Group included both clinicians and University personnel. Moreover, the Ad Hoc Group partnered with educators from the social work school to increase group work education at the school.

This advocacy effort demonstrates the power of a group to influence change; in this example a group of social workers was able to impact on changing the education at a social work school to include more group work content. Thus, for social workers who are committed to group work, this group advocacy effort may serve as an example of a way to impact on social group work education on a local level.

To engage in this type of advocacy effort, it was important to have effective planning as a group. Moreover, group composition (Kurland & Salmon, 1998) was a part of this planning as the group had the commonality of being alumni of the targeted program. Therefore, in planning this type of advocacy effort, one needs to consider the power of alumni as a group to affect change at their alma mater.

Organization and social context are also important for change efforts (Kurland & Salmon, 1998) and in this advocacy effort the organization had an administrative change and was undergoing curriculum change. As a result, the time was ripe to impact on the organization. This indicates that the group needs to evaluate the context to determine the possibility of change. At the present time, schools of social work are undergoing change as they reorganize to meet the new standards for CSWE. This may be an opportune time to impact on local institutions to enhance group work education.

It has been documented that there has been a decrease in social group work education, while the need for group work has increased (Sweifach & LaPorte, 2009). Social workers committed to group work need to recognize that they can impact this situation. This article demonstrates how one group of social workers had an impact on enhancing group work education. This can serve as an example for others to advocate change at the local universities.

References

Birnbaum, M.L., & Wayne, J. (2000). Groupwork in foundation generalist education: The necessity for curriculum change. *Journal of Social Work Education*, 36(2), 347-356.

Goodman, H. & Munoz, M. (2004). Developing social group work skills for contemporary agency practice. *Social Work with Groups*, 27(1), 17-33.

Gummer, B. (1987). Groups as substance and symbol: Group processes and organizational politics. *Social Work with Groups*, 10 (2), 25-39.

Kirst-Ashman, K. K., & Hull, G. H., Jr. (1997). *Generalist Practice with Organizations and Communities*. Chicago: Nelson-Hall.

Kurland, R. (1978). Planning: The neglected component of group development. *Social Work with Groups*, 1 (2), 173-178.

Kurland, R. & Salmon, R. (1998). *Teaching a Methods Course in Social Work with Groups*. Alexandria, VA: Council on Social Work Education.

Kurland, R, Salmon, R., Bitel, M., Goodwin, H., Ludwig, K., Wolfe Newmann, E., & Sullivan, N. (2004). The survival of social group work: A call to action. *Social Work with Groups*, 27(1), 3-17.

Maier, N. (1963). *Problem-Solving Discussions and Conferences: Leadership methods and skills*. New York: McGraw-Hill.

Sweifach, J. & LaPorte, H. H., (2009). Group work in foundation generalist classes: Perceptions of students about the nature and quality of their experience. *Social Work with Groups*, 32(4), 303-314.

Toseland, R. W. & Rivas, R. F. (2005). *An Introduction to Group Work Practice*. (5th ed.) Boston, MA: Pearson.

History

Based on a presentation at the XXVIII AASWG Symposium, San Diego, CA., 2006. First published in the Proceedings series in: Moyse Steinberg, D. (Ed.) (2010) *Orchestrating the Power of Groups: Beginnings, middles, and endings (overture, movements, and finales)*. London: Whiting & Birch (pp.17-26)

Notes on authors (at time of first publication)

Thelma Silver, PhD, LISW-S is Associate Professor in the Department of Social Work Youngstown State University, where she has taught group work. She is currently Co-Chair of the Education Committee of Northeast Ohio chapter of the AASWG.

Anna S. Fritz, MSSA was a former faculty member of the Mandel School of Applied Social Sciences at Case Western Reserve University where she taught group work. She was also actively involved in the Executive Committee of Northeast Ohio Chapter of the AASWG and was Chair of the Education Committee.

The metamorphosis of a university social group work club

Preface to the 2021 reprint

This article is about a group work club that I initiated as an Assistant Professor teaching group work courses at California State University, Long Beach (CSULB) School of Social Work. The purposes were to advance students' learning of social work with groups outside of the classroom, to connect participants to the International Association of Social work with Groups (IASWG), and to create a fun, supportive club for students, educators, and practitioners who had a passion for group work and wanted to share experiences and improve group work skills, knowledge and values.

As the article indicates, the group work club was very successful for many years, attracting students, faculty and practitioners. Faculty and practitioners often presented their group work scholarship and experience at the monthly meetings. Networking was a large component, and members advanced their careers and met group work friends. Group work skills were enhanced for all types of groups when experts presented and directed learning activities on their older adult, substance use, and children's groups among others. Evaluations were distributed at the end of each meeting so that Club improvements could be made from participant recommendations. Social action activities were part of the experience. For example, members created placards at one meeting and subsequently marched as a group for Gay and Lesbian marriages in California. The club also served meals to people who were homeless, raised funds for disease research by participating together in organized runs/walks, and made holiday cards for isolated people in nursing homes. In 2016 and 2017, as part of the IASWG Southern California Chapter, they held several wonderful events for people struggling with issues during the holiday season, where students facilitated talking circle groups in our community.

As a result of joining the club, many of the club members became members of IASWG, and some became IASWG leaders. Eventually the veteran IASWG Southern California Chapter members and leaders (who were mostly located in San Diego, California) asked the club located several hours away in Long Beach to take over the chapter. One of the club members, who helped initiate the club when she was a part-time BASW student, eventually earned an MSW and became the Southern California Chapter Chair. She went on to co-chair the IASWG Symposium on the Queen Mary in Long Beach. Another club member became an elected board member of IASWG, worked on the Long Beach symposium and then became the Southern California Chapter Chair. A third club member and the co-author of this article helped complete the evaluation research on the club, thereby honing her research and writing skills while documenting the club's process and progress.

The relevance of the article today is that it demonstrates how students, involved in an extra-curricular group work club in a social work academic program, can develop professionalism, leadership skills, and commitment to this effective social work modality and IASWG. Since the original publication, a number of journal articles discuss concerns about the decline of group work courses in academia and a lack of group work continuing education for field instructors who supervise student interns facilitating groups (Simon & Kilbane, 2014; Simon, Kilbane & Stollenberg, 2017; Skolnik, 2017). A contemporary article (Simon et al., 2017) found that only 33% of full time faculty teaching group work courses are members of IASWG, which may indicate minimal knowledge of the *Standards of Social Work with Groups* (IASWG, 2010). Unfortunately the idea of a group work club has not caught on or been documented in the literature beyond this program; nevertheless, IASWG and its local chapters are invigorated and inspired by social group work students who become members and are engaged in chapter meetings, annual symposiums and the bi-annual group work camp. I hope the reprint of this article will inspire group work faculty, in collaboration with social work students, to initiate group work clubs. It's imperative that social work students hone their group work practice methodology so that they can assist people who need diverse mutual aid groups to recover from or cope with mass shootings, natural disasters, illnesses, war zones, abuse, homelessness and many other adverse and normal circumstances that are part of our world.

Cheryl D. Lee

Cheryl D. Lee is Professor Emeritus at California State University, Long Beach and a board member of the Southern California Chapter of IASWG

References

International Association of Social Work with Groups (2010). *Standards for social work practice with groups,* 2nd ed. (2010). Retrieved from IASWG. org.

Simon, S.R. & Kilbane, T. (2014). The current state of group work education in U.S. graduate schools of social work. *Social Work with Groups,* 37:3, 243-256, DOI: 10.1080/01609513.2013.840821

Simon, S.R. & Kilbane, T. & Stoltenberg, E. (2017). Underexplored aspects of group-work education in MSW programs. *Social Work with Groups,* DOI: 10.1080/01609513.2017.1393370

Skolnik, S. (2017). Coming together: Factors that connect social workers to group work practice. *Social Work with Groups.* DOI: 10.1080/01609513.2017.1384948

The metamorphosis of a university social group work club

Cheryl Lee and Eliette Montiel

Introduction

This paper describes a follow-up study of a university social group work club that was created to meet the needs of students and practitioners to further group work expertise and foster mutual aid. The university group had a vision to empower students, practitioners and academics with discussions about group work; thus, it was named 'The Group Work Club' after the clubs that developed in settlement houses. Group work has its roots in the settlement house movement in England, the United States and Canada (Sullivan, Mesbur & Lang, 2009; Toseland & Rivas, 2009). Jane Addams visited Toynbee Hall, a settlement house in London in 1888, before creating Hull House in Chicago to serve new immigrants with adult discussion clubs, children's activity clubs, music, art, and sports clubs among other empowering group activities (Lee, 2009).

Review of the literature

Purpose of the club

The Group Work Club's purposes have roots in the literature. Bergart and Simon (2004) encouraged social group workers to form support groups when they feel isolated in their social work practices. Simon, Webster and Horn (2007) recommended connecting students to professional organizations such as AASWG to provide support, mentoring opportunities, and networking. The decline of social group work in curricula with the advent of generalist social work practice has been documented by Birnbaum and Wayne (2000) and Lee (2005), making it critical to supplement group work education. Sullivan (2006) noted the concurrent loss of members in the international social group work organization, the Association for the Advancement of Social Work and Groups (AASWG). AASWG is a professional organization dedicated to the promotion of group work and the use of ethical multi-cultural group work practice (Sullivan, 2006).

The Group Work Club's purposes address these identified needs. The purposes, which developed over the course of The Club's first year, became: (1) to nurture social group work in agencies; (2) to engage students, practitioners and academics in a collaborative educational group work experience; and (3) to link members to AASWG.

Conceptual framework

The literature is replete with discussion of group development and stages of group (Anderson, 1997; Berman-Rossi, 1993; Garland, Jones & Kolodny, 1965; Gitterman, 2005; Kurland & Salmon, 2005; Schiller, 1997; 2007; Shulman, 2009; Toseland & Rivas, 2009; Tuckman & Jensen, 1977). The Club's development is best described using Schiller's relational model (Schiller, 1997; 2002; 2007). In this model the stages of development are: pre-affiliation, establishing a relational base, mutuality and interpersonal empathy, challenge and change, and separation/termination. This feminist approach focuses on developing relationships and members connecting with one another. The majority of the members are women and members of different ethnic minority groups that have collectivist cultures in which harmony is valued.

During the first year of The Club, the facilitators and members planned for meetings, attracted members, met often, and developed close relationships with each other while forging a connection with the AASWG state chapter (which was experiencing difficulties) and the international organization. In the second year of The Club, mutuality and interpersonal empathy was evident at meetings. At the first meeting of the second year, a sharing and activity planning meeting, members provided peer consultation about groups they were facilitating. They also planned for upcoming group meetings on topics of interest: groups for victims of sexual assault, people experiencing alcohol and substance addictions, older adults, and social justice. At the social justice group meeting, members shared ideas about what social justice meant to them. They found commonalities and differences but were able to respect members' passions and learn from one another. This is the hallmark of the mutuality and interpersonal empathy stage when members can support others even when there are ideological differences (Schiller, 1997; 2007).

The Group Work Club experienced a challenge during the second year when the State Chapter's President and several board members wanted to resign their positions and dissolve the chapter due to a lack of available leaders. After much discussion among The Club members, consensus was reached to help the chapter by assuming leadership roles. Since it was the second year of The Club, many of the graduate student members of The Club had obtained their masters in social work (MSW degrees) and were practitioners in the community; therefore, they were eligible to serve on the state chapter board and run for office. A meeting was held with the former officers and members of the board who were delighted that The Club was able to keep the chapter alive (although it would be re-located several hours away in a different city). The metamorphosis of The Club into the state chapter is now complete with newly elected officers and board members. The process of transitioning from a university club to a state AASWG chapter fits with the fourth stage of Schiller's Relational Model, 'challenge and change' (Schiller, 1997; 2002; 2007). In this stage of a group's development, members are able to overcome conflict while maintaining connections.

Activities and educational programs

Programs and activities have major value for groups (Comer & Hirayama, 2009; Kurland & Salmon, 2005) and must be related to the group's purposes. The importance of activities was documented by Oborne and Maidment (2007), who wrote about a fathers' group that utilized activities such as indoor and outdoor team sports and an evening barbecue to foster cohesion among the group members as well as to strengthen relationships with their children. The Club had several meetings in which the major theme was activities. One session involved the creation of posters for the Gay and Lesbian Pride Parade. Members brought art supplies and shared their ideas and talents to create posters. A member who has led arts and crafts groups facilitated the activity group. Members not only enjoyed creating posters with a social justice theme but also furthered The Club's goals of providing support and mutual aid.

In addition, there is a need for group work educational programs which The Club provided. Birnbaum and Wayne (2000) documented that group work education has been in a state of decline. Goodman and Munoz (2004) conducted a study demonstrating that many agency supervisors knew little about social group work, and student interns were frustrated when comparing lessons learned in their group work classes. They suggested continuing education for agency personnel so that adequate group work is accomplished. Also, they recommended that educators stay involved with students through professional organizations. Over the course of the two years of meeting, many faculty members have spoken to The Club about different groups with which they have been involved. In addition, Club members have benefited tremendously from educational presentations made by group workers in the community.

Social justice

Social justice is central to empowerment in group work (Breton, 2004; Ephross, 2004; Toseland & Rivas, 2008). According to Breton, every social work group should have a social justice component that is not merely theoretical but results in activities that assist oppressed groups. In his famous book, *The Pedagogy of the Oppressed*, Freire (2007) discusses how teachers can learn much from students and members of other oppressed groups. During the first year of The Club, the members expressed interest in conducting social justice activities together; however, it was not until The Club's second year that they organized a social justice activity, marching in the Gay Pride Parade with signs denoting 'The AASWG Group Work Club', equality for all, and gay/lesbian marriage.

Methodology

Design

To evaluate The Group Work Club, a quantitative/qualitative longitudinal design was employed. The research questions were:

1. What was the satisfaction level of Club members during the second year of The Club as compared to the first year of The Club?
2. What were the strengths of the meetings?
3. What suggestions did members offer to improve The Club?
4. Was there an increase in AASWG's membership as a result of The Club's existence?

Instrument

No group work standardized instruments were found appropriate to evaluate The Group Work Club. Unfortunately, a current social group work instrument created by MacGowan (2003) was not a fit for The Club because it was geared toward treatment groups. Therefore, an instrument from an allied profession was used. The Client Satisfaction Questionnaire (CSQ-8, Attkisson, 1985) is an eight-question scale measuring consumer satisfaction with services rendered. One question was: 'To what extent has the program met your needs?' (4 = almost all of my needs have been met, and 1 = none of my needs have been met). Scores could range from 8 to 32, and higher scores equated with greater satisfaction with the services. The measure's reliability has ranged from .86 to .94 in previous studies (Attkisson, 1985). The reliability of the scale for this sample was excellent (alpha = .92). In addition, the CSQ-8 has good concurrent validity (Attkisson, 1985). A global question was also asked regarding the quality of the meeting: 'How would you rate the quality of tonight's meeting?' (1 = very poor to 5 = outstanding). The last two questions were: 'What were things that you liked about our meeting?' and 'What are your suggestions for future club meetings?'

Data collection and analysis

At the end of each meeting, the participants completed a questionnaire, which included the Client Satisfaction Questionnaire (CSQ-8, Attkisson, 1985) and open-ended questions developed by the researchers. Members were instructed to answer the questionnaire as it related to The Group Work Club. Demographic questions and AASWG records provided additional data.

The quantitative data was analyzed using the Statistical Program for the Social Sciences (SPSS 16). Satisfaction Scores were obtained as an aggregate for the entire sample as well as for individual sessions. Independent means t-tests were used to compare results from Year 1 versus Year 2. Themes were identified and tallied for the two open-ended questions. Two researchers reviewed the open-ended responses to establish inter-rater reliability.

Sample

The sample of those who evaluated the meeting over the eight sessions in the second year of The Club was 107. The general orientation/sharing group experiences and planning meeting for the second year included 13 members. Session 2 with a speaker on groups for victims of sexual assault included 15 members. For session 3, about alcohol and substance abuse recovery groups, there were 7 members. Session 4, sharing of group work experiences, included 13 participants. Session 5's topic was healthy aging groups for older adults; 18 Club members attended. Session 6 consisted of a group discussion about the meaning of social justice and included 12 members. At session 7, six members created placards to use at the Gay Pride Parade. At the culminating meeting/social justice activity, eight members marched together in the Gay Pride Parade, supporting equality for all and gay/lesbian marriages.

Year 2's Club membership had ethnic/cultural diversity (Table 1). Forty-six percent ($n = 49$) of The Club members were Caucasians/European Americans, 37% ($n = 40$) were of Latino descent, 6% ($n = 6$) were Asian Americans/Pacific Islanders, 6% ($n = 6$) were bi-ethnic, and 5% ($n = 5$) were African Americans. The majority of participants were females ($n = 83$, 78%), social work students ($n = 68$, 64%), and ages of members ranged from 21 to 61 ($M = 33$, $SD = 13$). Most of the members had previously facilitated groups ($n = 85$, 79%).

Table 1
Sample Characteristics (N = 107)

Variables	n	%
Gender		
Females	83	78
Males	14	22
Ethnicity		
European American	49	46
Latino (El Salvador, Mexico, Nicaragua, Peru)	40	37
Asian Americans/Pacific Islanders (China, Philippines, Vietnam)	6	6
Bi-ethnic/Bi-racial	6	6
African American	5	5

Results

Mean scores for the CSQ-8 were obtained for each of the eight sessions in Year 2 (Table 1). The means ranged from 28.38 (*SD* = 3.43) to 31.17 (*SD* = 1.33) out of a possible 32 points. Satisfaction scores were higher in Year 2 as compared to Year 1 (Y2 *M* = 29.85, *SD* = 2.86 vs.

Y1 *M* = 27.95, *SD* = 3.81, *t* = -4.05, p = .000). The global question assessing meeting quality resulted in mean scores of 5 out of a possible 5 points for seven of eight meetings. This rating indicates that members found the meetings to be of outstanding quality (Table 2).

Table 2
Member satisfaction with Group Work Club, Year Two (*N* = 107)

Session Number	CSQ-8			Meeting Quality Question		
	n	*M*	*SD*	*n*	*M*	*SD*
Session 1	13	31.08	1.26	13	5.00	0.00
Session 2	15	29.00	3.72	15	5.00	0.00
Session 3	7	31.14	1.86	7	5.00	0.00
Session 4	13	28.38	3.43	13	5.00	1.00
Session 5	18	29.61	2.87	18	5.00	1.00
Session 6	12	29.25	2.99	12	4.00	1.00
Session 7	6	31.17	1.33	6	5.00	0.00
Session 8	8	31.12	1.81	8	5.00	0.00

One qualitative question asked participants the strengths of the meetings. There were 107 responses to the strengths question (Table 3 overleaf) which were organized into themes. The strengths most frequently noted were: speakers (*f* = 31, 23%), sharing/mutual aid (*f* = 27, 20%), skills/knowledge (*f* = 13, 10%), social environment (*f* = 12, 9%), and networking (*f* = 12, 9%).

The 70 suggestions about meetings were grouped into the following themes: *speakers* on a variety of relevant topics who have group work experience; *activities* such as music and art activities and small group experiential exercises; *skills and techniques of group work* such as becoming a more effective facilitator; *social justice activities* such as feeding the homeless; *logistics,* changing day, time, or location; *attracting and maintaining new members; more processing; structure,* starting and ending on time; and *create a strategic plan.*

Table 3
Things you liked about the meeting

Strengths*	*f*	%
Speakers/presentations/topics *(having different speakers in the meetings, writing groups for older adults, groups for sexual assault victims, etc.)*	31	23.13
Sharing/mutual aid *(sharing experiences, helping each other)*	27	20.15
Skills/knowledge *(practice skills learned, Icebreakers, group work knowledge)*	13	9.70
Social environment *(welcoming, friendly, intimate, make friends, relaxing, fun, openness)*	12	8.96
Networking *(meeting new people, reconnecting with old members)*	12	8.96
Food	12	8.96
Participation in social justice activity *(reflections on social justice activity/gay pride parade)*	8	5.97
Cohesiveness *(unity of group)*	7	5.22
Processing	7	5.22
Structure/logistics *(i.e. meeting day and time)*	3	2.24
Link to AASWG *(discussing organization, conferences, etc.)*	2	1.49

*Multiple responses were possible.

In reviewing statistics regarding membership in AASWG, as a result of The Club's formation, AASWG's membership in the state increased by one-third or 17 members during the first year of The Club. Many of these members renewed their memberships. Five additional members joined in the second year.

The following quotes illustrate different members' meeting experiences:

My experience at The Group Work Club was a positive one. I did not know what to expect. However, when I arrived, everyone was welcoming. It is nice to know that there is a group on campus that encourages students to get together and share their experiences regarding group work. I also liked the fact that the Club provides guest speakers so that we can gain and enhance skills to be effective group work facilitators.

The discussion of social justice was very interesting because I was able to learn about each individual in the group. It highlighted the reasons we became social workers. We want to make our society just and that is why the group decided to participate in the Gay Pride Parade on May 17. The group has been working towards being a force in the community. Participating in this event will allow the group to bond and to stand up for social justice.

I loved the icebreaker exercise, as I thought it was a good way to acclimate the new people to a group setting. I felt as though people were able to relax and really show their personalities. As I looked around the room during the icebreaker, I felt as if I belonged here because of the great personalities in the room.

I was initially interested in attending The Club to learn more techniques and improve my clinical facilitation skills. I want to become exposed to other types of groups and I am eager to learn from the experiences of other practitioners. Much to my pleasant surprise the individuals who attended The Club meetings were of a diverse academic and professional background. The group appeared cohesive and members interacted well with one another. I decided to join AASWG, and I am looking forward to learning how to improve my skills so that I may better serve my clients. I think it is wonderful to have this recreational club as a way to provide practitioners education on group theory and facilitation.

Limitations

There were several limitations in this study. The CSQ-8 instrument was not specifically designed to evaluate group work or a group work club. No standardized instrument could be found that was appropriate for evaluating a group work club. Responses on the evaluations might have been influenced by social desirability. A comparison group could not be found. Qualitative data interpretation might be biased (Padgett, 1998); however, the two researchers who analyzed the qualitative data provided a check on each other.

Discussion

The goal of this manuscript was to document the longitudinal evaluation of The Group Work Club whose purposes were: to nurture social group work, to engage students, practitioners and academics in a collaborative educational group work experience, and to link members to an international social work organization AASWG. The first research question examined the satisfaction level of group members during The Club's second year. Members were highly satisfied, exceeding the satisfaction level measured in The Club's first year. This finding converges with the literature which reports that often group workers feel isolated in their practice and benefit from professional consultation, collaboration and support (Bergart & Simon, 2004; Simon et al., 2007). Simon et al. recommend linking students to professional organizations such as AASWG to provide them with support, mentoring opportunities and networking. Group workers benefit when there is ongoing education about group work and group process (Goodman & Munoz, 2004). Club members reported they gained group work knowledge and skills, provided mutual aid, and interacted with members who had similar passions.

The second research question inquired about the strengths of The Club. Members enjoyed the speakers who presented on different types of groups, such as substance abuse, sexual assault and healthy aging for older adults. Another strength was mutual aid and sharing. The group work literature notes the power of mutual aid in groups (Gitterman, 2005). A third strength found that members appreciated learning group work knowledge and skills. Birnbaum and Wayne (2000) and Lee (2005) discuss the decline of social group work in curricula making it imperative to supplement group work education in creative ways.

The third research question explored members' suggestions about The Club as a way to gain insight into hindrances to The Club's success. The number one suggestion was to bring more speakers with knowledge and experience about group work and varied groups. It is sometimes difficult for The Club to obtain volunteer speakers especially because it has a limited budget. The members suggested more activities. One activity that The Group Work Club experienced in the second year involved arts and crafts. Members created posters for the local Gay Pride Parade. This highly rated activity meeting corroborates findings in the literature that activities have value for groups (Comer & Hirayama, 2009; Kurland & Salmon, 2005). The literature also advises that activities should be related to the purpose of the group. The art activity and the marching for equality and gay/lesbian marriage in the gay pride parade aligned with the purposes of The Club and social group work in general. Breton (2004) and Ephross (2004) state that every social work group needs to include a social justice component.

The final research question addressed whether AASWG membership would increase as a result of The Club. Over the course of The Club's two-year existence, membership in the AASWG state chapter has increased due to Club members joining the organization.

Implications for social group work research, education, and practice

Research on group work has increased; yet, there is still a great need for researchers to evaluate the effectiveness of group work interventions (Doel, 2008; Hoyle, Georgesen, & Webster, 2001; McGowan, 2003; Toseland & Horton, 2008). By continuing to collect data and analyze group meetings, group processes will be better understood and evidenced-based practice will develop.

The results of this study suggest that social work departments and schools could greatly benefit by creating social group work clubs. Group work clubs can enhance students' group work education and experience. The Club also provides a place where practitioners can learn about group work from one another.

In addition, AASWG will grow by supporting the formation of group work clubs in schools and departments of social work. The organization needs to think about its future, and students provide new ideas that will insure its growth and sustainability (Freire, 2007). The AASWG state chapter in this community was not only able to survive but thrive due to the energy and leadership of The Group Work Club.

Authors' Note

This article describes a follow-up study to the first year's evaluation of The Group Work Club. For readers interested in learning more about the beginning formulation of The Club, see article by Lee, C.D., Montiel, E., Atchisson, J., Liza, J., Flory, P. & Valenzuela, J. (2009). An innovative approach to support social group work: A university group work club. *Groupwork: An interdisciplinary journal for working with Groups, 19*(3), 11-26.

References

Anderson, J. (1997). *Social work with groups: A process model.* NY: Longman.

Attkisson, C.C. (1985). Client satisfaction questionnaire (CSQ-8). In K. Corcoran & J. Fischer (Eds.), *Measures for clinical practice: A source book.* New York: The Free Press, 120-122.

Bergart, A. & Simon, S.R. (2004). Practicing what we preach: Creating groups for ourselves. *Social Work with Groups, 27*(4), 17-30.

Berman-Rossi, T. (1993). Empowering groups through understanding stages of group development. *Social Work with Groups, 15*(2), 239-255.

Birnbaum, M & Wayne, J. (2000). Group work foundation generalist education: The necessity for curriculum change. *Journal of Social Work Education, 36*(2), 347-356.

Breton, M. (2004). An empowerment perspective. In C.D. Garvin, L.M. Gutierrez & M.J. Galinsky (Eds.), *Handbook of Social Work with Groups.*

New York: The Guilford Press, 76-90.

Comer, E. & Hirayama, K. (2009). Activity: Use and selection. In A. Gitterman & R. Salmon (Eds.), *Encyclopedia of social work with groups* New York: Routledge, 62-63.

Doel, M. (2008). Assessing skills in groupwork: A program of continuing professional development. In C. S. Cohen, M. H. Phillips & M. Hanson (Eds.), *Strength and diversity in social work with groups: Think group.* NY: Taylor & Francis, 69-80.

Ephross, P.H. (2004). Social work with groups: practice principles. In Ephross & Grief (Eds.), *Group work with populations at risk.* (2nd ed.) New York: Oxford University Press, 1-12.

Freire, P. (2007) *The pedagogy of the oppressed.* NY: Continuum.

Garland, J.A., Jones, H.E. & Kolodny, R.L. (1973). A model for stages of development in social work groups. In S. Bernstein (Ed.), *Explorations in group work.* Boston: Milford House, 17-71.

Gitterman, A. (2005). Group formation: Tasks, methods, and skills. In A. Gitterman & L. Shulman, (Eds.), *Mutual aid groups, vulnerable & resilient populations and the life cycle.* (3rd ed.) NY: Columbia University Press, 73-110.

Goodman, H. & Munoz, M. (2004). Developing social group work skills for contemporary agency practice. *Social Work with Groups, 27*(1), 2004.

Hoyle, R.H., Georgesen, J.C. & Webster, J.M. (2001). Analyzing data from individuals in groups: The past, the present, and the future. *Group Dynamics, 5*(1), 41-47.

Kurland, R. & Salmon, R. (2005). *Teaching a methods course in social work with groups.* Alexandria, VA: Council of Social Work Education.

Lee, C.D. (2005). Nuggets of gold from Alex Gitterman. *Reflections: Narratives of Professional Helping, 11*(2), 4-21.

Lee, J.A.B. (2009). Jane Addams. In A. Gitterman & R. Salmon (Eds.), *Encyclopedia of social work with groups.* New York: Routledge, 13-16.

Macgowan, M.J. (2003). Increasing engagement in groups: A measurement based approach. *Social Work with Groups, 26*(1), 5-28.

Padgett, D.K. (1998). *Qualitative methods in social work research: Challenges and rewards.* Thousand Oaks, CA: Sage Publications.

Oborne, M. & Maidment, J. (2007). C'mon guys! A program to facilitate father involvement in the primary school environment. *Groupwork, 17*(3), 8-24.

Schiller, L. (1997). Rethinking stages of development in women's groups: Implications for practice. *Social Work with Groups, 20*(3), 3-19.

Schiller, L. (2002). Process of an idea – how the relational model of group work developed. *Social Work with Groups, 25*(1), 159-166.

Schiller, L. (2007). Not for women only: Applying the relational model of group development with vulnerable populations. *Social Work with Groups, 30*(2), 11-26.

Shulman, L. (2009). Beginning phase. In A. Gitterman & R. Salmon (Eds.), *Encyclopedia of social work with groups*. New York: Routledge, 112-114.

Simon, S., Webster, J. & Horn, K. (2007). A critical call for connecting students with professional organizations. *Social Work with Groups, 30*(4), 5-19.

Sullivan, N.E. (2006). President's pen: Why belong to AASWG?! *Social Work with Groups Newsletter*, 1.

Sullivan, N.E., Mesbur, E.S. & Lang, N.C. (2009). Group work history: Past, present, and future. In A. Gitterman & R. Salmon (Eds.), *Encyclopedia of social work with groups*. New York: Routledge, 3-6.

Toseland, R.W. & Horton, H. (2008). Group work. In T. Mizrahi & H. Horton (Eds.), *The encyclopedia of social work*. Washington DC: National Association of Social Workers.

Toseland, R.W. & Rivas, R.F. (2009). *An introduction to group work practice*. Boston: Pearson.

Tuckman, B. & Jensen, M.A. (1977). Stages of small group development revisited. *Group and Organizacional Studies, 2*(1), 419-417.

History

Based on a presentation at the XXX1 AASWG Symposium, Chicago, IL., 2009. First published in the Proceedings series in: Bergart, A.M., Simon, S.R., and Mark Doel, M. (Eds.) (2012) *Group Work: Honoring our roots, nurturing our growth*. London:Whiting & Birch (pp.194-208).

Notes on authors (at time of first publication)

Cheryl D. Lee, Ph.D., MSW, is Professor, School of Social Work, California State University, Long Beach. She teaches Social Group Work and HBSE. Research subjects include: Mentoring, Group Work, and Child Welfare. She is Chair of AASWG's Southern California Chapter and a member of its board, and was Chair of the Long Beach AASWG Symposium.

Eliette del Carmen Montiel, MSW, is a Psychiatric Social Worker, Los Angeles County Dept. of Mental Health.

De Wallonie et du Québec : réflexions sur les stratégies de formation visant à développer une culture de l'intervention de groupe chez les étudiants en travail social

Préface à la réimpression de 2021

Ce chapitre traite d'une étude réalisée entre 2010 et 2012 concernant la perception d'étudiants belges et québécois du travail social de groupe et des apprentissages faits sur le sujet. Les résultats indiquent que les étudiants apprécient de découvrir le travail social de groupe. Y être exposé et l'expérimenter développent de l'intérêt et le « goût de faire du groupe ». A contrario, les étudiants qualifient d'insatisfaisante la formation reçue : trop peu d'heures de formation, de lieux d'expérimentation et de superviseurs [1] de stage formés ou expérimentés. Ils déplorent un manque de passerelles entre les cours de travail social de groupe et les cours en travail social ainsi qu'une absence de transfert des notions apprises dans des tâches tel le travail en équipe.

Cette étude s'est continuée par une recherche-action (2013-2016) portant sur l'identification de leviers et de freins au développement d'une culture de l'intervention sociale de groupe chez les futurs travailleurs sociaux. À cet effet, la pertinence de l'implantation d'un *dispositif de formation axé sur l'aide mutuelle* auprès d'étudiants de deuxième année baccalauréat en formation pratique[2] et de maîtrise en travail social[3] a été évaluée. Neuf enseignants – 3 à la Haute École Libre Mosane, École Supérieure d'Action Sociale (l'ESAS), et 6 à l'Université du Québec à Montréal (l'UQAM) – et 147 étudiants (9 groupes à l'ESAS et 6 à l'UQAM) y ont participé. Les aspects suivants ressortent de cette implantation :

L'aide mutuelle et la posture de l'enseignant

Les témoignages des étudiants et des enseignants confirment que le dispositif d'aide mutuelle exige de la part de l'enseignant de passer d'expert de contenus à celui de facilitateur d'aide mutuelle. L'habitude de la posture classique de l'enseignant-expert et sa tendance à pratiquer de l'intervention individuelle en situation de groupe sont identifiées comme freins au développement de l'aide mutuelle dans les groupes d'apprentissage. Pointons aussi la peur de perdre le contrôle, la crainte de ne pas parvenir à « partager l'autorité et à favoriser la prise de décision dans le groupe ». Avec le temps et une meilleure compréhension de l'aide mutuelle et de la complexité du modèle, les enseignants ont su partager leur autorité, utiliser les ressources et les savoirs expérientiels du groupe, faire confiance au processus de groupe et devenir facilitateur d'aide mutuelle.

L'aide mutuelle dans les groupes d'étudiants

Les étudiants considèrent que cette posture de facilitateur leur permet de se sentir encadrés et stimulés à faire leur maximum tout en ayant une liberté d'expression, devenant favorable au développement du système d'aide mutuelle dans leur groupe-classe. Les étudiants ont aussi évalué les forces et limites de celui-ci. Cette auto-appréciation démontre une forte convergence sur la présence de deux dynamiques « partage d'information et d'idées et soutien émotionnel » et une divergence, selon les sites, sur le développement de la « confrontation des idées » et de « l'expérimentation de façons de penser, d'être faire et d'être ». L'avancement dans les études expliquerait cette divergence : les étudiants du bacc découvrant plutôt les bienfaits de la confrontation des idées dans un climat de bienveillance et de l'expérimentation des façons de penser, d'être et de faire. Les dynamiques « discussion de sujets tabous et potentiel de la force du nombre » sont peu développées, tout groupe confondu. Le développement de la dynamique « discussion des sujets tabous » demande une certaine maturité et l'exposition personnelle parfois importante qu'elle exige ne convient pas nécessairement à un contexte d'enseignement. Quant au « potentiel de la force du nombre », ce contexte pourrait aussi expliquer son faible développement.

Les résultats démontrent que l'utilisation d'un dispositif d'aide mutuelle en enseignement comporte des défis. Les enseignants sont confrontés à devenir facilitateurs, expérience déstabilisante qualifiée toutefois d'enrichissante. Reste à solutionner l'épineuse question du comment devenir un facilitateur d'aide mutuelle et rester évaluateur des apprentissages. Pour les étudiants, ceci exige un engagement important dans le groupe les conduisant à expérimenter un réel système d'aide mutuelle et les incitant à devenir acteurs de leurs apprentissages. Bref, ce dispositif en tant qu'expérience positive de l'aide mutuelle est un pas vers le développement d'une culture de l'intervention sociale de groupe chez les futurs travailleurs sociaux.

Preface to the 2021 reprint

The original chapter discusses a study carried out between 2010 and 2012 with Belgian and Quebec students that explores their perceptions of group social work and their education on the subject. The results indicate that students enjoy discovering group social work. Being exposed to and experiencing group social work develops their interest and their "taste for groupwork". Conversely, students describe the training received as unsatisfactory: not enough insufficient training hours, places to experiment groupwork placements and fieldwork instructors with training and experience in groupwork. They also deplore the lack of connections made between group social work courses and the rest of the social work curriculum, as well as the missed opportunities to integrate learned concepts into assignments such as teamwork.

A second action-research study was conducted (2013-2016) that aimed to identify factors driving and hampering the development of a culture of groupwork among future social workers. To this end, the study evaluated the relevance of implementing a *mutual-aid teaching method* with social work students in second-year undergraduate practical training[4] and in a graduate social work program.[5] Nine teachers – 3 at the School of Social Work, University College, Liège, Belgium (ESAS) and 6 at the University of Quebec, Montreal,Canada (UQAM) – and 147 students (9 groups at ESAS and 6 at UQAM) participated in this study. Two major themes emerged from this study:

Mutual Aid and the Role of the Educator

Testimonials from both students and educators confirm that the mutual-aid teaching method requires that educators shift from expert to facilitator of mutual aid. The tendency towards the traditional model of the teacher as expert, as well as the propensity to do individual intervention in group situations were identified as obstacles to fostering mutual aid in the student group. They also identify the fear of losing control and the fear of not being able to "share authority and favor group decision-making". Over time, and with a better understanding of mutual-aid and the complexity of the model, educators became better able to share their authority, use the resources and experiential knowledge of the group, trust the group process and become facilitators of mutual aid.

Mutual Aid in Student Groups

The students consider the role of facilitator as favorable to the development of mutual aid in the student groups; it allows them to feel guided and challenged while having the freedom to express themselves. The students also evaluated the strengths and limitations of the mutual-aid system in the group. This self-assessment shows a strong convergence of the presence of two dynamics "the sharing of information and ideas" and "mutual support". There was a divergence of perceptions, according to the sites, about the presence of "the confrontation of ideas" and "experimenting ways of thinking, doing, and being". The level of education could explain this divergence: undergraduate students discovered to a greater extent the benefits of these two dynamics within the context of a safe space. There was little development of the dynamics "discussion of taboo subjects" and "potential of strength in numbers" in any of the groups. The development of the dynamic "discussion of taboo subjects" requires a certain maturity, and the significant level of personal exposure that is required is not necessarily compatible with an academic context. As for the "potential in the strength of numbers," this context could also explain its weak development.

The results illustrate that the use of a mutual-aid teaching method presents its own challenges. Educators are confronted with becoming facilitators, a destabilizing experience that is also described as enriching. The difficult question remains to be solved: *How to become a facilitator of mutual aid while also remaining an evaluator of learning?* For students, this requires an important commitment to the group that allows them to experience a real system of mutual aid and encourages them to become actors in their learning process. In summary, this teaching method, as a positive experience of mutual aid, is a step towards the development of a culture of groupwork among future social workers.

Ginette Berteau and Louise Warin

Ginette Berteau is a social worker and has been a professor of group social work at the University of Quebec at Montréal, Canada, for 20 years

Louise Warin has been working with women's groups for 20 years and was teacher at HELMo ESAS (School of Social Work, University College, Liège, Belgium)

Notes

1   Superviseurs de stage ou référents de stage
2   ESAS, HELMo, Liège, Belgique
3   École de travail social, UQAM, Montréal
4   ESAS, HELMo, Liège, Belgique
5   École de travail social, UQAM, Montréal

De Wallonie et du Québec : réflexions sur les stratégies de formation visant à développer une culture de l'intervention de groupe chez les étudiants en travail social[1]

Ginette Berteau et Louise Warin

Summary

This chapter addresses the results of a joint study of students registered in courses on social work with groups at a Canadian school of social work (Montreal, Quebec) and a Walloon university college (Liège, Belgium) in fall 2010 and 2011. The authors discuss the role of the facilitators and the obstacles to the development of a group work culture among social work students. As the editors of this volume, we are pleased to respond to the request of the authors that this chapter be presented in French.

Introduction

Cet article présente les résultats et les perspectives suite à une recherche menée conjointement dans une École de travail social québécoise (Montréal, Canada) et dans une Haute École wallonne (Liège, Belgique) auprès d'étudiants inscrits dans un cours sur le travail social auprès des groupes durant les automnes 2010 et 2011. Le but de cette étude s'inscrit dans une réflexion globale sur les possibilités de développer une culture d'intervention de groupe chez les étudiants de baccalauréat en travail social. Une première étape de cette réflexion a été de mener un sondage et des groupes de discussion auprès d'étudiants ayant suivi le cours de travail social de groupe durant les automnes 2010 et 2011. L'article est divisé en sections. La première fait état du contexte de la problématique et des contextes d'enseignement spécifiques. La seconde partie présente sommairement le modèle d'aide mutuelle, modèle de référence commune pour l'enseignement du travail social auprès des groupes. La troisième présente la méthodologie utilisée alors que la quatrième expose les résultats. Dans la cinquième section, le lecteur trouvera l'analyse de ces résultats. Le tout se termine par une réflexion à deux voix qui permet de tirer des conclusions générales et surtout des pistes de réflexion sur les enjeux entourant le développement d'une culture de travail social de groupe chez les étudiants de baccalauréat.

Contexte d'émergence de la problématique

Dans un contexte social d'incertitude et de crise, que ce soit en Europe ou en Amérique, l'intervention sociale de groupe présente plusieurs potentialités pour contrer l'isolement social et développer des réseaux de solidarité et de proximité. Malgré la reconnaissance du groupe comme mode d'aide sur les plans personnel et social, les pratiques d'intervention sociale auprès des groupes restent des initiatives isolées. Partout à travers le monde, la formation à l'intervention de groupe reçoit peu d'attention (Berteau et Warin 2011; Lindsay, Roy, Turcotte et Labarre, 2010; Birnbaum et Wayne, 2000; Knight, 2000). Les recherches mettent aussi en évidence que les intervenants se disent insuffisamment formés avec comme résultat que les pratiques de groupe s'apparentent davantage à des interventions de travail social individuel à l'intérieur de groupe et/ou à des pratiques d'animations ponctuelles. Les processus à l'œuvre au sein du groupe sont peu exploités comme potentiel de changement pour ses membres.

Dans le cadre de symposiums internationaux, deux enseignantes francophones (Liège, Belgique et Montréal, Québec) en travail social de groupe ont partagé ce constat : d'entrée de jeu, les étudiants ne s'inscrivent pas en travail social avec l'intention de développer une pratique de groupe. Ces enseignantes observent, dans le cadre de cours sur le travail social de groupe, que les étudiants arrivent avec une représentation limitée et des présomptions parfois négatives de ce mode d'intervention. Elles constatent aussi qu'une pédagogie appropriée fait diminuer leurs craintes par rapport à cette pratique et que leur intérêt grandit au fil de l'apprentissage. Toutefois, le nombre insuffisant de superviseurs formés et à l'aise dans cette pratique a pour conséquences de limiter les offres de stage dans l'expérimentation de ce mode d'intervention (Knight 2000). La formation pratique étant un élément central dans la construction de l'identité professionnelle, les étudiants ne développent pas suffisamment la culture de cette pratique pour en faire un incontournable dans leurs futures interventions.

Fortes de ces constats, ces enseignantes ont décidé de se saisir de ces enjeux en menant dans le cadre de leur cours respectifs, une recherche conjointe sur la perception des étudiants des deux écoles au sujet de leurs représentations initiales, du développement de leurs connaissances et de leurs habiletés suite au cours sur le travail social de groupe et sur leurs intentions de réaliser un stage en travail social de groupe.

Avant de décrire la méthodologie utilisée, arrêtons-nous sur les caractéristiques de chacun des établissements d'enseignement.

Pour la Haute École Libre Mosane située à Liège en Belgique (HELMo), la formation initiale des assistants sociaux de type non universitaire s'étend sur 3 ans. Elle comprend notamment 385 heures de cours sur les méthodologies de l'intervention sociale et 720 heures de stage et séminaire d'analyse des pratiques. En Bac 1, le cours d'Introduction à la dynamique de groupe de 30 heures se poursuit en Bac 2, par le cours de travail social auprès des groupes obligatoire et qui compte 30 heures. En Bac 3, les étudiants ont la chance de suivre un cours de travail social de groupe optionnel de 20 heures.

À l'École de travail social de l'Université du Québec à Montréal (UQAM), la formation initiale est de niveau universitaire s'étend aussi sur 3 ans. Elle comprend 270 heures de cours sur les méthodologies d'intervention sociale, 750 heures de formation pratique : bénévolat, stage et séminaire d'analyse des pratiques. En début de deuxième année, le cours de travail social auprès des groupes est obligatoire et est d'une durée de 45 heures.

L'enseignement du travail social auprès des groupes

Que cela soit en Belgique ou au Québec, le modèle privilégié pour former les étudiants au travail social auprès des groupes est le modèle d'aide mutuelle de Steinberg (Steinberg, 2004; Steinberg & Lindsay, 2008). Ce modèle vise l'instauration d'une dynamique d'aide mutuelle en amenant les participants à être dans une position aidé-aidant et à devenir des ressources les uns pour les autres. Il place les participants d'un groupe dans une position d'acteurs les incitants à agir sur leur environnement personnel et social. L'intervenant est considéré comme un facilitateur, ce qui le conduit à partager son pouvoir.

Dans le cadre des cours donnés en travail social auprès des groupes dans les deux sites, les étudiants sont d'abord initiés aux fondements de l'aide mutuelle. En cohérence avec le modèle, les étudiants sont aussi instruits à l'importance du processus d'intervention (phase prégroupe, début, travail et fin) ainsi qu'à l'utilisation des processus à l'œuvre dans le groupe comme conditions facilitantes à l'émergence des dynamiques d'aide mutuelle. Pour favoriser l'apprentissage, une pédagogie active dans laquelle les étudiants sont appelés à expérimenter partiellement ou entièrement les phases du processus d'intervention dans une perspective d'aide mutuelle.

Dans le cadre du cours obligatoire en Bac 2 à l'ESAS, les étudiants sont appelés à planifier un projet d'intervention sur base de populations réelles. Toutefois, 30 heures de cours ne suffisent pas à le mettre en application. Dès lors, certains étudiants proposent ces projets aux référents de stage. Le cours donné à l'UQAM étant d'une durée plus longue (45 heures) permet aux étudiants d'expérimenter, depuis 10 ans, l'ensemble du processus d'intervention par l'expérimentation d'un projet d'intervention de groupe axé sur l'aide mutuelle de quatre rencontres avec des personnes nouvellement arrivées au Québec.

Sondage et groupes de discussion

Méthodologie utilisée (2010-2012)

Désirant poursuivre une réflexion commune sur l'évolution des apprentissages réalisés dans ces deux cours de travail social auprès des groupes axés sur l'aide mutuelle ainsi que sur l'évolution de l'intérêt à l'égard de ce type d'intervention, les deux professeures ont décidé d'entreprendre une recherche non subventionnée. Entre décembre 2010 et mai 2012, trois sondages ont été administrés et quatre groupes de discussion ont été organisés auprès des étudiants ayant fréquenté le cours obligatoire de travail social de groupe à Liège et à Montréal. Cette méthodologie à la fois quantitative et qualitative s'étant modifiée au cours du processus, nous présentons celle-ci chronologiquement.

Les sondages

Sur le plan quantitatif, un questionnaire de type sondage a été conçu en décembre 2010. Ce sondage a été structuré en cinq sections. Les trois premières avaient pour but de cerner les représentations du travail social de l'étudiant avant son entrée dans les programmes de formation, l'évolution de celles-ci ainsi que les éléments déclencheurs de ce changement. La quatrième section a porté sur ces représentations de la spécificité du travail social auprès des groupes ainsi que sur les apprentissages faits dans le cours. La cinquième section a été consacrée à identifier les habiletés acquises et qui restent encore à développer après le cours. Cette section a été construite à partir d'un répertoire d'habiletés (Berteau, 2006) qui comprend quatre catégories d'habiletés soient : les habiletés permettant de stimuler les interactions, d'encourager la responsabilité du groupe à l'égard de son processus de groupe, de développer le système d'aide mutuelle et de stimuler la réalisation de la cible commune.

Le questionnaire était de type fermé, avec choix multiples. Quelques questions ouvertes ont été posées en vue de recueillir des commentaires. Les étudiants étaient libres de participer à ce sondage. Ils ont signé à cet effet un formulaire de consentement.

À l'automne 2010, le sondage a été complété en fin de cours, tandis qu'en 2011-2012, après un enrichissement de la section sur les habiletés (phases prégroupe et de début), il a été administré en début et fin de cours. À l'ESAS, 62,5 % de la cohorte des étudiants, soient 195 étudiants, âgés en moyenne de 20,2 ans y ont participé. Du côté de l'UQAM, 25 % des étudiants pour un total de 71 étudiants, âgés en moyenne de 27,5 ans ont complété les trois sondages. Dans les deux sites, la très grande majorité des participants étaient des jeunes femmes (80 % et plus).

Les groupes de discussion

Quatre groupes de discussion eurent lieu. Les trois premiers ont eu lieu au printemps 2011 et avaient pour but d'approfondir les résultats du sondage de 2010. L'échantillon sélectionné de manière aléatoire était constitué d'étudiants ayant répondu au sondage. Chaque groupe devait accueillir au minimum un garçon. Deux de ces groupes eurent lieu à l'ESAS (6 et 7 étudiants) et un à l'UQAM (5 étudiants).

Au printemps 2012, un groupe de discussion a été réalisé à l'ESAS auprès de 5 étudiants de 3e année de baccalauréat pratiquant une intervention de groupe en stage. Il avait comme objectif de récolter les opinions des étudiants sur la qualité du cursus de formation à l'intervention sociale de groupe et plus particulièrement sur le nouveau cours optionnel proposé depuis septembre 2011 en Bac 3.

Résultats des sondages

Les résultats sont traités à partir de la compilation des données chiffrées des sondages et des commentaires libres exprimés lors des sondages.

Les représentations du travail social

Une première question interpellait les étudiants au sujet de leurs représentations du travail social. Cette question voulait vérifier si les étudiants inscrivaient dans leurs représentations, le travail social auprès des groupes. Les résultats du sondage de 2011 (avant le cours) ont clairement laissé entrevoir que cette perspective était déjà présente chez les étudiants des deux sites. La comparaison avec les résultats du sondage après (2011) indiquait suite au cours, une augmentation de 10 % de répondants insérant une perspective de travail social de groupe dans leur perception du travail social.

Cependant, des différences de résultat entre les deux cohortes étaient relevées. À l'ESAS, sur deux ans, 21,5 % des répondants ont eu tendance à situer davantage le travail social comme étant un travail avec les individus et les groupes alors que 56,7 % de deux cohortes de l'UQAM ont positionné le travail social auprès des groupes dans une perspective intégrée, c'est-à-dire qu'ils considéraient que le travail social est à la fois du travail social avec les individus, les groupes et la collectivité. Remarquons aussi qu'au point de départ, que pour plus de la moitié des étudiants, tout site confondu, percevaient que le travail social de groupe utilise les mêmes techniques que l'intervention individuelle.

Les résultats ont aussi mis en évidence, pour les étudiants des deux sites, les mêmes éléments déclencheurs du changement de représentation du travail social. Ces éléments déclencheurs étaient par ordre d'importance : les cours (en particulier les cours de méthodologie de l'intervention), l'exposition à la pratique (stage d'observation, bénévolat, rencontres de professionnels et d'enseignants, l'expérimentation), l'échange avec les pairs (rencontres, discussions et travaux de groupe entre étudiants) et les lectures.

Perception des apprentissages réalisés

Nous avons aussi demandé aux étudiants quels étaient les apprentissages majeurs réalisés dans les cours respectifs. Voici sous forme de tableau la perception des apprentissages que les répondants ont considéré avoir faits :

De façon générale, les répondants de l'UQAM ont semblé avoir retiré davantage d'apprentissages que ceux de l'ESAS, l'écart étant plus important en ce qui concerne la préparation de l'intervention et l'utilisation du modèle d'aide mutuelle.

Une question qualitative portait sur le principal apprentissage fait dans ce cours. Pour les deux sites, l'apprentissage le plus annoté se rapportait à la découverte de la richesse de l'aide mutuelle et à l'importance

Tableau I
Perceptions des apprentissages réalisés

Perceptions des apprentissages	UQAM (Montréal) 2010 2011	ESAS (Liège) 2010 2011
Comprendre les fondements de l'aide mutuelle	87,5 % 90	85 % 77,5
Préparer une intervention de groupe	90 % 90	77,5 % 77,5
Utiliser le modèle de l'aide mutuelle	80 % 87,5	70 % 67,5

des quatre phases d'intervention. Pour les étudiants de l'ESAS, les commentaires furent plus nombreux concernant l'apprentissage de la phase prégroupe et pour l'UQAM, ceux sur l'apprentissage de la phase de travail ont occupé une place prépondérante. Cet écart dans les résultats peut s'expliquer par les différences de contexte d'enseignement.

Perception du développement d'habiletés

Lors du sondage de 2011, nous avons aussi demandé aux étudiants leur perception sur l'importance qu'ils accordaient aux habiletés de la phase prégroupe et de début. Cette récolte de données s'est faite à l'aide d'une question ouverte. De façon spontanée, les cohortes interrogées ont semblé réaliser la complexité de la phase prégroupe et l'importance de préparer minutieusement le groupe. Les répondants ont semblé avoir retenu la nécessité de cerner la problématique et les besoins communs, de définir le but initial, les objectifs et la composition du groupe en fonction de ces besoins communs, de réfléchir à la structuration du groupe et de formaliser le projet d'intervention. Par ailleurs, les étudiants des deux sites ont peu noté l'influence du contexte organisationnel sur les pratiques de groupe.

Par rapport à la phase de début, à l'UQAM tout comme à l'ESAS, les étudiants ont nommé aisément la nécessité lors de cette phase de mettre en oeuvre des habiletés favorisant un climat de confiance, de sécurité afin de mettre en place un cadre propice à la cohésion du groupe et à l'émergence de l'aide mutuelle.

Par contre, malgré l'insistance dans les deux cours sur la clarification du but, des objectifs et des normes du groupe avec le groupe ainsi du rôle de l'intervenant, les répondants des deux sites n'ont pas identifié ces habiletés comme importantes.

Puis, à l'aide du répertoire d'habiletés (Berteau 2006), les étudiants avaient à indiquer leur degré d'aisance face à l'acquisition d'habiletés suite au cours. Du côté de l'UQAM, les habiletés avec lesquelles les étudiants ont semblé à l'aise après le cours (2010-2011) étaient, par ordre de priorité, les suivantes : énoncer et favoriser la création de normes et de règles d'organisation démocratique, inviter les membres à construire sur les idées des autres, favoriser l'interaction entre les membres du groupe et entre le groupe et l'intervenant, encourager la participation collective, favoriser la cohésion, tenir compte de la culture du groupe, rechercher des terrains communs, susciter des points de vue différents, structurer un programme d'activités selon les besoins et établir des buts avec le groupe. Dans les commentaires qualitatifs, plusieurs ont mentionné l'importance de ne pas se positionner comme expert du groupe.

Du côté de l'ESAS, les étudiants semblent avoir identifié la nécessité de développer, par ordre de priorité, ces habiletés : rechercher les éléments communs, encourager la participation collective, énoncer et favoriser la création de normes et de règles d'organisation démocratiques, tenir compte de la culture du groupe, encourager les activités et les actions collectives, renforcer l'importance du travail de groupe, renforcer et souligner les comportements d'aide mutuelle, inviter les membres à construire sur les idées des autres, établir des buts avec le groupe et laisser le groupe agir par lui-même.

Les répondants des deux lieux d'enseignement avaient aussi à repérer les habiletés qu'ils considéraient ne pas avoir suffisamment développées. Pour l'ensemble des cohortes, des habiletés telles que soutenir les efforts d'inclusion et protéger les membres contre de possibles attaques du groupe et être réceptif aux communications voilées et les rendre claire. Notons toutefois que les étudiants de l'UQAM ont nettement identifié après le cours que l'utilisation de stratégies permettant l'expérimentation à l'intérieur et à l'extérieur du groupe leur paraissait particulièrement difficile. Les résultats ont dénoté aussi plus clairement leur malaise en ce qui concerne la gestion de conflit et la recherche de consensus. Par contre, les résultats concernant les habiletés davantage reliées au travail sur le but commun ne sont pas ressortis clairement. À titre d'exemple, à l'UQAM, en 2010 et 2011, seulement 12 % des répondants y ont fait allusion au moment de cocher la progression des apprentissages faits dans les cours.

Les répondants de l'ESAS, quant à eux, appréhendaient dans une future pratique les habiletés suivantes : traduire le processus de groupe au groupe, stimuler l'établissement de normes qui favorisent la contribution des membres et le développement de l'aide mutuelle, généraliser les besoins particuliers dans le but d'établir des terrains communs, savoir saisir le thème commun derrière les messages indirects du groupe, utiliser de façon appropriée la révélation de soi de la part de l'intervenant et à l'intérieur du groupe, appuyer les exigences et les attentes du groupe lorsqu'elles appuient la cible commune du groupe et l'émergence du système d'aide mutuelle, créer un espace sur le plan émotif et physique pour chaque membre, permettre la remise en question de la cible commune et identifier les normes informelles et utiliser des stratégies permettant l'expérimentation à l'intérieur et à l'extérieur du groupe.

Perception des retombées du cours

Les enseignantes ont aussi demandé aux répondants des deux sites s'ils avaient l'intention de faire un stage en travail social de groupe et comment ils envisageaient de réutiliser ce qu'ils avaient appris dans le cours. Le tableau 2 illustre les résultats à ce sujet.

Tableau 2

	UQAM 2010 2011	ESAS 2010 2011
Envisager le transfert du système d'aide mutuelle dans d'autres activités de formation	92 % 90 %	87,5 % 70,10 %
Projeter de faire un stage en travail social de groupe	57,5 % 54, 2 %	57,5 % 33 %
Se sentir prêt à effectuer une intervention de groupe en stage	76,5 % 75 %	57,5 % 65 %

Ce tableau met aussi en évidence que les étudiants de l'UQAM ont semblé davantage prêts à expérimenter l'aide mutuelle dans d'autres contextes tout de suite après le cours. Ces résultats ont peu varié d'une année à l'autre. Par contre, les étudiants de l'ESAS se sont dits moins prêts à expérimenter l'aide mutuelle dans d'autres contextes. Au contraire des étudiants de l'UQAM, un écart important entre les résultats obtenus dans les deux années surtout sur le plan de la projection de faire un stage en intervention de groupe, est observé. Manifestement, les résultats illustraient que même s'ils se sentaient prêts, ils n'avaient pas l'intention de faire un stage en intervention de groupe.

Commentaires sur les résultats des sondages

Les réflexions suivantes sont à partager quant aux résultats des sondages : de façon convergente, le fait que des étudiants en travail social suivent un cours sur le travail social auprès des groupes contribue à ancrer celui-ci dans leurs représentations du travail social. Les étudiants des deux sites considèrent que le cours leur permet de bien comprendre les fondements de l'aide mutuelle, ce qui est au point de départ, un aspect positif. Ils sont aussi d'accord pour reconnaître la complexité de l'intervention de groupe, l'importance et la nécessité de la phase prégroupe et sont en mesure de reconnaître les habiletés clés liées la phase de début.

Par contre, les autres résultats ont démontré constamment un écart dans les perceptions des deux cohortes, et plus particulièrement lorsqu'il s'agit de parler de la progression des apprentissages liée aux habiletés d'intervention. C'est le cas pour les apprentissages concernant la préparation de l'intervention et l'utilisation du modèle mutuelle, pour la perception du développement des habiletés de même que pour l'intention d'utiliser l'aide mutuelle dans d'autres contextes. Cette différence dans les résultats est selon nous attribuable au fait que les étudiants de l'ESAS ne sont pas, en fin de cours en Bac 2, formés à la phase de travail et à la phase de fin d'intervention tandis que ceux de l'UQAM ont la chance d'expérimenter un court projet d'intervention qui les confrontent à l'ensemble des phases. Il est clair aussi que les étudiants du site québécois ont pu commencer à intégrer des habiletés centrales liées à la stimulation des interactions et au développement de l'aide mutuelle. De plus, lorsque ces mêmes étudiants identifient comme habileté difficile, celle d'utiliser de stratégies permettant l'expérimentation à l'intérieur et à l'extérieur du groupe, les enseignantes pensent que ceux-ci commencent aussi à réaliser la complexité des moyens pour atteindre les objectifs du groupe et leur transfert à l'extérieur du groupe.

Il est aussi intéressant de constater que les étudiants des deux sites traitent de la nécessité de définir le but initial du groupe lors de la phase prégroupe, mais reprennent peu la notion du travail avec le groupe sur le but commun lorsqu'ils commentent la phase de début et les habiletés de la phase de travail.

Résultats des groupes de discussion

Pour affiner le sens de ces résultats et pour pouvoir développer une stratégie permettant de consolider la place de l'enseignement du travail social auprès des groupes, nous avons organisé dans chacun des lieux des groupes de discussion à divers moments de la recherche.

Les groupes de discussion suite au sondage de 2010 et qui avait comme but de faire réagir aux résultats du sondage ont confirmé les données recueillies dans le sondage. Les étudiants ont réitéré leur appréciation du cours et leur intérêt pour le travail social auprès des groupes. Le modèle d'aide mutuelle est attractif pour eux. Clairement, l'expérimentation du projet d'intervention à l'UQAM est ressortie comme un élément catalyseur d'apprentissage. Les participants au groupe de discussion de ce site ont noté aussi que la formule a permis à chacun de développer ses habiletés en fonction de son évolution. Par contre, les répondants de l'ESAS ont mentionné comme limite de ne pas pouvoir expérimenter la phase-travail par le biais d'un projet d'intervention.

Tant au Québec qu'en Belgique, les participants à ces deux premiers groupes de discussion se sont dits intéressés à transférer l'aide mutuelle dans différentes situations telles que les travaux en équipe. Selon leur milieu d'appartenance, ils ont perçu que l'aide mutuelle pourrait être utilisée dans d'autres contextes. Ainsi, les étudiants de l'ESAS ont identifié que des cours comme les séminaires d'analyse des pratiques pouvaient être des lieux propices à l'utilisation de l'aide mutuelle. Pour leur part, les étudiants de l'UQAM ont repéré que certains cours avaient des concepts apparentés (ex. intervention avec les familles et leurs proches et interculturalité). Dans les deux sites, tous considéraient que le contenu du cours sur le travail social auprès des groupes pouvait être transféré en stage. Enfin, les étudiants de l'ESAS ont dit regretter la référence prédominante au travail social individuel dans les contenus des cours généraux. Ces répondants ont aussi repéré des interprétations différentes de la notion d'aide mutuelle chez les enseignants.

Un troisième groupe de discussion s'est tenu en 2012, mais uniquement à l'ESAS a rassemblé cinq des étudiants Bac 3 ayant suivi un nouveau cours optionnel sur le travail social auprès des groupes faisant suite au cours obligatoire, cours consacré à la phase de travail et davantage axé sur des mises en situation. Ces étudiants pratiquant tous une intervention de groupe en stage ont confirmé la nécessité de l'expérimentation pour mettre en oeuvre les habiletés liées au processus du groupe et aux conflits et pour approfondir une réflexion sur la position d'intervenant.

Lors de ce groupe de discussion, les étudiants ont mentionné plusieurs types de freins au réinvestissement des notions apprises dans les cours du travail social de groupe. Parmi ceux-ci, la durée du stage limitée à 340 heures et les caractéristiques du lieu de stage sont nettement ressorties : comment mettre en pratique un groupe axé sur l'aide mutuelle lorsque le milieu de stage a une mission d'aide sous contrainte ou comment, en l'absence d'intervention sociale de groupe dans un lieu de stage, intervenir auprès d'un groupe sans modèle professionnel?

Plusieurs étudiants ont manifesté l'intérêt pour inclure des moments d'autoévaluation des apprentissages dans le cadre du cours de groupe de Bac 2. Ce processus renforcerait par le développement de leurs habiletés et de leur confiance en leur capacité d'intervenir en groupe.

Des étudiants de ce groupe de discussion ont observé que l'intervention auprès des groupes n'est pas toujours reconnue à sa juste valeur par l'ensemble des enseignants et que la qualité de la collaboration entre les superviseurs de stage et enseignants pouvait être un élément d'influence sur le développement d'un projet d'intervention de groupe. La discussion a mis en évidence des besoins en formation et d'accompagnement en stage de travail social auprès des groupes différents selon le profil de l'étudiant en terme d'expérience d'animation de groupe et en fonction du niveau d'anxiété ressentie par celui-ci.

Réflexions à deux voix

De ces diverses investigations, nous apprenons que le fait d'être exposé au modèle d'aide mutuelle crée un engouement pour chez les étudiants qu'ils soient d'origine belge ou québécoise. L'expérimentation dans le cadre d'un cours en travail social auprès des groupes fait naitre un début d'aisance face au travail social auprès des groupes contribuant à désirer s'engager dans une pratique de groupe. Les étudiants des deux sites deviennent aussi conscients de la complexité de l'intervention ainsi que du rôle de l'intervenant. Toutefois, comme plusieurs caressent le rêve de faire leur stage en travail social auprès des groupes, cette complexité ne semble pas trop effrayer.

Les groupes de discussion mettent en évidence que les cours sur le travail social auprès des groupes sont appréciés et éveillent les étudiants à la richesse de l'aide mutuelle. Dans les deux sites, les étudiants détectent les incohérences dans les programmes de formation et le peu de place donné au travail social auprès des groupes. Ils souhaiteraient une meilleure articulation entre les contenus de cours ainsi qu'une approche intégrée dans l'enseignement des cours de méthodologie d'intervention. Les étudiants de la Belgique sont aussi conscients de trois obstacles importants pour permettre une réelle expérimentation : la durée du stage ne permet pas toujours de mettre en place un projet d'intervention de groupe, le travail social auprès des groupes est une pratique minoritaire et les superviseurs de stage ne sont pas toujours préparés à les accompagner dans l'expérimentation de ce mode d'intervention.

Ces constats mettent en évidence que les cours et les stages ne suffisent pas à développer les pratiques de groupe et une culture de l'intervention sociale auprès des groupes chez les futurs travailleurs sociaux. Plusieurs freins sont identifiés : d'abord dans le contexte d'enseignement actuel, le travail social auprès des groupes n'est pas suffisamment reconnu, ce qui cause une rareté d'offres de stage ou encore de lieux de stage proposant aux étudiants des opportunités d'expérimenter des interventions de groupe. Cette rareté est surtout évidente quand les pratiques de travail social auprès des groupes restent une pratique minoritaire. Or, nous le constatons à travers les sondages et les groupes de discussion, l'expérimentation est un déclencheur du « goût de faire du groupe ». Enfin, la peur d'une pratique « inconnue » et le sentiment de ne pas disposer de suffisamment de compétences pour la pratiquer ont un impact sur le désir de pratiquer des interventions de groupe et nécessairement freinent le développement d'une culture de travail social de groupe. Ces freins persuadent de la nécessité d'une vision globale et à long terme de la formation au travail social auprès des groupes qui conçoivent des actions à plusieurs niveaux si l'on veut encourager le développement d'une culture de travail social auprès des étudiants, et soutenir des pratiques qui renforcent les liens sociaux.

Stimulées par ces constats, les deux enseignantes ont décidé de poursuivre la recherche. Une nouvelle étape a débuté à l'automne 2012 et a pour but d'approfondir l'analyse des leviers et des freins au développement d'une culture de l'intervention sociale auprès des groupes. Cette recherche-action comprend deux volets : le premier est de mettre en place un dispositif d'aide mutuelle comme modalité pédagogique dans les Séminaires d'analyse des pratiques à Liège et dans des supervisons de groupe offertes aux étudiants réalisant un stage en intervention sociale de groupe à la maîtrise à Montréal. La pertinence de ce dispositif sera évaluée en collaboration avec les enseignants et les étudiants.

Puis, le deuxième volet consiste à élargir l'action menée en offrant dans chacune des deux villes une formation en travail social auprès des groupes en milieu de pratique. Suite à cette formation, les intervenants intéressés seront invités à accompagner des étudiants désireux d'expérimenter le travail social auprès des groupes en stage. Ces intervenants seront alors sensibilisés aux craintes et aux réactions des étudiants à une première exposition à un réel travail de groupe ainsi qu'à la diversité de leurs besoins de formation sur le sujet. Comme aboutissement à ces formations, la mise en place de communautés de pratiques en travail social auprès des groupes sera stimulée.

Ces différentes actions sont un premier pas vers la consolidation de la formation initiale, du renforcement des pratiques existantes, d'une meilleure articulation entre les milieux de formation et les milieux professionnels. Toutes ces stratégies desservent la même fin : celle de développer une culture de travail social auprès des groupes chez les étudiants. Si ces stratégies sont efficaces, le travail social auprès des groupes deviendra une pratique plus vivante et plus répandue. Le travail social auprès des groupes contribuera ainsi de façon plus active à sortir de leur isolement et de leur impuissance, les populations marginalisées.

Enfin, il importe ici de signaler les limites de cette recherche. D'abord, le fait qu'elle se déroule en Belgique et au Québec nécessite de relever plusieurs défis : la distance, le décalage-horaire, la différence de culture et de systèmes scolaires demandent moult ajustements exigeant de la souplesse et un appel la sensibilité interculturelle. La création d'un sondage commun en est un bon exemple puisqu'il a fallu tenir compte de la structure différente des cours et de la façon de concevoir la notion d'habiletés et de compétences. Le petit nombre d'étudiants ayant participé aux groupes de discussion est une seconde limite. Les enseignantes sont conscientes que ces résultats ne peuvent être généralisés. L'absence de financement de cette recherche constitue une troisième limite puisque sur ce plan, les enseignantes doivent assumer l'ensemble de la démarche. Par contre, la richesse des échanges, les ressources spécifiques de chacune, la passion commune et la volonté de faire progresser le travail social auprès des groupes viennent amenuiser ces obstacles. Dans l'ensemble, cette démarche contribue à sortir les enseignantes de leur isolement comme professeures et comme travailleuses sociales de groupe et leur permet d'actualiser leur passion commune : le travail social auprès des groupes.

Note

Culture : ensemble de connaissances acquises qui permettent de développer le sens critique, le goût et le jugement. (*Petit Robert*, 2003, p. 611)

Bibliographie

BERTEAU, G. (2006). La pratique de l'intervention de groupe : perceptions, stratégies et enjeux. Ste-Foy : PUQ.

BERTEAU, G. ET WARIN, L (2011). *Former à l'intervention sociale auprès des groupes : une responsabilité collective pour contrer la fragilisation des liens sociaux.* 4e congrès de l'AIFRIS, Genève.

BIRNBAUM, M., WAYNE, J. (2000). Groupwork and foundation generalist education. The necessity of curriculum change, *Journal of Social Work Education*, 36 (2), pp. 347-356.

KNIGHT, C. (2000). Critical content on group work for the undergraduate social work curriculum. *Journal of Baccalaureate Social Work*, 5, pp. 93-112

LINDSAY, J., ROY, V., TURCOTTE, D. et LABARRE, M. (2010). Tendances actuelles au sujet de la formation en service social des groupes. *Intervention*. N° 132, pp. 15-24.

STEINBERG, D. M. (2004). *A mutual-aid approach to working with groups: Helping people help one another* (2nd ed.). Binghamton, NY: Haworth.

STEINBERG, D. M., LINDSAY, J. (2008). *Le travail de groupe : Un modèle axé sur l'aide mutuelle pour aider les personnes à s'entraider.* Québec : Presses de l'Université Laval.

WARIN, L. (2010). Intéresser les étudiants au travail social de groupe : récit d'une pratique belge. Intervention, la revue de l'Ordre des travailleurs sociaux et thérapeutes conjugaux et familiaux du Québec, Numéro 133.

History
Based on a presentation at the XXXIV IASWG Symposium, Long Island, NY., 2012. First published in the Proceedings series in: Tully, G.J., Bacon, J., Dolan-Reilly, G., & Lo Re, A. (Eds.) (2013ß) *Group Work: An international conversation highlighting diversity in practice.* London: Whiting & Birch (pp.116-132).

Notes on authors (at time of first publication)
Ginette Berteau, is a social worker and professor at the School of Social Work at the University of Quebec, Montreal (UQAM, Canada) where she has worked for 13 years. She has always been a passionate believer in social group work, and this enthusiasm has led her to do group work, train and supervise group work social workers and students, earn a PhD in the skills specific to group work, and to publish a book on the subject.

Louise Warin is a social worker, a trainer at FOPA (open university), and an educator at HELMo ESAS (School of Social Work, University College, Liège, Belgium) for the past 13 years. She has been working with women's groups for 20 years. She shares her passion for group work by teaching future social workers. Her interest in training students to do social work with groups led her to work with the UQAM school of social work.

Index

Teasley, M. 46–7
technology, CSSP groups 108
teen pregnancy and sexual health, CSSP groups 113
Terizan, M.A. 37, 38–9
termination, video 26, 29–30
textbooks 78–9, 80
'The American Black History Month Project' 142–4
The Pedagogy of the Oppressed (Freire) 219
theory and skills, training requirement 19
therapy, use of reflecting teams 4–6
three-step sequence 4–5
Thyer, B.A. 1–2
tolerance, effects of 44
Torres, R.-M. 155
Toseland, R. 20, 27, 28–9, 37, 47, 66, 71–2, 209, 210, 211
Toynbee House 216
Truell, R. 150–1
Truelove, Y. 46
trust, and mentoring 190, 191–2
Trygged, S. 155
Tutu, Archbishop D. 60

universals 160

values, clarification 69–70
video
   beginning stage 24
   cohesion 25, 28
   concepts 24
   concepts clearly addressed 27–9
   concepts inadequately addressed 29–30
   confidentiality 24, 27–8
   conflict/resistance 25, 28–9
   context and overview 19
   developments since first publication 17–18
   under-emphasized concepts 26–7
   ending stage 25–6
   goal formation 26–7, 29
   group participation 24–5
   homework 25
   ice-breakers 24
   implications for group work education 27
   introductions 24
   literature review 19–20
   method 20–1
   middle stage 24–5
   non-verbal language 28
   pre-group interaction 26, 30

The Symposia and Proceedings

Each year the IASWG convenes a symposium held in a different location. Key papers related to social group work theory, practice, education and research are selected through a juried process. Over the years the proceedings have been published as special editions of the journal, *Social Work with Groups*, or as books. Proceedings from the 25th Symposium onwards (apart from Cologne) have been published by Whiting & Birch. Some of the Proceedings from earlier years are now out of print.

All Proceedings by year and location

38th and 39th Symposia, 2016 & 2017 (New York City, USA) *Group work around the globe: Creating transformative connections in challenging times.* Edited by Christine Wilkins, Mark Doel, Sari Skolnik, John Genke, and Lorrie Greenhouse Gardella. London: Whiting & Birch

37th Symposium, 2015 (Chapel Hill, NC, USA) *Group work: Creating space for all voices.* Edited by Lorrie Greenhouse Gardella and Greg Tully. London: Whiting and Birch

36th Symposium, 2014 (Calgary, Alberta, Canada) *Unity in diversity: Embracing the spirit of group work.* Edited by William Pelech, Karen Ring, and Sarah LaRocque. London: Whiting and Birch

35th Symposium, 2013 (Boston, MA, USA) *Revitalizing our social group work heritage: A bridge to the future.* Edited by Mark Gianino and Donna McLaughlin. London: Whiting and Birch

34th Symposium, 2012 (Long Island, NY, USA) *Group work: An international conversation highlighting diversity in practice.* Edited by Gregory J. Tully, Jean Bacon, Georgianna Dolan-Reilly, and Alexandra Lo Re. London: Whiting and Birch

33rd Symposium, 2011 (Long Beach, CA, USA) Lee, C. (2011) *Social group work: We are all in the same boat.* Edited by Cheryl D Lee. London: Whiting and Birch

32nd Symposium, 2010 (Montreal, Quebec, Canda) *Strengthening social solidarity through group work: Research and creative practice* Edited by Sacha Genest Dufault, Valérie Roy, and Ginette Berteau. Strengthening social solidarity through group work: Research and creative process. Proceedings of the 32nd International Symposium on Social Work with Groups, London: Whiting and Birch.

31st Symposium, 2009 (Chicago, IL, USA) *Group work: Honoring our roots, nurturing our growth* Bergart. Edited by Ann M. Bergart, Shirley R. Simon, and Mark Doel. London: Whiting and Birch.

30th Symposium, 2008 (Köln, Germany). *Mensch.* (CD only)

29th Symposium, 2007 (Jersey City, New Jersey, USA) *Groups: Gateways to growth.* Edited by Gregory J Tully, Kathleen Sweeney, & Susanne E Palombo. London, England: Whiting & Birch

28th Symposium, 2006 (San Diego, CA, USA) *Orchestrating the power of groups: Beginnings, Middles, and Endings (overture, movements, and finales).* Edited by Dominique Moyse Steinberg. London, England: Whiting & Birch.

27th Symposium, 2006 (Minneapolis, MN, USA)*Group work: Building bridges of hope.* Edited by Carol F Kuechler London, England: Whiting & Birch.

26th Symposium, 2004 (Detroit, MI, USA) Not published as a separate volume. Some papers this event were included as a supplement to the 2013 Procedings.

25th Symposium, 2003 (Boston, MA, USA) *Creating connections: Celebrating the power of groups.* Edited by Lucia Berman-Rossi, Marcia B. Cohen, and Holly Fischer-Engel. London, England: Whiting & Birch.

24th Symposium, 2002 (New York City, USA) *Think group: strength and diversity through group work.* Edited by Carol S. Cohen, Michael H. Phillips and Merdith Hanson. New York : Routledge.

23rd Symposium, 2001 (Northeast Ohio, USA) *Growth and development through group work.* Claudia J. Carson, Anna S. Fritz, Elizabeth Lewis, John H. Ramey, and David T. Sugiuchi, Editors. 2004. Binghampton, NY: Haworth.

22nd Symposium, 2000 (Toronto, Ontario, Canada) *Social Work with Groups: Social Justice Through Personal, Community, and Societal Change.* Edited by Nancy Sullivan, Ellen Sue Mesbur, Norma C. Lang, Deborah Goodman, and Lynne Mitchell. Binghampton, NY: Haworth.

21st Symposium, 1999 (Denver, Colorado, USA) *Mining the gold in social work with groups.* Edited by Sue Henry, Jean East, and Cathryne Schmitz. Binghampton, NY: Haworth.

20th Symposium, 1998 (Miami, FL, USA) *Strengthening resilience through group work.* Edited by Timothy B. Kelly, Toby Berman-Rossi, and Susanne Palombo. Binghampton, NY: Haworth.

19th Symposium, 1997 (Quebec City, Canada) Separate French and English volumes. Plenary papers are the same (in English or French according to the language of the volumes), other selected papers are in their original French or English in the respective language volumes.

French: *Groups Symposium 1997,* Sous la direction de René Auclair, Jocelyn Lindsay et Daniel Tourette. Published in *Service social,* Volume 46, Numbers 2 et 3, 1997. Quebec : Faculté des sciences sociales de l'Université Laval.

English: *Crossing Boundaries and Developing Alliances Through Group Work. Edited by* Jocelyn Lindsay, Daniel Tourette, and Estelle Hopmeyer. Binghampton, NY: Haworth.

18th Symposium, 1996 (Ann Arbor, Michigan, USA) *Rebuilding communities: Challenges for group work.* Edited by Harvey Bertcher, Linda Farris Kurtz, and Alice Lamont.

Binghampton, NY: Haworth.

17th Symposium, 1995 (San Diego, CA, USA) *From prevention to wellness through group work*. Edited by Joan K. Parry, Editor, 1997. Binghampton, NY: Haworth.

16th Symposium, 1994 (Hartford, Connecticut, USA) *Voices from the field: group work responds*. Edited by Albert S. Alissi and Catherine G. Corto Mergins. Binghampton, NY: Haworth.

15th Symposium, 1993 (New York City, USA) *Group work practice in a troubled society: Problems and opportunities*. Edited by Roselle Kurland and Robert Salmon. Binghampton, NY: Haworth.

14th Symposium, 1992 (Atlanta, GA, USA) *Social group work today. and tomorrow: Moving from theory to advanced practice*. Edited by Benj. L. Stempler, Marilyn Glass, with Christine M. Savinelli. Binghampton, NY: Haworth.

13th Symposium, 1991 (Akron, OH, USA) *Capturing the power of diversity*. Edited by Marvin D. Feit, John H. Ramey, John S. Wodarski, and Aaron R. Mann. Binghampton, NY: Haworth.

12th Symposium, 1990 (Miami, FL, USA) *Working from strengths: The essence of group work*. Edited by David Fike and Barbara Rittner. Center for Group Work Studies

11th Symposium, 1989 (Montreal, Quebec, Canada) *Innovation – tradition: Social work with groups and the challenge of change / Le service social des groupes et le défi dechangement societal*. (2 volumes) Edited by The Coordinating Committee of the 11th Annual Symposium on Social Work with Groups, with the assistance of Jocelyn Lindsay and Jean-Pierre Landriault. Montreal [Papers printed in original English or French as presented]

10th Symposium, 1988 (Baltimore, MD, USA) *Social work with groups: Expanding horizons*. Edited by Paul H. Ephross, Stanley Wenocur, and Thomas V. Vassil. Binghampton, NY: Haworth. [Also published as *Social Work with Groups*, Volume 16, Numbers 1/2 1993]

Ninth Symposium, 1987 (Boston, MA, USA) *Reaching out: People, places and power*. Edited by James A. Garland. Binghampton, NY: Haworth. [Also published as *Social Work with Groups*, Volume 15, Numbers 2/3, 1992]

Eighth Symposium, 1986 (Los Angeles, CA, USA) *Theory and practice in social group work: Creative connections*. Edited by Marie Weil, Kenneth Chau, and Dannia Sutherland. Published as Supplement #4, *Social Work with Groups*. Binghampton, NY: Haworth.

Seventh Symposium, 1985 (New Brunswick, NJ, USA) *Roots and new frontiers in social group work*. Edited by Marcos Leiderman, Martin L. Birnbaum, and Barbara Dazzo. Published as Supplement #3, *Social Work with Groups*. Binghampton, NY: Haworth

Sixth Symposium, 1984 (Chicago, IL, USA) *Social group work: Competence and values in practice*. Edited by Joseph Lassner, Kathleen Powell, and Elaine Finnegan. Published as Supplement #2, *Social Work with Groups*. Binghampton, NY: Haworth.

Fifth Symposium, 1983 (Detroit, MI, USA) *Innovations in social group work: Feedback from practice to theory*. Edited by Marvin Parnes. Published as Supplement #1, *Social Work with Groups*. Binghampton, NY: Haworth

Fourth Symposium, 1982 (Toronto, Canada) *Patterns in the mosaic: Patterns and issues in contemporary practice: purpose, context, and technology.* (2 volumes) Edited by Norma C. Lang and Christine Marshall. Toronto, Canada: Committee for the Advancement of Social Work with Groups

Third Symposium, 1981 (Hartford, CN, USA) *Reaping from the field: From practice to principle.* (2 volumes) Edited by Norman N. Goroff. Hebron, CN: Practitioners Press

Second Symposium, 1980 (Arlington, TX, USA) *Group Workers at Work: Theory and Practice in the '80s.* Edited by Paul H. Glasser and Nazneen S. Mayadas. Totowa, NJ: Rowman and Littlefield

First Symposium, 1979 (Cleveland, OH, USA) *Social work with groups: Proceedings 1979 Symposium.* Edited by Sonia Leib Abels, and Paul Abels. Committee for the Advancement of Social Work with Group

Proceedings published by Whiting & Birch

Group work around the globe:
Creating transformative connections in challenging times
(2016 & 2017 New York)

Eds. Christine Wilkins, Mark Doel, Sari Skolnik, John Genke, Lorrie Greenhouse Gardella

http://www.whitingbirch.net/cgi-bin/indexer?product=9781861771452

January 2010, ISBN 9781861771452, 324 pages, US$45.00/£35.00/€40.00

Group Work:
Creating space for all voices (2015 Chapel Hill)
Eds. Lorrie Greenhouse Gardella and Greg Tully

CONTENTS: *A Tribute to Maeda J. Galinsky* Marilyn Ann Ghezzi and Anne C. Jones ✦ *Patterns of Entry and Exit in Open-Ended Groups* Maeda J. Galinsky and Janice H. Schopler ✦ *Groupwork as the Georgian Association of Social Workers' Approach for Promoting Collective Action* Natia Partskhaladze ✦ *Actualizing the Global Agenda for Social Work and Social Development through Social Group Work* Carol S. Cohen, Alexis Howard, Kyle McGee, and Erin Nau ✦ *On Getting Over Oneself and Creating Space for All Voices in Group Work with Adolescents* Andrew Malekoff ✦ *A Place in History: Adelphi NY Statewide Breast Cancer Hotline and Support Program* ✦ *A Group Work Challenge to Maintain Group Purpose in an Open-Ended Group* Patricia Ki and Adina Muskat ✦ *Using Focus Groups to Inform Suicide Prevention Efforts on Campus* Willa J. Casstevens and Karen J. Miller ✦ *Professional Development: An MSW Course Based on Group Work Principles and Opportunities* Shirley R. Simon ✦ *Remembering Jim Garland: Loneliness in the Group* Lorrie Greenhouse Gardella

http://www.whitingbirch.net/cgi-bin/indexer?product=9781861771469
June 2019, ISBN 9781861771469, 150 pages, US$39.95/£24.95/€28.00

Unity in diversity:
Embracing the spirit of group work (2014 Calgary)
Eds. William Pelech, Karen Ring, & Sarah LaRocque

CONTENTS: *Global Group Work Plenary: The Future of Social Group Work* ✦ *Sacred Science of Circles: An Inclusive Approach to Social Work Practice* Betty Bastien ✦ *Next Steps in the Investigation of Mutual Aid Processes* Charles Garvin ✦ *Cat's Cradle: Managing and (Maybe Even) Enhancing the Complexities and Diversity of Groups in Human Service Organizations* Jane Matheson ✦ *How Did You Get Here? Engagement in Social Justice Journeys Through Pechakucha* Liza Lorenzetti & Joan Farkas ✦ *Developing Facilitator Self-Awareness: Introducing Mindfulness Practices to the Helping Classroom* David Delay & Jennifer Martin ✦ *The Theory of Trauma-Informed Approaches for Substance Use: Implementing a Seeking Safety Group* Rachael V. Pascoe ✦ *The Use of Dream Groups for Developing Professional Self-Care and Spiritual Well-Being* Karen Ring ✦ *Culturally Relevant Group Work With Barbadian Adolescent Males in Residential Care* Sadie K. Goddard-Durant & Nicole N. Lynch ✦ *Validating the Borderlands: Group Work with Queer Latinas* Jayleen Galarza ✦ *La supervision combinée comme soutien à l'apprentissage du travail social de groupe d'étudiants à la maîtrise en travail social* Ginette Berteau, Sylvie Cameron, et Étienne Guay ✦ *"Without Them, I Probably Wouldn't Be on This Planet": Benefits and Challenges of Groups for Parents of Children with Disabilities* Alice Home ✦ *An Inventory for Enhancing Cross-Cultural Group Work* Tomasz Michal Rapacki

& Dawn Lorraine McBride ✦ *Strengths-Based Group Supervision with Social Work Students* Mari Alschuler, Linda McArdle, and Thelma Silver ✦ *A New Group Worker Learns and Practices* Samantha Swift ✦ *Psychoeducational Groups: Do They Meet the Diverse Needs of Women Who Have Been Abused by a Partner?* Stephanie L. Baird ✦ *Group Dynamics in the Classroom: Comparing the Applicability of Group Stage Models* Kyle McGee ✦ *The Chrysalis Model: Mutual Aid in "Peer Juries," School-Based Restorative Justice Groups* Rebecca Witheridge ✦ *The Mind–Body Connection and Group Therapy* Rachel Seed

http://www.whitingbirch.net/cgi-bin/indexer?product=9781861771384

June 2015, ISBN 9781861771384, 324 pages, US$39.95/£27.95/€35.00

Revitalizing our social group work heritage:
A bridge to the future (2013 Boston, with papers from 2004 Detroit)
Eds. by Mark Gianino and Donna McLaughlin

CONTENTS: *The Power of Groups for Healing at a Time of Great Anxiety and Fear* Hubie Jones ✦ *Social Determinants of Health and Parent Coffee Hour* Jessy Benjamin ✦ *Challenges & Opportunities for Applying Group Work Principles to Enhance Online Learning in Social Work* Marcia B. Cohen, Shirley R. Simon, Donna McLaughlin, Barbara Muskat, and Mary White ✦ *Attachment and Recovery: Combining 12-Step Programs and Group Psychotherapy to Treat Addiction* Santiago Delboy ✦ *Challenges and Rewards of Facilitating Support Groups in an Under-Resourced County Jail* Kerry Dunn, Erin Daigle, Ariane Bowie, Kristen Cianelli, Erika Gilbert, and Elisa Orme ✦ *Social Workers Collaborating with Faith Based Organizations to Create a Group Mentoring Program for African American Youth* Anthony C. Hill ✦ *Theatre Workshops as a Group Format for Promoting Intercultural Understanding* Claude Olivier and William Dunn ✦ *Participant Observation of an Online Task Group Process: A Narrative* Mamadou Seck ✦ *Integration of Strengths and Empowerment into Group Work Practice* Thelma Silver, Charlla Allen, and Linda McArdle ✦ *Finding Focus: Adolescents Experiencing Major Mental Illness Explore Their Photographic Realities* Kyle Taylor Ganson ✦ *Ethnic Nonprofit Organizations During the Economic Recession: An Examination of the Role of Organizational Capacity and Leadership Building for Long-Term Sustainability* Biswas Pradhan and Dale Asis ✦ *Groupwork Interventions for Women and Children Experiencing Domestic Abuse: Do They Work & Do They Last?* Stephanie Holt, Gloria Kirwan and Jane Ngo ✦ *Group Work with Mothers with Multiple Sclerosis: A Second True Self Emerges* Rebecca Halperin ✦ *An Evaluation of a Psycho-Educational Program for Pregnant Women Living with HIV in Toronto, Canada* Simone Shindler, Stephanie Bell, and Mary Tangelder ✦ *"Why do WE Have to Come in Here?": Using Group Work to Reduce Conflict and Stigma Among Boys in a Youth Development Setting* Dara Kammerman ✦ *Things I Didn't Learn in Graduate School: A Survival Guide for Leading Involuntary Groups* Francis S. Bartolomeo

Papers from the XXVI Symposium, Detroit, October 21st-24th, 2004 'Group Work Reaching across Boundaries: Disciplines, Seasons of Life, Practice Settings, Cultures and Nations' Edited by Alice Lamont and Dale Swaisgood ✦ *Reducing Inter-Group Conflict Through the Use of Group Work* Charles Garvin and David Bargal ✦ *Groups as a Medium for Reducing Sex Offender Recidivism* Steven Hartsock and Karen V. Harper-Dorton ✦ *Grandparent Caregivers: Implications for Groupwork* Jessica Rosenberg ✦ *Exploring Group Work Concepts Presented on Video in an Undergraduate Social Work Practice with Small Groups Course* John Mansfield, Debrah Cuda, Pamela Oliver and Amy Sill ✦ *Blueprints for Awakening Desire The 'Girl Talk' Healthy Sexuality Group Program* Maura McIntyre and Naomi Mitchell

http://www.whitingbirch.net/cgi-bin/indexer?product=9781861771391

June 2016, ISBN 9781861771391, 376 pages, US$45.00/£32.00/€39.00

Group work: An international conversation highlighting diversity in practice (2012 Long Island)

Eds. Gregory J. Tully, Jean Bacon, Georgianna Dolan-Reilly, Alexandra Lo Re

CONTENTS: *Diversity in group work practice: An obstacle or opportunity?* William Pelech & Robert Basso ✦ *Examining the relationship between leader behavior and group climate for aggressive adolescents in group intervention: A pilot study* Marisa D. Mahler & Eva Feindler ✦ *Recovering together: multiple family group therapy in work with adolescent chemical abusers* Loretta Hartley-Bangs & Colleen Egan ✦ *Effects of peer group intervention on sexual addiction treatment in Iran* Masoomeh Maarefvand & Maryam Sadat Mirmalek Sani ✦ *Under the influence of Katy: Foundational contributions of Dr. Catherine P. Papell and other greats* Reverend Judith A.B. Lee ✦ *Walking the talk: Utilizing group work in social work education gatekeeping* Mary Wilson ✦ *Developing a white anti-racism identity: A psycho-educational group model* Kathryn K. Berg & Shirley Simon ✦ *De Wallonie et du Québec : réflexions sur les stratégies de formation visant à développer une culture de l'intervention de groupe chez les étudiants en travail social* Ginette Berteau & Louise Warin ✦ *Group work with KEG Cards: Keys to emotional growth* W. J. Casstevens, L. Cloninger, & E. Avinor ✦ *Understanding the refugee experience: Culturally sensitive group work with resettled Burmese male refugees* P. Matthew Lozano ✦ *Group based parental skills training: Parents' view* Jorūnė Vyšniauskytė-Rimkienė ✦ *Tuckman goes backpacking: Training outdoor student leaders in group work theory and practice* Emily Wilk ✦ *Homicide survivors: Supporting victims' loved ones through groups* Lauren Phillips ✦ *Roots and Wings: Reflections on AASWG* Dr. Ellen Sue Mesbur

http://www.whitingbirch.net/cgi-bin/indexer?product=9781861771346

June 2013, ISBN 9781861771346, 212 pages, US$39.95/£24.95/€28.00

Social group work:
We are all in the same boat (2011 Long Beach)

Ed. Cheryl D. Lee

CONTENTS: *All in the same boat—but where is the flotilla?* Mark Doel ✦ *Defining moments in groups: My personal journey* Alex Gitterman ✦ *Groups as anchors in times of turbulence: The centrality of group dynamics in transforming human service agencies into learning organizations* Michael J. Austin ✦ *Academic mentoring of social work faculty: A group experience with a feminist influence* Alana B. Atchinson, Lisa M. Murphy, Maria A. Gurrola, Cheryl D. Lee, and Shirley R. Simon ✦ *Balancing it all: A group initiative for college students with learning disabilities* Lorraine Ruggieri ✦ *Using a reflecting team as a small group exercise in the social work classroom* Willa J. Casstevens and Marcia B. Cohen ✦ *Single-session groups in healthcare: Two approaches to program evaluation* Barbara Muskat and Joanne Sulman ✦ *Self-hypnosis groups for teaching relaxation and dealing with stress* Kay Goler Levin ✦ *A men's support group: An adjunct for men in psychotherapy* Ernest M. Gunderson ✦ *Group member engagement in domestic abuse treatment: A mixed-methods study of two urban programs* Michael George Chovanec ✦ *Harnessing the promise of diversity in group work practice* Robert Basso, William Pelech, and Edcil Wickham

http://www.whitingbirch.net/cgi-bin/indexer?product=9781861771360

June 2014, ISBN 9781861771360, 200 pages,US$39.95/£24.95/€28.00

Strengthening social solidarity through group work:
Research and creative practice (2010 Montréal)

Eds. Sacha Genest Dufault, Valérie Roy, & Ginette Berteau

CONTENTS: *Solidarity and universal democracy* Jean Bédard ✦ *The importance of altruism for mutual aid group initiation and sustainability* Victor Hainsworth ✦ *The Model A Continuum of Connecting the Classroom and Community: Utilizing group work* Brenda Exum and Mary Yanisko, ✦ *Pedagogy without Pretense: Preparing non-social workers to facilitate social work groups* Dana Grossman Leeman ✦ *Introduction of a model of social work peer consultation groups* Kathleen M. Walsh ✦ *Managing ethical issues in social work with groups* Allan E. Barsky ✦ *Increasing diversity competence in social work students through group research projects* Stephen J. Yanca ✦ *Group work at the heart of hospital social work practice: Creating inclusion and solidarity in the acute care environment* Joanne Sulman, Lieve Verhaeghe, Catherine Coulthard, Kristy MacDonell, Amber Oke, Aviva Werek Sokolsky, Trish Woodhead, Sue Worrod ✦ *Challenges, strategies and rewards of an adaptation of trauma systems therapy for newly arriving refugee youth: School-based group work with Somali adolescent boys* Amanda Nisewaner and Saida Abdi ✦ *Men in India: Eliminating gender-based violence* Sanjay Singh and Madhu Kushwaha ✦ *Group intervention work with aboriginal youth preparing for adult living* Stéphane Grenier, Martin Goyette, Andrée-Anne Lemay and Alexis Pearson ✦ *French-Canadian version of the Wellness Recovery Action Plan (WRAP): Preliminary report of its validity for mental health patients in a community teaching and research hospital* Jean-Philippe É. Daoust,

Valérie Lemieux, Gilles Fleury, Danielle Perron-Roach and Diane Lavallée ✦ *Research with and about groups: Overcoming obstacles to creativity and solidarity*, Alice Home ✦ *Research! What we can do to advance it in social work with groups* Mark Macgowan ✦ *Some Ethical and Legal Challenges in Researching Groupwork Practice* Michael Preston-Shoot

http://www.whitingbirch.net/cgi-bin/indexer?product=9781861771261

June 2014, ISBN 9781861771261, 244 pages,US$39.95/£24.95/€28.00

Group work: Honoring our roots, nurturing our growth (2009 Chicago)

Eds. Ann M. Bergart, Shirley R. Simon, & Mark Doel

CONTENTS: *AASWG at Hull House for tea* Catherine P. Papell · *Testing the applicability of the Boston Model: Worker perceptions* Susan Ciardiello · *Going back to our roots: Social group work, the ideal method for youth development* Helene Filion Onserud · *The use of program and activities: Purpose, planning and structure* Alison H. Johnson · **Part two: Our present** · *The power of group work and community organizing in the 2008 U.S. Presidential race* Gerald Kellman · *The use of group work to fight external threats to a community-based organization during harsh economic times* Andrew Malekoff · *Group work in graduate social work education: Where are we now?* Shirley Simon and Terri Kilbane · *Global group work: Honouring processes and outcomes* Carol S. Cohen, Mark Doel, Mary Wilson, Deirdre Quirke, Karen A. Ring, and Sharima Ruwaida Abbas · *The 'Rainbow Nation' way of teaching sensitivity to diversity for social work with groups* Reineth Prinsloo · Alzheimer's disease and dementia sufferers access their inner artist: Maintaining connections rather than becoming strangers Lorraine Ruggieri ✦ **Part three: Our future** · Group work and technology: Embracing our future Shirley R. Simon and Kathleen W. Stauber ✦ *Communicating the values of social work with groups by talking in the idiom of the other: Implications for practice* Dominique Moyse Steinberg and Robert Salmon · *The metamorphosis of a university social group work club* Cheryl Lee and Eliette Montiel · *Generalist social work practice with groups: Sharing the past, present, and future* Stephen J. Yanca and Louise C. Johnson · **Part four: Abstracts of poster and workshop presentations** ✦ *Poster presentations at the 2009 AASWG Symposium* · *When internal processes go astray: Turning points in group: A workshop* Alex Gitterman ✦ Clements and Samuel R. Benbow

http://www.whitingbirch.net/cgi-bin/indexer?product=9781861771254

September 2012, ISBN 9781861771254, 270 pages,US$39.95/£24.95/€28.00

Groups: Gateways to growth (2007 New Jersey)

Eds. Gregory J Tully, Kathleen Sweeney, & Susanne E Palombo

CONTENTS: *My love affair with stages of group development* Toby Berman-Rossi ✦ *Revisiting 'joyful noise': Gateways from Singing the Blues to the Hallelujah Chorus. Talking in the idiom of the other: A necessary skill for responding to the current crisis in social work practice* Dominique Moyse Steinberg and Robert Salmon ✦ *Reflective practice and mutual aid in educational groups: A gateway to constructed knowledge* Barbara Hogan✦ *Teaching social work from a group-as-a-whole perspective: A classroom case study* James J. Canning ✦ *Gate keepers, gate crashers, and gateways in group work with kids: A group work mystery story* Andrew Malekoff ✦ *Transgenerational groups: Rediscovering our legacy* Scott P. Anstadt and Deb Byster ✦ *The Silver Foxes group: Growing older and living with HIV/AIDS* Erin McGarry, Nadja Kane and Ling-Wai Fung ✦ *Welcome to the family: A group work model for new staff orientation* Sandra Radzanower Wolkoff ✦ *When is a group not a group?* Mark Doel ✦ *Connecting students and professional associations: A curricular approach* Shirley R. Simon ✦ *Dealing with small group conflict: Seven keys for helping people to make meaning of their differences, take two* Dominique Moyse Steinberg

http://www.whitingbirch.net/cgi-bin/indexer?product=9781861771247

June 2012, ISBN 9781861771247, 198 pages, US$39.95/£24.95/€28.00

Orchestrating the power of groups: Beginnings, Middles, and Endings (overture, movements, and finales) (2006 San Diego)

Ed. Dominique Moyse Steinberg

CONTENTS: *Mutual aid: Back to basics* Alex Gitterman ✦ *Orchestrating the power of a group of AASWG members in partnership for change with colleagues at a university social work program* Thelma Silver and Anna Fritz ✦ *Mentoring in group* Cheryl D. Lee and Eliette del Carmen Montiel *A magical mystery tour: Education and social work with groups across borders* Ellen Sue Mesbur ✦ *The facilitator 411 on phone groups: When caller ID isn't enough* Vicki Hallas ✦ *Groupwork researchers as 'temporary insiders'* Mark Doel and Kim Orchard ✦ *Dancing towards wholeness: The impact of conflict on patterns of interpersonal coordination in a small treatment group* William Pelech and Robert Basso ✦ *Using the research process to develop group services for older persons with a hearing disability* Timothy B. Kelly, Debbie Tolson, Tracy Day Smith, and Gillian McColgan ✦ *Participatory research and evidence-based practice for rape survivor groups: Implications for practice and teaching* Shantih Clemans & Susan Mason ✦ *Relevance of group work's humanistic values and democratic norms to contemporary global crises* Urania Glassman ✦ *A critical call for connecting students and professional associations* Shirley R. Simon, Joyce A. Webster, Karen Horn

http://www.whitingbirch.net/cgi-bin/indexer?product=9781861771278

Dec. 2010, ISBN 9781861771278, 212 pages, US$39.95/£24.95/€28.00

Group work:
Building bridges of hope (2005 Minneapolis)
Ed. Carol F Kuechler

CONTENTS: *More than sixty years with social group work: Personal and professional history* Catherine P. Papell ✦ *Settlement houses and neighbourhood houses: Groupwork and community work: Have they a future in the 21st century?* Luke Geoghegan • *Community social service projects: Working in task groups to create change* ✦ Marilyn D. Frank ✦ *Constructing a bridge between research and practice: A reflection on cooperative group learning* • Annette Gerten ✦ *Best practices in group work: Assessment and monitoring of group processes* ✦ Kendra J. Garrett ✦ *Exploring group work concepts presented on video in an undergraduate group work course* ✦ John Mansfield and Patrick Hull ✦ *Male Sexuality Group: Understanding sexual expression in a long term care facility* • Liese Mittiga Zilberleyt and Ling Wai Fung ✦ *Group work with children of divorce: The use of tactile-related techniques for anger management* ✦ Lisa Tobias and Angela Chierek Bratcher ✦ *Bridging the gap: New group workers and adolescents finding their voice* • Brianna Cashman Loop & Amirthini Ambrose Keefe ✦ *Lost homeland, lost childhood: Group recovery from trauma* • Carol Irizarry ✦ *Bridging professional and indigenous cultures through group work: An aboriginal empowerment program* • Kim Clare and Kathy Jones ✦ *The Hamburg mask making approach: Bridges to group work* • Jürgen Kalcher and Otto Luedemann ✦ *When words are not enough: Facilitating angels in the funzone!* Mary Wilson and Deirdre Quirke

http://www.whitingbirch.net/cgi-bin/indexer?product=9781861771230

April 2011, ISBN 9781861771230, 212 pages, US$39.95/£24.95/€28.00

Creating connections:
Celebrating the power of groups (2003 Boston)
Eds. Lucia Berman-Rossi, Marcia B. Cohen, & Holly Fischer-Engel

CONTENTS: *Common elements in philosophy and method: A brief history of social group work in the United States* Janice Andrews-Schenk ✦ *Innovations in groupwork with abusive men: Theories that promote engagement and empowerment* Michael George Chovanec ✦ *'I have a dream': A visioning group for adolescent First Nations girls* Arielle Dylan ✦ *Using literature groups to teach diversity* Mari Ann Graham ✦ *The use of 'twelve-step' concepts of recovery in group work with mentally retarded and developmentally disabled adults* Juli Kempner ✦ *Group supervision: Motivation for social action* Carol F. Kuechler and Jennifer Schwartz ✦ *'As if by magic': Women with breast cancer, dragon boats and healing in a group* Paule McNicoll ✦ *'SAVE' Students Against Violence at Emery. A whole school initiative: A small group approach* Lynne Mitchell and Dianne Cullen ✦ *Group work with refugee children in a multicultural bereavement program* David Prichard ✦ *Creating connections among disadvantaged youth: Toward participation in policy development for social change* Nancy E. Sullivan and E. Michelle Sullivan

http://www.whitingbirch.net/cgi-bin/indexer?product=9781861771216

June 2010, ISBN 9781861771216, 168 pages, US$39.95/£24.95/€28.00